Acknowledgments

WHILE MANY KITCHENS are pictured in this book, two projects are featured in process. The kitchen renovation of David Long and Jackie Davidson appear in many photos of details and methods. The builder was Dave Larson of Turkey Mountain Woodcrafters in Addison, Vermont. He and his crew—Chris Day, John Lafountain, and Jason Betourney—were extremely helpful and patient with our photo work.

The primary example of how a kitchen design evolves is the renovation of Kit Gates and Mark Yorra's kitchen, designed and built by Iron Bridge Woodworkers of Plainfield, Vermont, the company I work for. Thanks to both families and both builders.

Many other people also allowed us to photograph their homes and kitchens. These include Mary Niebling and David Spence, Sara Lisniansky and Ruth Coppersmith, David Palmer and Jean Lathrop, Jeff and Kellie Merrell, Michael Birnbaum and Karen Seeger, Alexis Smith, John and Jenny Warshow, Bob and Sue Goodby, Michael Horowitz and Kerrin McCadden, Maury Martin and Susan Miller, Leda Schubert and Bob Rosenfeld, and David Scheckman and Julie Hackbarth. Many thanks.

Andrew Kline of Afterimage Photography in Montpelier, Vermont, took hundreds of photos. He was a great partner, always flexible and attentive, often rising at dawn for the long drive to the job site. Thanks also to the designers listed on the previous page.

Many of my friends in the building business here in Vermont answered technical questions. These include: Stanley Martin of Country Floors in Marshfield, Steve Noyes of East Montpelier Home Center, Judy Maurice of Allen Lumber Co. in Barre, and Matt Grundy of Builder Specialties in Montpelier. Charlie Cerutti, of Ormby's TV and Appliance in Barre, spent a morning giving me a lesson on the current appliance scene. Bill St. Cyr of St. Cyr Plumbing and Heating in Montpelier explained plumbing mysteries. Lawrie Morrison of The Gallery of Cabinets in East Montpelier showed me how computer-design systems can add to kitchen design and provide artwork as examples. Bob Miller and Sean Ward of Home Depot in Williston explained how their end of the kitchen marketplace works. Keja MacEwan researched online kitchen design programs. Rebecca Stahlnecker made CADD plans and elevations. Ray Tricozzi of Sears in South Burlington provided parts on an emergency basis for my geriatric Sears table saw. Paul Morrison of Morrison and Clark, in South Barre Vermont, provided information on and samples of laminated flooring. Further afield, Anne Remby of The Kitchen Works in Arlington, Massachusetts explained how independent kitchen designers work. Tom Worthen of Fireslate 2 provided lots of technical information along with the counters for the Long/Davidson project. Thorsten Horton provided key information on wiring and lighting.

David Palmer, Barney Carlson, David Scheckman, Aaron Kyle, and Jean Lathrop, my colleagues at Iron Bridge Woodworkers, helped in many ways—but in particular allowed me to abandon the business for seven months to work on the book, and arrive at the job site late during repeated revisions. A lot of what I know I learned from them over many years and many projects.

I worked closely with two talented editors. Andy Wormer got the project going and guided it through the first version. Rick Mastelli of Image & Word in Montpelier, Vermont, took it from there, laying out the book, as well.

Contents

Taunton's

BUILD LIKE A PRO®

Expert Advice from Start to Finish

REMODELING A
KITCHEN

Expert Advice from Start to Finish

REMODELING A
KITCHEN

SAM CLARK

The Taunton Press

The Taunton Press, Inc., 63 South Main Street, P.O. Box 5506, Newtown, CT 06470-5506

e-mail: tp@taunton.com

Distributed by Publishers Group West

EDITOR: Rick Mastelli

COVER AND INTERIOR DESIGN: Lori Wendin

LAYOUT: Rick Mastelli

ILLUSTRATOR: Mario Ferro

Taunton's Build Like a Pro® is a trademark of The Taunton Press, Inc.,
registered in the U.S. Patent and Trademark Office.

Library of Congress Cataloging-in-Publication Data

Clark, Sam.
   Remodeling a kitchen / Sam Clark.
          p. cm. -- (Taunton's build like a pro)
Includes index.
   ISBN 1-56158-482-7
   1. Kitchens--Remodeling. I. Title. II. Series.
   TH4816.3.K58 C53 2003
   643'.3--dc21

                                         2003007245

Printed in the United States of America

10 9 8 7 6 5 4 3 2

The following manufacturers/names appearing in *Remodeling a Kitchen* are trademarks: Franke®, Studor®, Ikea®, Bally®, Good Stuff®, Formica®, Corian®, Gibralter®, Avonite®, Fireslate®, Livos®, Sheetrock®, Durabond®, KitchenAid®, Viking®, Garland®, Thermador®, Wolfe™, DCS™, Sub-Zero®, Conserve®, Broan-/Nu tone®, Allurer®, Gaggenau®, UPS®, Andersen®, Marvin®, Channellock®, Cat's Paw®, Prazi®, Bigg Lugg ™, Durabond®, Hyde®, QUICK-GRIP®, American Tool Companies®, Swanson Speed® Square, Polyseamseal®, Phenoseal®, Bosch®, Miele®.

The author wishes to thank all the designers whose work is featured in this book:
Lawrie Morrison of Gallery of Cabinets; Barbara Feeley; Sundance Design; Robert Orr of Robert Orr and Associates; David Palmer, David Scheckman, and Iron Bridge Woodworkers; Alexis Smith; Paul Weiner of Paul Weiner Design and Building Consultants, Inc.; Eric Gazley of Gazley, Plowman, Atkinson Architects; Martha B. Finney and Garrett Finney; Ross Chapin; Peter Twombley of Estes/Twombley Architects; Nathan Rome; Anne Remby of The Kitchen Works; Kerrin McCadden and Michael Horowitz; Gerry Copland; Paul D. Voelker; Brad Sills of Whirlwind Homes Ltd.; John Seibert of Birdseye Building Company; Jan Regis of Binns Designer Kitchens; David Roessler; Jenny Warshow; Jim Tolpin; Clark and Duberstein; Fred Jordan of Artageddon.com; and Adam Smith.

Introduction

THIS BOOK SURVEYS the process of remodeling a kitchen from start to finish, including design, carpentry, mechanical systems, and cabinet installation. There is also an overview of making your own cabinets. The emphasis is on good planning, how to work effectively with people you may hire, and practical technique.

A kitchen renovation is one of the most challenging and rewarding projects you can take on. It involves almost every trade: carpentry, electrical work, plumbing, tilework, cabinetmaking, and usually others as well. The planning is a challenge, too, because a kitchen is complex, expensive, and often involves many people.

The rewards, however, are as great as the challenges. First, there's lots of room to be creative as you design, outfit, and detail your kitchen. But the creative opportunities often go further. Many older homes, despite their charms, have problems that extend beyond an outdated kitchen. They may be too dark or the rooms too small. They often will be poorly organized, particularly for the way families live today. Few older homes are energy efficient, and structural problems are not uncommon. These problems may have been compounded

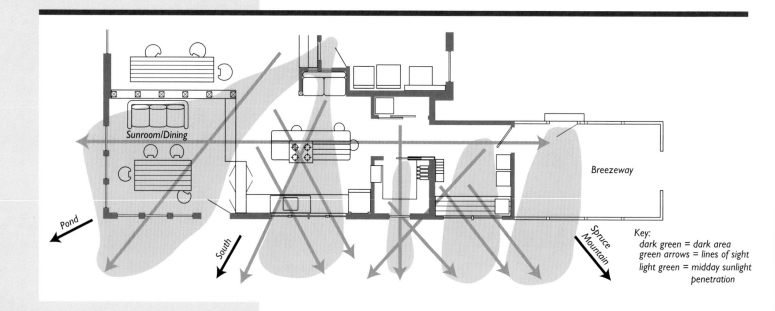

Sunroom/Dining

Breezeway

Pond

South

Spruce Mountain

Key:
dark green = dark area
green arrows = lines of sight
light green = midday sunlight
penetration

by inept renovations by previous owners. Your kitchen renovation may be the best opportunity to address these issues. Often, by remodeling the kitchen, you transform the house around it.

There is more design information here than in other books on the kitchen. Creating a thorough, detailed design makes all the difference in how well a kitchen will work when it's done. In my experience, getting the carving knife, trash can, and spices in just the right places, where you can put them to use effortlessly, is more important than having fancy appliances or high-end cabinets. Locating the new window at just the right height can have as much impact as new flooring. Professional designers use a broad variety of design tools, resources, and techniques to get both plan and details right. I think these methods will be equally useful to you.

There's another reason for a thorough discussion of design ideas. Not every reader will have the resources to purchase expensive appliances, fixtures, or other amenities. But every reader can invest time into the kitchen design. Having the perfect stove is great, but it can be costly. Having your stove in exactly the right place is no less valuable and usually adds no cost to your project. Your kitchen is your

workshop. I've found that careful design is your most powerful tool for making that workshop efficient and tailoring it to your particular ways of cooking. Such a kitchen can be a great joy to work in, every day.

How to Use This Book

IF YOU'RE READING THIS, you're a doer who is not afraid to take on a challenging project. We've designed this book and this series to help you do that project smoothly and cost effectively.

Many doers jump in and do, reading the directions only if something goes wrong. It's much smarter (and cheaper) to start by knowing what to do and planning the process step by step. This book is here to help you. Read it. Familiarize yourself with the process you're about to undertake. You'll be glad you did.

Planning Is the Key to Success

This book contains information on designing your project, choosing the best options for the results you want to achieve, and planning the timing and execution. We know you're anxious to get started on your project. Take the time now to read and think about what you're about to do. You'll refine your ideas and choose the best materials.

There's advice here on where to look for inspiration and how to make plans. Don't be afraid to attempt drawing your own plans. There's no better way to get exactly what you want than by designing it yourself. If you need the assistance of an architect or engineer, you'll find advice in this book on why and how to work with those professionals.

After you've decided what you're going to undertake, make lists of materials and a budget for yourself, both of money and of time. There's nothing more annoying than a project that goes on forever.

Finding the Information You Need

We've designed this book to make it easy to find what you need to know. The main part of the book details the essential parts of each process. If it's fairly straightforward, it's simply described. If there are key steps, they are addressed one by one, usually accompanied by drawings or photos to help you see what you will be doing. We've also added some other elements to help you understand the process better, find quicker or smarter ways to accomplish the task, or do it differently to suit your project.

Alternatives and a closer look

The sidebars and features included with the main text are there to explain aspects in more depth and to clarify why you're doing something. In some cases, they are used to describe a completely different way to handle the same situation. We explain when you may want to use that method or choose that option, as well as detail its advantages. The sidebars are usually accompanied by photos or drawings to help you see what the author is describing. The sidebars are meant to help, but they're not essential to understanding or doing the process.

Heads up!

We urge you to read the "Safety First" and "According to Code" sidebars we've included. "Safety First" gives you a warning about hazards that can harm or even kill you. Always work safely. Use appropriate safety aids and know what you're doing before you start working. Don't take unnecessary chances, and if a procedure makes you uncomfortable, try to find another way to do it. "According to Code" can save you from having trouble with your building inspector, building an unsafe structure, or having to rip your project apart and build it again to suit local codes.

There's a pro at your elbow

The author of this book, and every author in this series, has had years of experience doing this kind of project. We've put the benefits of their knowledge into quick tips that always appear in the left margin. "Pro Tips" are ideas or insights that will save you time or money. "In Detail" is a short explanation of an aspect that may be of interest to you. While not essential to doing the job, it is meant to explain the "why."

Every project has its surprises. Since the author has encountered many of them already, he can give you a little preview of what they may be and how to address them. And experience has also taught the author some tricks that you can only learn from being a pro. Some of these are tips, some are tools or accessories you can make yourself, and some are materials or tools you may not have thought to use.

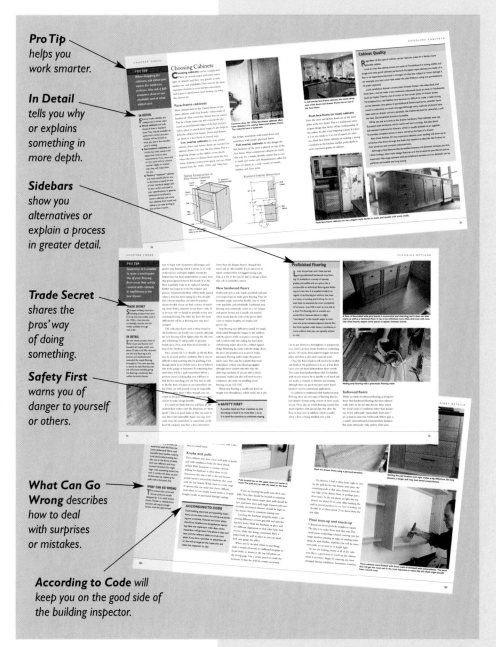

Pro Tip helps you work smarter.

In Detail tells you why or explains something in more depth.

Sidebars show you alternatives or explain a process in greater detail.

Trade Secret shares the pros' way of doing something.

Safety First warns you of danger to yourself or others.

What Can Go Wrong describes how to deal with surprises or mistakes.

According to Code will keep you on the good side of the building inspector.

Building Like a Pro

To make a living, a pro needs to work smart, quickly, and economically. That's the strategy presented in this book. We've provided options to help you make the best choices in design, materials, and methods. That way, you can adjust your project to suit your skill level and budget. Good choices and good planning are the keys to success. And remember that all the knowledge and every skill you acquire on this project will make the next project easier.

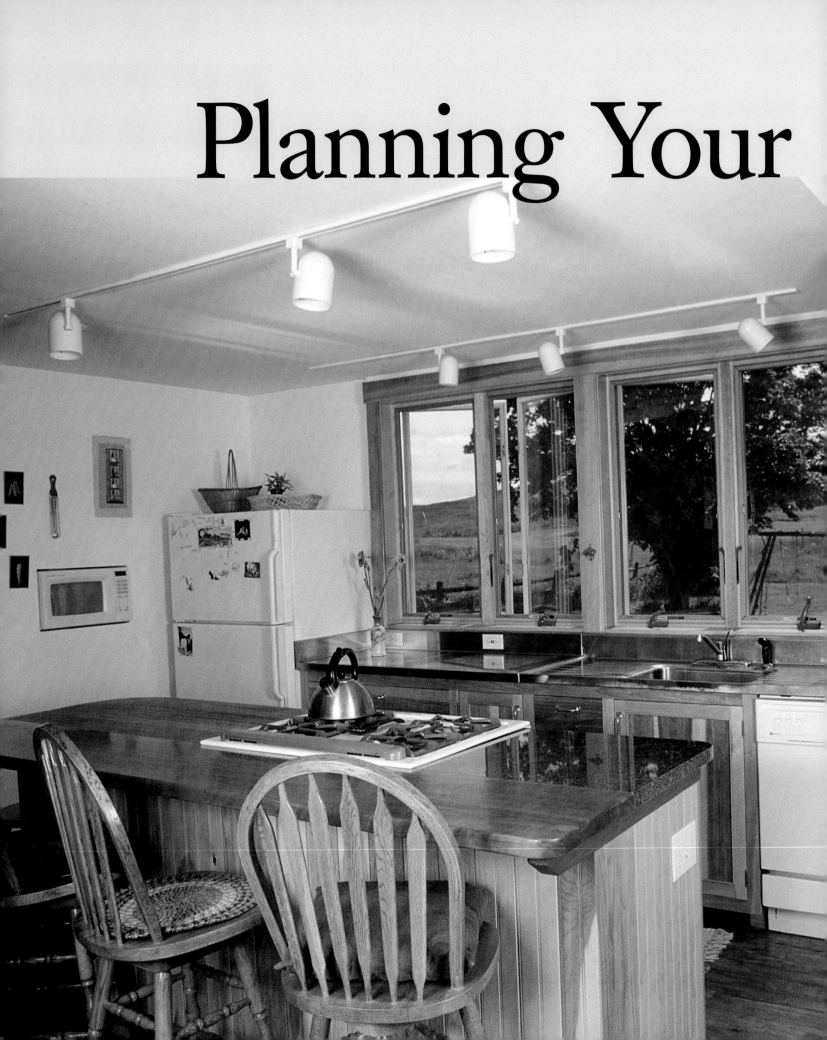

Planning Your

CHAPTER ONE
Kitchen

Sometimes a kitchen renovation is simple. When the existing layout works well, the project may concentrate on replacing cabinets, appliances, and finishes, making only minor adjustments to the layout. But when the existing kitchen doesn't reflect how the family lives today, a kitchen renovation provides an opportunity to make major changes.

This chapter begins with methods that professional designers use to understand their clients' needs, to define a project's goals, and to draw up floor plans that describe the existing conditions. Then the chapter introduces concepts central to all good design: circulation, light, orientation, relating the indoors to the outdoors, and principles of layout.

Kitchen layout is often oversimplified. As a result, some new kitchens aren't nearly as convenient and pleasant to work in as they could be. The methods presented here will help you to design a kitchen that not only looks great but also is a pleasure to use.

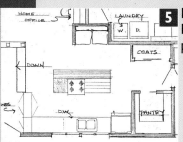

TRADE SECRET

Before starting any project, I make a drawing of the existing conditions, including the walls, windows, doors, existing cabinets, and many other details. This plan also encompasses all the areas that may be involved in the redesign, including the dining room and any entries, porches, or decks that are nearby. I also like to show the compass points, which will usually influence where windows and other features are located, and any important views.

Using the right tools makes drafting easier: triangles, tape, drafting pencils, erasers, drafting brush to sweep the erasure dust away, plastic templates, and an architect's scale. I use a parallel rule in place of the usual T-square.

Preliminary Design

In design, jumping to conclusions is a common and tempting trap. You've probably thought about your kitchen project for a long time, and you've seen some inspiring kitchens in friends' houses or in books or magazines. You know a lot about what you want in terms of layout, appliances, colors, and finishes. But sometimes the eagerness to move ahead can keep you from exploring other options that may prove far better. Professional designers use a variety of methods to elicit and sharpen the goals for a project, generate design concepts, and compare and evaluate alternative designs. Often it comes down simply to asking the right questions and giving yourself time to find your way to the best answers. Adapting the methods that designers use will help you develop a better overall plan for your kitchen. This is preliminary design.

When the details are carefully thought out, your kitchen can be a pleasure to use as well as a pleasure to see.

This kitchen was very dark, and the work areas were cramped and awkward. The counters felt too low, particularly at the sink. These kinds of problems are listed on the design program.

Your design program

Begin by creating a design program, which is simply a detailed list or statement of your goals and priorities for the project. Your program will sharpen your thinking and serve as a standard against which to measure the designs you develop.

Express these ideas in the form of goals to be reached or problems to be solved, not in the form of solutions. For example, rather than write "new commercial stove," your goal might more accurately be stated as, "ability to do effective wok cooking." Rather than simply writing "island layout," put down the goals you think an island layout might achieve, such as "see and chat with family and friends while cooking." That way, you won't jump to conclusions. You might find out that you can do wok cooking with one of the newer domestic stoves, saving the expense of the commercial model. You might find that a peninsula layout will meet your needs better than the island you initially envisioned.

I don't use any particular format or question-naire when making a program, though some kitchen books and magazines offer them. Develop your program in the format that works for you. Just remember to look at the problems you have with the current kitchen, the functional improvements you hope to make, the ways your family will use the space, and the larger architectural issues, such as circulation, natural light, views, and the way the kitchen space relates to the rest of the house. These larger issues can be keys to how successful your new design will be.

Include a budget that assesses the money you can comfortably spend. Also consider the amount of work you realistically can do yourself.

Also think about scheduling. A kitchen renovation often takes four to twelve weeks. If you do much of the work yourself, it can take far longer. That's a long time to eat pizza or to cook on a

The Design Program

This is the design program for the project featured in this chapter. The categories apply to most kitchens, though you should adapt or expand this format to your own situation and needs.

1. **Problems with existing kitchen**
   - Cabinets in bad shape; drawers don't work
   - Hard to access items in back of base cabinets
   - Cramped feeling at frequently used work centers
   - Poor task lighting
   - Poor storage for oversize plates and other large items
   - Awkward, unattractive entry to house
   - No room for two cooks
   - Counter too low for tall people, particularly at sink

2. **Functional improvements wanted**
   - More counters, in better relationship to appliances
   - Higher counters, if possible, particularly at sink
   - Improved storage for everything
   - Upgraded floor and wall finishes
   - Walk-in pantry, if feasible

3. **Activities to be included in kitchen**
   - Phone/message
   - Better visiting with guests/family
   - Home office
   - Recycling
   - Comfortable seating right in kitchen

4. **Dining and seating arrangements**
   - Simple way to eat in kitchen, if possible; tall stools for 4–5 people

5. **Architectural considerations and special features**
   - More light, better windows
   - Better relation to main part of house
   - Simple design
   - Close off hall to bathroom
   - Storage for sports gear

6. **Budget and scheduling**
   - Total cost: approximately $30,000
   - Client will do all painting/varnishing
   - Demolition to be done while family on vacation (January)

PRO TIP

To keep drawings neat, use your drafting brush to sweep erasure dust and other dirt off the drawing as you work.

IN DETAIL

Here's a list of drafting tools and supplies basic to designing a kitchen:

- Drafting table, work table, or a smooth piece of plywood about 30 in. by 42 in.
- Parallel ruler or long T-square
- Soft and hard pencils (I use 2H and 4H drafting pencils and ordinary #2½ pencils)
- Erasers
- Plastic drafting triangles: 45-degree, 30-60-90-degree, and adjustable
- Soft drafting brush for sweeping away erasure mess
- Masking tape for securing paper to board
- 11-in. by 17-in. or 18-in. by 24-in. vellum
- 18-in.-wide roll of white tracing paper for sketching ideas

camp stove. In consultation with your family, try to assess the best time to do the work in terms of weather, vacations, and school schedules. It may be possible to schedule vacation time so that you can either do more of the work yourself or (if you are hiring a builder) go away for part of the project.

When I'm designing for others, I rely not only on what they say about their kitchen needs but also on what I observe when I'm there. I might see something important that the family no longer notices: A tall person might stoop uncomfortably while doing dishes. People bump into each other as they work. The dishwashing routine is needlessly time consuming. I record these observations in my notes and address them in the design. I suggest you do the same for your own kitchen as you watch others use the space.

Making scale floor plans

The layout—or floor plan—is usually the heart of a design. If the plan is well thought out and elegant, the whole design will be; details will fall into place. If the layout is awkward, even high-end equipment or fancy fixtures won't make the kitchen work well.

The first step toward a great layout is to make (or find) a measured floor plan of existing conditions. Usually floor plans are drawn in a scale of ¼ in.=1 ft. If your space—or the part of it that might change—is relatively small, a scale of ½ in.=1 ft. will show details more clearly. The cabinet drawings later may be in ½ in.=1 ft. scale.

You can use graph paper for your kitchen plans, but if you choose this approach, be sure to get graph paper with 4 or 8 boxes per inch, rather than 10 boxes per inch, as is used in engi-

As is often the case, the kitchen (viewed from the southeast) renovation for this house involved redesigning the circulation to and through the kitchen. The original floor plan appears on the facing page.

Plan of Existing Conditions

A plan of the existing layout, in scale, shows basic features, including cabinetry, major furniture, doors, and windows. Also note window heights, ceiling heights, compass points, views, and other information that may influence your design.

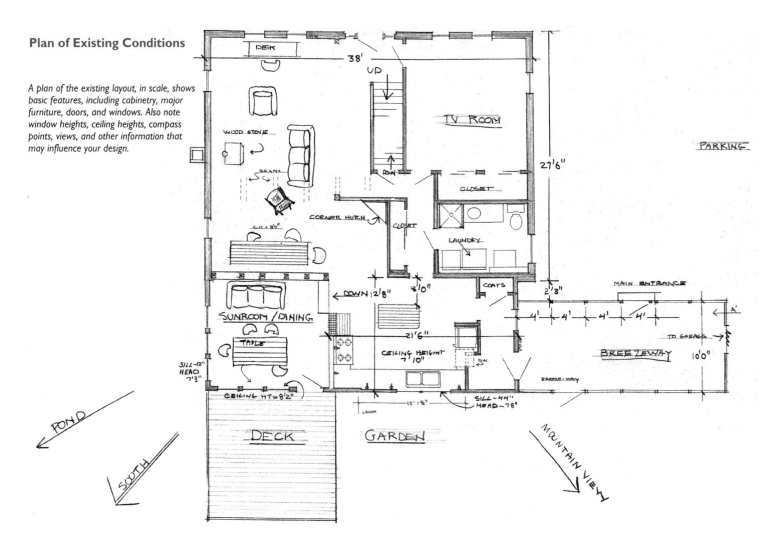

neering. While graph paper works okay, it doesn't handle small dimensions well or provide a convenient way to represent angles or curves.

I find it simplest to make these drawings on large pieces of drafting vellum (a heavy-duty tracing paper) using a drawing board fitted with traditional drafting tools. For larger-scale projects, such as the one shown here, 18 in. by 24 in. is a good size. You'll probably have to get this large size copied using the diazo (blueprint) process at an architectural supply company or architect's office. For most projects, use 11-in. by 17-in. vellum, which can easily be photocopied.

Vellum and ordinary tracing paper have one very important advantage: You can use them for tracing. This can save enormous amounts of drawing time, both during preliminary design

phases and later, when you will generate elevations (side views) from your floor plans.

The basic approach is to draw very lightly at first, with a fine pencil such as a drafting 2H or 4H. I usually don't include all the dimensions; since the drawing is large and in scale, the dimensions are implicit. If I know a dimension to be particularly critical, I'll add it. At each window, I write in the height from the floor to the bottom of the window (the sill) and to the top (the head). At this stage, I ignore the trim.

I try to draw to the nearest ½ in., as it is difficult to get much more accurate. As the plan takes shape, I use a blacker pencil (such as a 2B) to darken the lines representing the walls, and shade in between them to make the drawing easier to read. All the lines need to be dark enough to read

PRO TIP

Brainstorm layout possibilities with family members and friends, who may have good new ideas.

TRADE SECRET

Even if you use graph paper, an architect's scale will become one of your handiest and most indispensable drafting tools. It allows you to measure or draw dimensions in all of the common scales, such as ¼ in. = 1 ft. It's tricky to use at first be-cause the inches are indicated separately at the end, and each edge contains two separate scales. Don't buy an engineer's scale; it has the wrong scales for kitchen design.

An architect's scale allows you to draw dimensions in the proper scale.

Computer-Generated Kitchen Plan

clearly. Otherwise, they will be impossible to duplicate. Be sure to show cabinets, tables, appliances, and other features in scale. (Use the templates on p. 199.) You can also buy useful Plastic templates at drafting-supply houses or art-supply stores.

It's becoming increasingly popular to make kitchen drawings on your computer using computer-assisted design programs (CAD). If you enjoy computer work or want to avoid hand drafting, this may work well for you. These menu-driven programs are powerful and rela-tively easy to learn, but they also impose some limits on your design. See p. 58 for further discussion of CAD.

Develop alternative layouts

Designers make a practice of developing several options—sometimes many options—even when the solution appears obvious. At first, these alter-native designs are quick freehand sketches made by placing tracing paper over the plan of existing conditions (even if your "existing conditions" is a CAD drawing).

The big problem with the house shown in the drawing on p. 11 was the corkscrew entry hall, which used up a lot of valuable space. All of the alternative layouts shown on the facing page addressed this issue:

- Plan A is a U-shaped kitchen opposite the existing work area with a table under the window.
- Plan B moves the entry door, so people can walk straight into the kitchen. The corkscrew hallway becomes a narrow pantry. The island is moved closer to the windows to make the existing 3-ft. passageway less cramped. The entry door in the breezeway is moved closer to the kitchen.
- Plan C is a variation on Plan B. The refrigerator is positioned on the exterior wall, which allows the pantry to get bigger. That pushes the stove out into the island. A window seat along the passageway provides a place for people to chat with the cook or read the paper.

This is only paper. Don't be afraid to try out some radical ideas, showing massive changes or ideas that seem improbable or impossible at first.

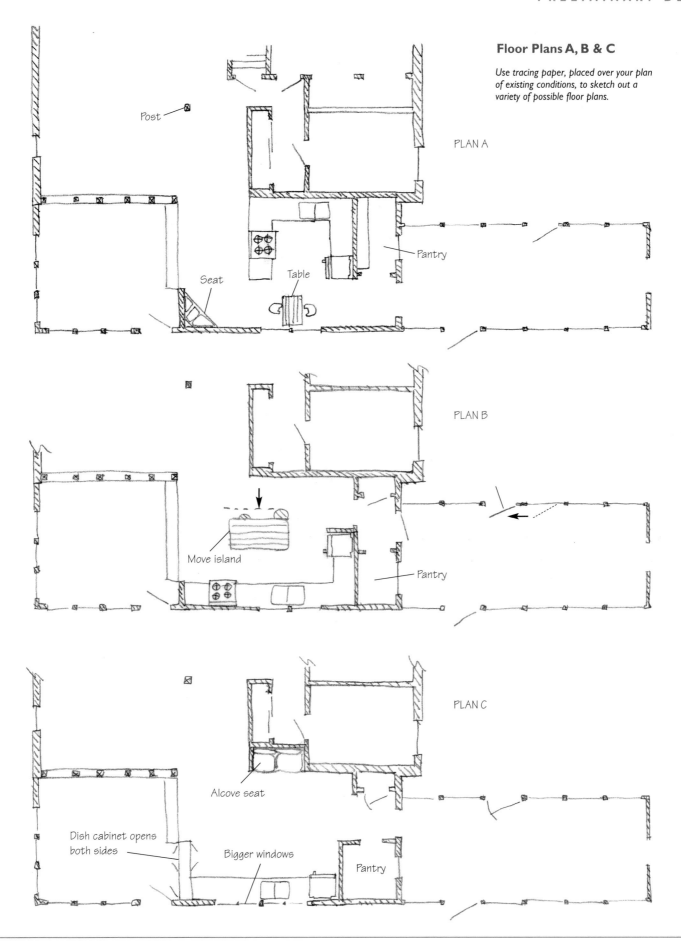

Floor Plans A, B & C

Use tracing paper, placed over your plan of existing conditions, to sketch out a variety of possible floor plans.

PLAN A

Post

Pantry

Seat

Table

PLAN B

Move island

Pantry

PLAN C

Alcove seat

Dish cabinet opens both sides

Bigger windows

Pantry

PRO TIP

Lever handles are much more convenient than round knobs; when carrying groceries in, you can open the door with your arm or elbow.

IN DETAIL

Here are planning guidelines for doors:

- Carefully study which way each door swings.
- Exterior doors come both in-swing or out-swing; usually people choose in-swing to leave room for a screen or storm door.
- Exterior doors are usually 36 in. wide; 32 in. is a minimum.
- Interior doors should be at least 30 in. wide; 32 in. is even better.
- 36-in. doors are standard for accessible or universal design.
- Consider some glazing for every entry door.
- Insulated steel entry doors are usually the best value for the money.
- Sliding and bifold doors work well for closets.
- Pocket doors can work where door swings will create a problem.

Always develop more than one schematic layout. On this project several options were developed. Plan C (p. 13), almost an afterthought, proved the best.

I've worked on many projects where we actually moved the kitchen into a different space. In the example here we looked at two such solutions (see the drawing on the facing page). In one, the work area moves toward the door; in the other, it moves down into the sunroom. The sunroom idea didn't make much sense, but the other version had some nice features. Even if you reject these concepts right away, you may get some ideas you can use in the design you do pick. And you may find a great solution that you wouldn't otherwise have considered.

These alternative layouts are schematic studies. Post them on the wall, think about them over time, and write responses right on the drawings. Often a few days or even weeks of casual study leads to insights a quick or concentrated review will not yield. Friends or visitors may have insightful observations, too.

A built-in seat makes the passage through the kitchen more interesting and provides a place to sit and visit with the cook. Interior windows above let light into the hallway behind.

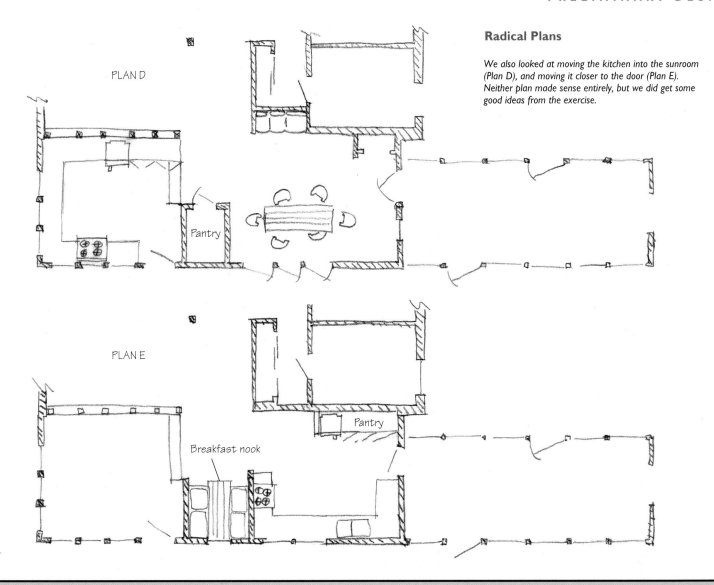

PLAN D

Pantry

Radical Plans

We also looked at moving the kitchen into the sunroom (Plan D), and moving it closer to the door (Plan E). Neither plan made sense entirely, but we did get some good ideas from the exercise.

PLAN E

Breakfast nook

Pantry

Planning Guidelines for Windows

- Above countertops, casements are easier to operate than double-hung windows.
- Consider lines of sight both seated and standing.
- Don't make the windows too small—taller is usually better; a bit wider can seem a lot wider.
- South-facing glazing is good, but don't overdo it.
- For economy, consider wood-tilt double-hung windows.
- There may be good single units available at considerable savings at your home center's "bargain" area.
- If you reuse a window, make sure it's in good shape and double glazed.
- If you're buying new windows, remember that you get what you pay for.

Casement windows above counters are easier to operate; with careful layout, they can come right down to the backsplash.

PRO TIP

If possible, keep house-hold traffic separate from the kitchen work area. If not, the passageway should be at least 5 ft. wide.

IN DETAIL

In passive-solar design, fairly large windows face south for solar gain. Sometimes the kitchen will be placed in the east corner for morning sun. If the dining room is placed toward the west, people can watch the sun set over dinner. In renovation you have fewer choices than in new work, but being aware of where the sun is at different times of day is still important. A diagrammatic "light plan" that is similar to a circulation plan will help you get a handle on light, lines of sight, views, and solar orientation (see p. 19).

Guidelines for Effective Layout

Next, review your schematic plans with reference to your program, and then begin a series of revisions. As you refine your design or designs, you'll be making progressively more careful and more detailed drawings. Let's look at the basic design principles that should guide these refinements. Most designers apply these concepts to any design problem, not just kitchens.

Circulation patterns

Circulation refers to the pathways in a design. These include halls, walkways through rooms, staircases, entries, and the corresponding paths outdoors that connect to them. The circulation plan is the skeleton of the layout, the structure that makes your design work. A good circulation plan will be relatively simple and compact. It will have a logic that reflects how you want to live and will help organize the space to meet your needs. It will connect spaces that should be linked, and separate those that should be separate. At best, the circulation spaces themselves,

Weiler House Plan

Here's an example of a good circulation plan. At one end of this house is the master bedroom and bath, a separate, quiet, private zone, with its own small hidden deck. At the opposite end is a wing for guests, including grandchildren. The common area and kitchen are in the middle, along with a big deck. This is the meeting ground. The path to the master bedroom skirts the living room, and is separated from it by a simple bookcase.

such as hallways and foyers, will also be as thoughtfully developed and as beautiful as the rooms they link.

The house shown in the drawing on p. 11 is a good example. Among the problems in the existing plan:

- Entering is awkward and circuitous.
- The entry hall itself is cramped and dark and is a catchall. It wastes a lot of space.
- The path through the breezeway is long and cuts the space in half, making it less useful than it could be.
- The bathroom seems too close to the kitchen.
- The stools at the island obstruct the walkway into the main part of the house.

A major consideration of the redesign, as resolved in Plan C, was to correct these problems. Switching the position of the entry door and a window in the wall between breezeway and house, a relatively economical alteration, changes everything. It creates a place for a pantry.

Bubble Diagrams

Sometimes designers use "bubble diagrams" to explore how activities can be grouped. It's a particularly useful way to think more loosely, with fewer preconceptions, about how your remodeled spaces should be organized.

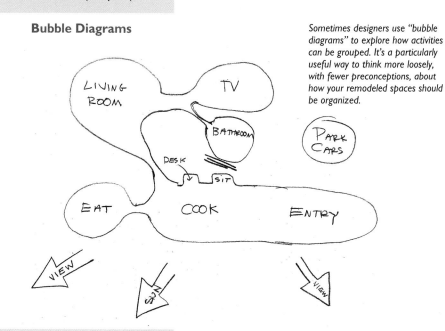

Before

After

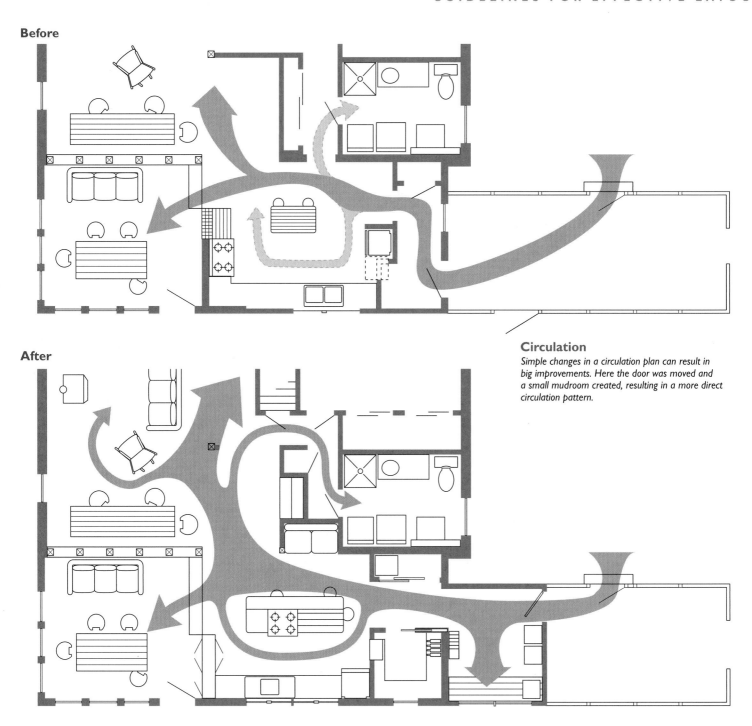

Circulation

Simple changes in a circulation plan can result in big improvements. Here the door was moved and a small mudroom created, resulting in a more direct circulation pattern.

You can walk straight into the kitchen now. Moving the main entrance shortens the path through the breezeway, making access to the kitchen even more direct. It also makes the breezeway more useful for bike repair, storage, and other family uses. Reconfiguring the kitchen island increases the width of the walkway through the kitchen, leaving more space for the stools. And blocking the path to the bathroom provides room for a built-in seat, which makes the circulation space more interesting and accommodating. These are small changes, but they completely transform the kitchen and make the whole house work better.

PRO TIP

Provide for alternative activities in the layout, and they won't disrupt the cook or clutter up the counters.

IN DETAIL

Here are some activities that might be included in your kitchen plan:

- Big meals
- Small meals
- Kid's play area
- Home office/sorting mail/paying bills
- Comfortable seating, couch, built-in seats
- Greenhouse/plant area
- TV/music/computer
- Homework or project area
- Laundry or sewing area
- Recycling
- Phone/message area
- Hobbies or sports activities

Light and orientation

Good natural light is often the difference between an okay design and a great one. There are many devices to get the most out of the daylight available. Most obvious are windows, glazed doors, skylights, and dormers. Light-colored paint, half-walls, interior windows, and even well-placed mirrors can also put daylight where you want it. I spend a lot of time observing where the light is, finding windows that are just the right size and type, and locating them in just the right place.

People designing new houses often orient the house toward the south, to maximize potential sunlight and solar gain. The east windows bring in morning sun, and the west face the sunset. In a renovation, observe the sun patterns, and let more of that south, east, and west light in. Of course, in hot climates one might locate windows so as to limit solar gain, especially from western (afternoon) exposure.

Lines of sight are important. I want a couple of places in the house where I can see from one end to the other and out to a view. I want to avoid dark dead ends or turns in hallways. I try to put a window in such places, or if not that, a transom light, a mirror, or even a nice painting of a window. Small changes like these make the house seem bigger, more friendly, and bright in the broadest sense.

The existing house had plenty of potential sun, but kitchen windows were small. The corkscrew entry was very dark. Potential views were blocked. We widened the windows over the sink counter and added windows in the new pantry. We installed a new fully glazed entry door. Although functionally unnecessary, this extra glass helped the feeling of the space greatly. Internal windows behind the built-in seat let a hint of daylight into the hall by the bathroom. We made the cabinets themselves light in color.

A small dormer lets in south light and expands the space.

Added together, these relatively simple changes infused the whole area with light. The difference in light penetration is shown before and after in yellow in the top drawing on the facing page. There are fewer dark areas (dark green).

These changes increased the "lines of sight" in the space (shown in green). In the before version, you can see to the pond, garden, and mountain from several places. In the revised plan, you can see out everywhere. Even the pantry has a view of Spruce Mountain. This makes the whole house seem larger and happier.

The vertical dimension of a window is just as important as its location on the plan. Many houses have windows that may be too low at the top to let the sun in, or too high at the bottom to see the garden or lower views. Make sure the windows provide sunlight and lines of site appropriate to their locations.

Light Plan

Before

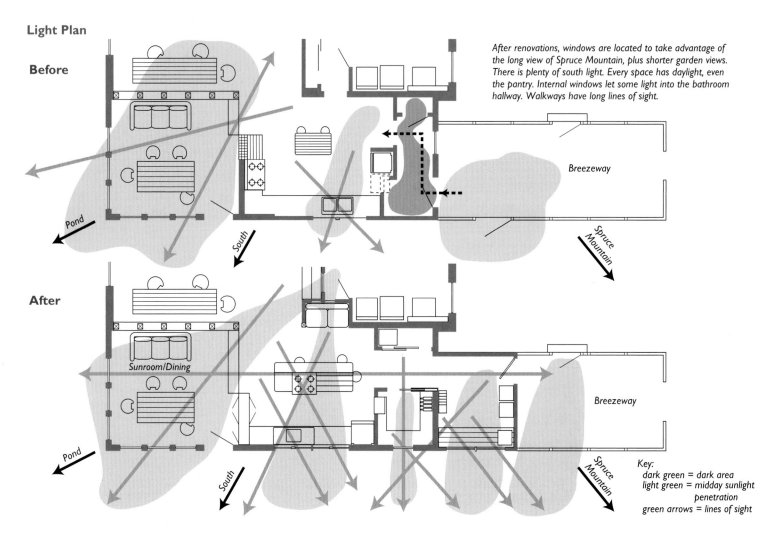

After renovations, windows are located to take advantage of the long view of Spruce Mountain, plus shorter garden views. There is plenty of south light. Every space has daylight, even the pantry. Internal windows let some light into the bathroom hallway. Walkways have long lines of sight.

Breezeway

Pond

South

Spruce Mountain

After

Sunroom/Dining

Pond

South

Breezeway

Spruce Mountain

Key:
dark green = dark area
light green = midday sunlight penetration
green arrows = lines of sight

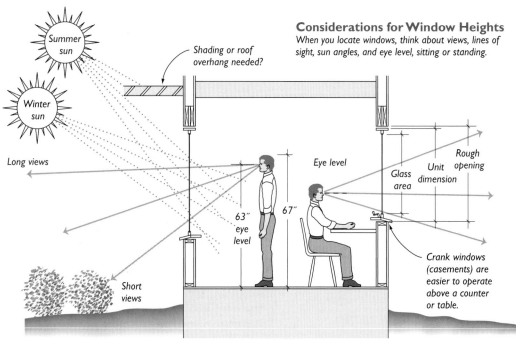

Summer sun

Winter sun

Shading or roof overhang needed?

Considerations for Window Heights
When you locate windows, think about views, lines of sight, sun angles, and eye level, sitting or standing.

Long views

Eye level

Rough opening

Glass area

Unit dimension

63″ eye level

67″

Short views

Crank windows (casements) are easier to operate above a counter or table.

19

PRO TIP

Provide a small shelf or bench outside by the door to put things on as you find your keys and open the door.

IN DETAIL

The entrance to the kitchen, as well as being convenient, should provide a graceful transition from the busy world outside to a more tranquil, private world indoors. A garden path, some flowers, a gateway, or a little deck can make coming into the house an aesthetic experience. A convenient seat can provide a place to collect your thoughts, perhaps while contemplating a small garden view, before entering.

This idea, "entrance transition," is an example of ideas from *A Pattern Language* by Christopher Alexander, et al. For more, see Resources on p.196.

When possible, design both the inside and the outside spaces. Easily accessible "outdoor rooms" can extend the use of your home and property. Photos by Rick Mastelli

Indoor/outdoors

Often, the best renovations find ways to integrate the outdoors into the design. Windows and doors, decks and porches, patios, pathways, arbors, fences, and even window boxes create a physical link between life inside and life outside.

It helps to think of the floor plan and circulation plan as encompassing both inside and outside spaces. Pathways inside extend out onto porches and garden paths. For example, in one of my recent projects, two decks, a little entry, an arbor, and the pathways up to the house were planned at the same time as the house. Each deck serves to extend the interior space that accesses it and creates a transition to the outside. Along with the arbor, they create "outdoor rooms" that expand the life of the house and integrate it with the land around it (see the top drawing p. 16). (For more information, see Resources on p.196)

Your way of living

The kitchen is for cooking, but almost any other family activity can also happen there or in adjacent spaces. My own kitchen has a couch and a nice easy chair right next to the workspace. I have a friend whose office is right off the kitchen. In my family's house at the lake, long ago, we had a daybed in the kitchen, and it was a great place to read or sleep.

A kitchen office: Many different activities can find a home in your kitchen.

Your Kitchen Plan: Five Layout Tools

As you begin to make more detailed plans from your preliminary sketches, you want to be sure you will be making a highly functional kitchen, one that will be pleasant, efficient, and physically comfortable to work in. Finding good-quality and appropriate cabinets, appliances, doors, and other items is important. But putting them in just the right configuration, with just the right dimensions, is even more crucial. Kitchen researchers and designers, beginning in the 1920s, developed some useful concepts for making these choices. Here are some of the ideas that I have found most useful.

1. The "work center" concept

Perhaps the most important of these concepts is that of the work center, which goes back to the early days of industrial engineering and the work of Frank Gilbreth. The basic idea is that any work station—whether a carpenter's bench or a kitchen work area—should be set up to accommodate the specific details of the work to be performed. Work surfaces should be placed at the correct height and made of the most appropriate materials. Tools and supplies that go with the work should be handy but not in the way. And the best and most convenient storage locations should be allocated to the tools and supplies used most frequently.

Early kitchen researchers defined three primary kitchen work centers reflecting three different sorts of kitchen work: cleanup, mixing, and cooking. The cleanup center includes the sink, a place to stack dirty dishes, probably a place for a drainboard, cleaning supplies, and often storage for everyday dishes. Today, the cleanup center would usually include a dishwasher. A trash can is essential, and the countertop should be waterproof or water-resistant. A cleanup center may

also be a place for good preliminary recycling. The mix center (or food-preparation center) should be organized around the premier work counter, with easy access to favorite knives, utensils, bowls, and small appliances, as well as to the most frequently used supplies, such as oil, salt, flour, and such. Sometimes butcher block is used here, though many people prefer movable chopping boards. The cooking center includes the stove, another counter, a heatproof place to set down hot dishes, and tools and supplies used primarily at the stove, such as pots, pans, lids, spatulas, pot holders, and perhaps spices.

Today we cook very differently than early researchers did, but these three basic and relatively distinct work areas are still helpful design building blocks. Many designers rightly add a fourth function, the serving center, which is often near the table. It has a place to set hot pans, and it houses serving dishes, perhaps the good tableware, and napkins. Many cooks also define other centers for inclusion, particularly a baking center. A message center might be as simple as a wall phone with a pad of paper, but

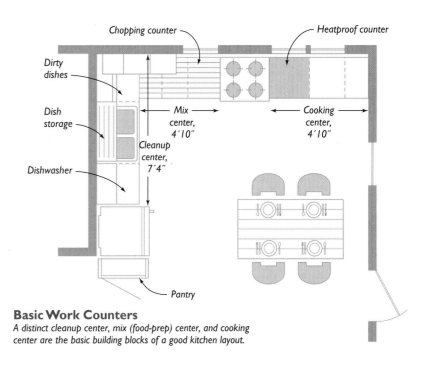

Basic Work Counters
A distinct cleanup center, mix (food-prep) center, and cooking center are the basic building blocks of a good kitchen layout.

IN DETAIL

In a tight space, inches matter. A 30-in.-wide mix-center counter feels much bigger than a 27-in. one, and a 33-in. one feels positively huge. If passageways are narrow, recessing the refrigerator 3 in. can make a big difference. Taking pains over small dimensions will definitely pay off.

WHAT CAN GO WRONG

Often a tight kitchen layout will work perfectly for most meals but show its limitations when cooking an elaborate meal for a big group. If so, sometimes a drop-leaf or a rolling cart can be mobilized for more work area, or the kitchen table can become a temporary workplace.

A kitchen can have a simple phone and message area.

it could be large enough to include a desk with a computer for doing homework and paying bills. Your kitchen might be large enough to include a recycling center, where newspaper, bottles, and other recyclables can be organized on their way out of the house. As I survey and evaluate any kitchen layout, locating the basic work centers on the plan, I have a specific range of dimensions in mind.

Cleanup center: I often start with the cleanup center. It has, of course, a sink, usually (but not always) 25 in. or 33 in. wide. There is at least a 2-ft.-wide counter on one side for dirty dishes, and a similar 20-in. or wider counter on the other side for a drainboard. A dishwasher is 24 in. wide; in most new kitchens, a space for it will be needed beneath one of these side counters.

Mix center: For some very tidy cooks, this food-prep center can be as little as 30 in. wide but more often is 36 in. to 60 in. wide. It should be handy to both sink and stove. It might be an island, but it's often a counter between cleanup

and cooking. It can't be the same as the counters at the sink, which are routinely covered with dishes, nor any other counter that's occupied by a microwave, big mixer, or other gear.

Cooking center: Most stoves are 30 in. wide, though some commercial models are 36 in. or more. If a hood is desired, it's helpful (though not essential) to have the stove on or near an outside wall. The cooking center should have its own counter. This counter should be at least two feet wide, preferably more. It is often the place where a second cook can work.

Don't position the side of a stove right up against a wall. The heat from the burners can burn the wall. Also, avoid a location adjacent to a hallway or walking space, where kids or others walking by might accidentally knock over a hot pan. If the stove is in an island or a peninsula, make sure it is protected at the rear, either with a raised back or by a counter at least 9 in. wide.

The refrigerator: Although the refrigerator is sometimes included with one or another work center, it makes more sense to think of it as a separate element. A refrigerator is big and bulky, so it doesn't work well in the middle of a run of cabinets. It's usually placed at the end of a run, sometimes in combination with a tall pantry unit of some kind (see the drawing on p. 21). It's important to have some counter space nearby to place shopping bags on for loading the fridge.

If I can include all of these essential elements on my plan, I know a good layout will be possible.

2. The food-flow idea

When possible, it's good to locate the work centers in the right sequence, based on the way food is processed. To oversimplify, food comes in the back door, gets stored in a pantry or the fridge, gets taken out again, is washed up at the sink, chopped up at the mix center, cooked, then served. If the work centers are more or less in that order, kitchen work will be easier, with fewer wasted steps.

3. Standard kitchen layouts

Most of us are familiar with the standard kitchen layouts that have evolved: the U, L, galley, one-wall, island, and peninsula. The peninsula, I suppose, is simply any layout without a wall behind some of the cabinets, while both the peninsula and island schemes can be thought of as variations on the U-layout. Although there are endless variations and elaborations, most kitchens fall into one of these models.

U-layouts make a lot of sense. They concentrate a complete work area in a compact space, with little through traffic. The peninsula and island versions allow for sociability, and they often connect the workspace to the dining or family space nearby. The L-layout is simple, handy, and efficient. It's also compact in a special sense. Where the U-layout requires a distinct space of its own, an L-shaped kitchen can be simply the edge of a larger space. For that reason a small space often calls for an L-layout. The galley layout is quite efficient if the aisle is 3 ft. to 5 ft. wide. The disadvantage is that the aisle is usually a traffic lane, which can disrupt the cook. The one-wall layout is not ideal; it results in a lot of walking and would be used where a better option is impossible.

4. The work-triangle test

The work triangle, devised in the early 1950s as a test for kitchen layouts in government-financed housing, specifies an optimal relationship between the sink, stove, and refrigerator. The idea is that if these are too far apart, there will be needless extra steps while cooking. If they are too close together, work centers will overlap, and you'll have to constantly walk around the appliances to get to your work area.

The Food-Flow Idea

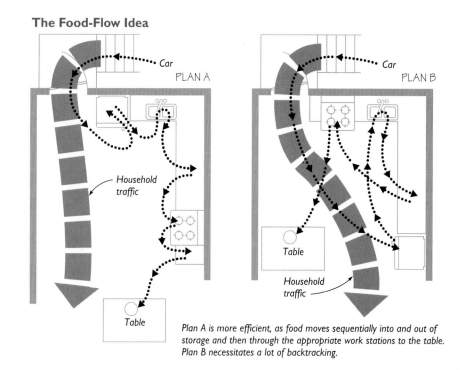

Plan A is more efficient, as food moves sequentially into and out of storage and then through the appropriate work stations to the table. Plan B necessitates a lot of backtracking.

Standard Kitchen Layouts

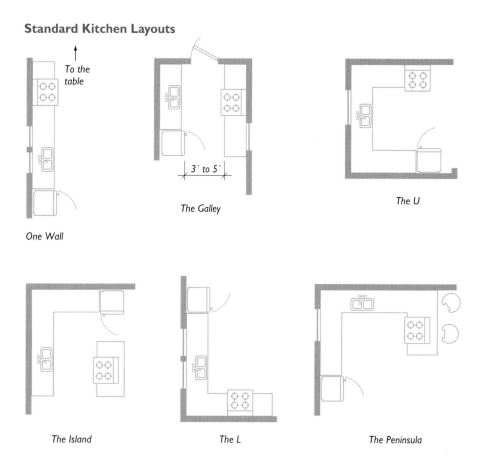

23

IN DETAIL

Sometimes storage can be recessed into walls. For example, a pantry can be as little as 5 in. to 7 in. deep. A pantry this size can be buried in the wall. I have often recessed refrigerators, shelf units, and microwaves into walls to save space.

Recessing the microwave saves counter space.

5. The power-kitchen idea

In kitchen remodeling, it's sometimes impossible to devise a perfect layout. This has been true of many of the houses I've lived in and fixed up. But there is another insight from kitchen research that I've found useful. Most of the little journeys in cooking are from the sink to the mix center and back, from the stove to the mix center and back, or between the sink and stove. There are significantly fewer trips to the fridge, table, pantry, or back door. That means that if you can establish a mix center or main work counter that is within about two or three steps of both sink and stove, and maybe even directly between them, the kitchen can be efficient, even if other features of the layout are less than ideal.

Put another way, you can live with having the fridge, pantry, or table a short walk away, or having the basic units out of the ideal "food-flow" order. But if the main work counter is a hike from the sink or stove, or if those appliances are too widely spaced, your kitchen will be inconvenient to use no matter what else you do.

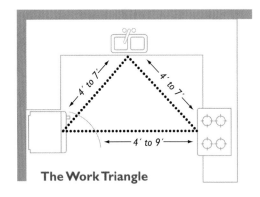

The Work Triangle

Design Devices for Tight Layouts

Many houses don't have space for a large kitchen. A carefully designed compact kitchen can work just as well as a large kitchen and even has a couple of advantages. Besides being less expensive to build, it may be easier to work in because there are fewer steps to take. Beyond the five basic layout tools, there are several ways to make a tight layout work.

First, combine the kitchen with dining and living areas to make one large space, with a single eating area. A small work area, a modest dining area, and a decent sitting area taken together can make for an ample, gracious room.

Consider an L-layout, which saves space in two ways. First, it's not a separate rectangle or square of floor space but just a 2-ft. margin along the wall. Second, it can share circulation space with an adjacent table or walkway. If you use an

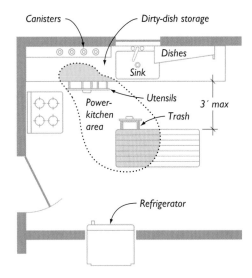

Power-Kitchen

An imperfect layout can work as long as there is a nice generous counter space handy to both sink and cooktop. Here there is no counter space at the stove, the left sink counter is cramped, and the refrigerator is too far from the food prep-area. But the main food prep counter—the power-kitchen area—is big enough, is very handy to both sink and stove, and has supplies, tools, and a trash can near at hand. So it is still quite an efficient kitchen to work in.

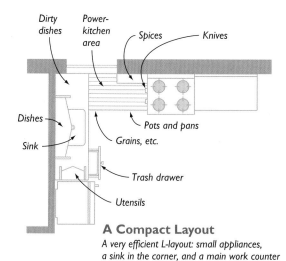

A Compact Layout
*A very efficient L-layout: small appliances,
a sink in the corner, and a main work counter
a half-step to both the sink and stove.*

An L-layout is often the most space efficient. Here the table is about 6 ft. from the counters, which is plenty of room.

L-layout, the sink should probably go at the corner. That way the dirty-dish part of the cleanup center can be the inside corner, saving more accessible counters for better uses.

Another option is to use slightly smaller appliances. Companies such as Franke® (800-423-5247, www.irc.parts.com) make standard 25-in. single-bowl sinks with huge basins that I've used in many tight layouts. Use a 24-in., 27-in., or 30-in. refrigerator instead of the popular 32-in. to 36-in. sizes. Stoves and cooktops are also available smaller than the standard 30-in. size. If you have a microwave, it should be small. In fact, for a small kitchen, everything that can be small should be, and seldom-used items should be eliminated or stored elsewhere.

Clean lines, light colors, good light, and simple detailing also will help a small kitchen seem bigger and make it look better as part of a large public space.

Dining Area Guidelines

Experiment in your drawings with different sizes and shapes of dining tables to find the most comfortable, spacious, and appealing scheme. Draw the tables and chairs right on your floor plans. Use the templates (see p. 199) for round and rectangular tables and cut these out to place on your drawings, or trace the shapes onto the drawings as you experiment. Remember to leave room to pull the chairs back. I like to leave a 3-ft. margin around a table for this.

Since tables, chairs, people, and the meals they prepare vary so much, it's best to mock up the shape you are considering. If you have the table in question, set it with chairs in position. If you don't have the table, mark a similar area on the floor, and set that as you would a table. It's possible to set plates as close as 22 in. (from the center of one plate to the center of the next), but 24 in. or 26 in. is much more comfortable, and for everyday family use, 30 in. is gracious.

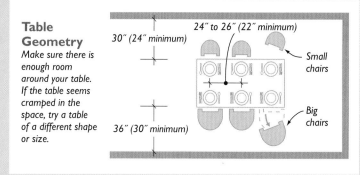

Table Geometry
Make sure there is enough room around your table. If the table seems cramped in the space, try a table of a different shape or size.

30" (24" minimum)

24" to 26" (22" minimum)

Small chairs

36" (30" minimum)

Big chairs

PRO TIP

Sometimes minor layout adjustments can eliminate the need for costly changes in plumbing or heating location.

IN DETAIL

A bar-stool arrangement can be great for snacks or informal meals. Be sure to leave knee room, as well as room enough for table settings. A breakfast nook saves space by doing without the space usually allotted to back up the chair and walk to it. Instead, people slide in from the end. If possible, mock up booths and stool setups to make sure they will be comfortable for you.

Geometry of Stools

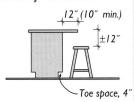

12" (10" min.)

±12"

Toe space, 4"

Stools require adequate knee space. Whatever the counter height, stools should be about 12" less in height.

Geometry of Booths

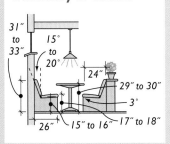

31" to 33"

15° to 20°

24"

29" to 30"

3°

26"

15° to 16"

17" to 18"

Reviewing Your Floor Plan

You now have one or preferably more than one viable schematic plan. Your next step is to evaluate or "review" your schematic floor plans, find the one that seems best, and then draw it more accurately, improving and fine-tuning it along the way.

In our example (see the drawings on pp. 13 and 15), schematic Plan A seems congested: There isn't a lot of counter space, and the pantry is very narrow. Plan D has some nice features—like the breakfast nook—though the traffic cuts through the work area. Plan E is a nonstarter: It's too radical for too little improvement (if any). Plan B seemed workable, but the counter space and the seating at the island are tight.

Plan C tucks the fridge onto the outside wall and puts the stove in a greatly enlarged island. The result seems much more spacious and open.

Accessible Layout and Universal Design

The idea of "universal design" is that houses should be designed so that anyone can inhabit, visit, and use them conveniently, whatever their physical abilities. In renovation, it's often not practical or necessary to achieve this standard, but I try to incorporate as many accessible features into all my designs as possible. This does mean thinking about the needs of wheelchair users and others with major disabilities. But universal design also recognizes that people vary greatly in height, reach ranges, arm and hand strength, range of motion, energy, vision, hearing, and other characteristics, and that every person's abilities change with age.

If we design with the variety of human capacities in mind, we can make our homes comfortably usable by almost everyone without significant added cost. It turns out that many of the features recommended for universal design also make a home or kitchen more convenient for all users.

Examples include wide hallways and doors, drawers with full-extension hardware, big D-shaped pulls on drawers and doors, and appliance knobs that are easy to see and grab. Dimensions are important, too. If overhead cabinets are positioned a little lower than standard, and counters are tailored to the height of their users, a kitchen can be much more comfortable to use.

The drawing below shows some of the layout characteristics commonly found in universal or accessible design. Some of the details are included in later chapters.

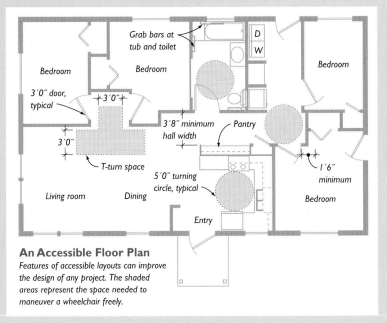

Grab bars at tub and toilet

Bedroom

Bedroom

Bedroom

D

W

3'0" door, typical

3'0"

3'8" minimum hall width

Pantry

T-turn space

3'0"

5'0" turning circle, typical

1'6" minimum

Bedroom

Living room

Dining

Entry

An Accessible Floor Plan
Features of accessible layouts can improve the design of any project. The shaded areas represent the space needed to maneuver a wheelchair freely.

Plan C-2

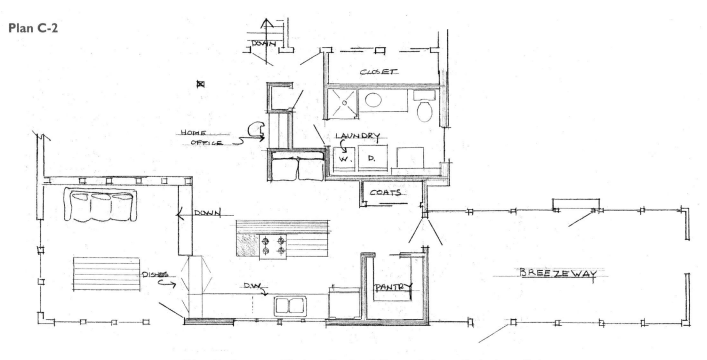

This revision is more carefully drawn. The closet is bigger, and a home office has been added.

There is more seating at the island. The pantry is much bigger; it would be easier to move around inside it. The seating alcove adds a really nice place to sit and read the paper. The dish storage, accessible from both sides, is convenient to the dining space in the sunroom and also to the everyday eating spot on the island. After extensive discussion, Plan C seemed the most attractive.

But several goals of the program remained to be addressed. There is no home office. The coat closet is small, and no provision is made for the family's massive collection of skis, bike helmets, boots, and other sports gear.

Also review the circulation and light of your plan. Here, the main pathway through the kitchen is much improved, but the tangle of swinging doors at the entry could be a constant irritation. Two areas become very dark: the new pantry and the closed-off hallway by the bathroom.

With this analysis in mind, I made revision C-2. This version enlarged the coat closet and tucked a home-office area right next to the kitchen. To reduce the door confusion, the closet

gets a pair of sliding doors, and the pantry gets a pocket door.

We're now passing beyond the sketching stage. C-2 is a more carefully drawn, accurate, ruled pencil drawing that will eventually become the "final" floor plan. It's drawn in pencil, though, because there will be many further revisions before we're done.

It always makes sense give yourself time to ponder and consider the design. Make copies and post them on the wall. As you walk by, note your comments right on the copies. Show them to friends—who often have great suggestions. If you have a friend who is a designer, he or she will have good ideas.

The entry is a crucial element in any design. It should be graceful, pleasant, and convenient. Although Plan C-2 improved things a lot, the entry was still awkward and abrupt. The breeze-way was a long, narrow catchall. There was no place to take off boots.

Our solution (Plan C-3, shown in the top drawing on the facing page) was to turn about

IN DETAIL

The size of the chairs you use can make a big difference in a small dining area. We used to have nice big Windsor dining chairs, but they jammed the space when we had guests and crowded the room generally. Now we use some smaller old pine chairs, and it's surprising how much more room there is.

8 ft. of the breezeway into a heated entry, known in New England as a mudroom. This would provide added storage and a place to take off winter gear. It would be a pleasant space, too, with big windows and a view. The windows to be taken out of the kitchen would fit perfectly. Since the mudroom would be heated, the entry door from Plan C-2 could be eliminated altogether, making the whole space more open, with even longer lines of sight. At the same time, we added a window to the pantry, and the wall to the left of the seating alcove was opened up.

The next step is to confirm that your layout will function well. Later, every detail of the work areas will be studied and finessed, but for now review the overall scheme with reference to the layout tools mentioned above.

Make sure that your layout is well organized for the three basic work centers: cleanup center, mix center (primary food prep), and cooking center. We could see that Plan C-3 had an obvious problem with its "cleanup center". With the sink down by the refrigerator, and the dish storage way down at the other end by the sunroom/dining space, the cleanup center was effectively divided in half. Clearing the table, putting dishes away, and other tasks would be awkward, involving a lot of extra steps. So right away we pushed the sink down toward the left, to create Plan C-4. Here the cleanup center is distinct and compact, including the sink, dishwasher, a place for dirty dishes, and dish storage directly convenient to the dining space. The counter on the other side of the sink becomes a huge 5-ft.-plus mix center/food-prep area. The counter to the right of the stove becomes the cooking center and secondary food-prep area. The counter to the left of the stove—with a heatproof top—becomes a serving center.

The food-flow criterion—an important one, I think—works well. You bring in the food, place it on the island, and both the fridge and pantry can be easily loaded up. The mix center comes next, handy to sink and stove. Cooking comes next. Then the serving center provides a handy place to put hot dishes, adjacent to the dining space in the sunroom and also the eating counter on the island itself. Setting and clearing the table also involve a minimum of steps.

Using the work-triangle criterion, the sink/stove combination and the stove/refrigerator combination are just barely close enough. But I wouldn't rule out a layout that didn't conform to

Passageway Widths

Passageways	Min.	Opt.	Max.
Front door	32"	36"	
Entry to kitchen	36"	40"+	
Kitchen to dining	36"	40"+	
Between cab. rows	36"	40"–60"	72"
Cab. row to island	30"	36"–48"	60"
Halls	36"	40"+	

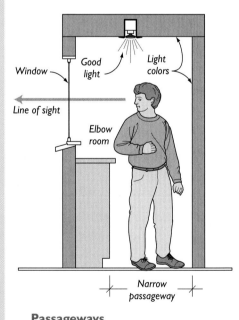

Passageways
When a passageway must be narrow, extra width at eye level, windows, lines of sight, and windows will make the passage seem more spacious.

Plan C-3

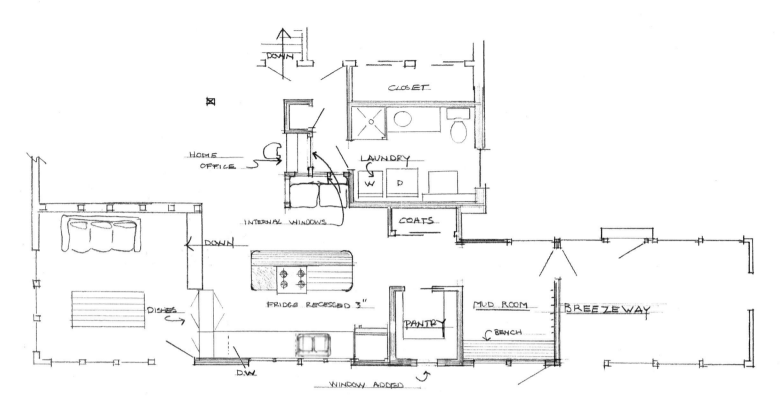

More improvements: add a mudroom, add a window in the pantry, recess the fridge, and round-over the corners of the island counter to widen the passageway.

Plan C-4

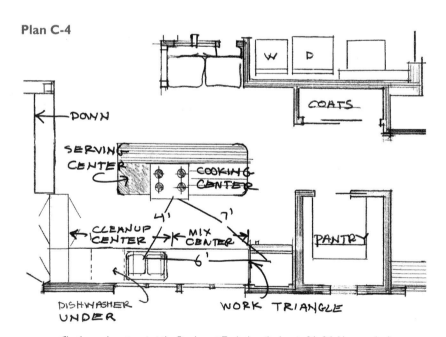

this criterion, particularly if it passes the power-kitchen test: Is the main work counter or food-prep area convenient to both sink and stove? Here I could well imagine the cook using either the mix center or the cooking center as the favorite food-prep zone. In either case, sink and stove will be just a step or two away. With about 42 in. between the two counters, the route is easy to traverse, but there's room also for two people to cook at once.

As to standard layouts, I suppose this could be considered an island kitchen. It's not important that your kitchen conform to one of these patterns exactly. The important thing is that it works for you.

Check your layout against the Five Layout Tools described on p. 21–24. Here, we had to move the sink toward the dining area to create a coherent "cleanup center."

Detailing Your

CHAPTER TWO

Design

A well-organized floor plan that suits the way your household lives is the key to a successful kitchen renovation. But the details of the design are just as important. I try to subject the size of every drawer, the height of every counter, and the location of every switch and outlet to the same careful analysis devoted to larger-scale issues. This chapter looks at the design concepts you can use to turn a good basic plan into a really first-rate, comprehensive design. It also covers the many design considerations for lighting, wiring, plumbing, and heating, which are not only crucial to the design but also can entail major expenses. A good place to start is with basic ideas that apply to the design of any work center but particularly to your kitchen work centers.

31

PRO TIP

Knives, spices, oil, salt, utensils, and the trash can are used constantly. Give them the best storage locations.

IN DETAIL

Kitchen researchers developed elaborate techniques in their research, but they came down to a basic tool anyone can use: observation. As you use your old kitchen and plan your new one, notice what tasks go well and which ones are awkward. If your back hurts as you work at your sink, take note. If something you use frequently is hard to reach, take note of that, too. Also notice how the kitchen works for others who use it. Keep a list of such observations as you design your work centers.

Designing Work Centers

The modern study of kitchen design began with the work of Frank and Lillian Gilbreth in the 1930s and culminated in the Cornell Kitchen Studies of the early 1950s. The concepts these pioneers developed still form the basis of good kitchen work-center design.

Perhaps the most fundamental idea that the Gilbreths emphasized—apart from the work-

Therbligs

Frank Gilbreth was an industrial designer who developed "Therbligs" ("Gilbreth" spelled backwards) as an alphabet of motion, a way to measure and describe any work activity. Therbligs are useful for observing how you do things and refining your work-center design.

- Search (manual or visual)
- Select
- Transport empty (moving a hand or other carrier toward a desired object)
- Grasp
- Transport loaded (moving an object with hand, or by dragging, rolling, etc.)
- Hold
- Release hold
- Position (orient an object in preparation for the next step)
- Pre-position (position for later use)
- Inspect
- Assemble
- Use
- Unavoidable delay
- Avoidable delay
- Plan
- Rest to overcome fatigue

One-motion storage: Store the things used most often where they can be retrieved with a minimum number of easy, quick motions. Here, favorite knives can be put to use with a single motion.

center concept itself—is the idea of *storage at point of first use.* Usually kitchen stuff is stored by category: knives go with knives; bowls go with bowls. But different knives or bowls have different uses and often are needed at different places in your work area. I use my paring knife near the sink, so I store it here. I use my carving knife near the stove, so I store it there. It's a simple idea, but few people apply it thoroughly.

There are two corollaries. The first is to give the best storage to the things you use the most frequently. The second corollary the Gilbreths called "one-motion storage." If my favorite knife is kept in a drawer, I have to step back, grasp the drawer handle, pull the drawer open, locate the proper knife, grasp it, take it out, reposition it in my hand, and close the drawer before I can use the knife. That adds up to many separate motions for a task done often. But if the knife is kept in a slot in the counter right in front of me, I can reach out, grab the knife using the same grip I use to chop, and start working. That's the ideal: *one-motion storage.* Of course, not everything can be retrieved in one motion. But as you detail your kitchen, visualize the tasks you will do repeatedly, and imagine the *number* of motions, their *difficulty,*

Body Dimensions, Reach Ranges, and Counter Heights (inches)

Height	Eye level	High reach	Counter height	Low reach	Table height
	36	-	28		
70	66	78	38	-	30
72	67	80	39	-	31
Wheelchair users					
63	46	55	32	17	31
66	48	57	32.5	15	31
68	49	59	33	13	31
73	51	68	34	10	31

Standard Dimensions vs. Ergonomic Dimensions (inches)

	Standard	Ergonomic
Table height	30	29
Kitchen counter height	36	varies
First upper shelf	55	48–50
Top shelf	75+	70
Outlet height	12–18	24
Switch height	48	44
Door width	30–32	34–36

their *length*, and even their *gracefulness or awkwardness*. Without any added expense, you will be able to make major improvements in your design simply by locating things in an optimal way.

A number of key features can put these basic principles to work in your kitchen. Not long ago, it was difficult to find some of these elements in affordable manufactured cabinets made in this country. But more and more, they have been widely adopted by the kitchen industry.

Countertops can be different heights

Although the standard kitchen counter is 36 in. off the floor, different tasks can call for different counter heights. Sometimes a sink counter should be higher because the user is actually working down *inside* the sink. Often, bakers like a lower counter for kneading bread or rolling out pastry because it allows them to put more weight behind the movement of kneading or rolling.

Different counter heights for different tasks: Here the homeowners determined by experimentation that a lowered section would be more comfortable for chopping and other food-preparation tasks.

IN DETAIL

Designing your own kitchen allows you to accommodate specific items, devising dividers, racks, or other special features that make retrieving them easier.

Slots were dimensioned to match the items stored.

WHAT CAN GO WRONG

Pullout shelves behind doors make little sense. Better to make drawers and avoid the superfluous motion of opening the door to get at the pullouts.

A 36-in.-high counter is really designed for a 5-ft. 6-in. or 5-ft. 7-in. user. Although it works fine for many people, if you are short or tall, have a bit of arthritis or other disability, or are simply fussy about your kitchen, consider your needs carefully. Counters that are too low can lead to back strain; too-high counters can strain arms and shoulders. Perfect counter heights make work more pleasant, less fatiguing, and more fluid. Also, you may find that different members of a household will prefer different counter heights, and that you can detail work areas accordingly.

The charts on p. 33 give guidelines, but experiment to find what will be best for you by using work surfaces of different heights. Sometimes you can mock up a counter that is higher or lower than standard to try out your ideas.

Storage should be specific to contents

Design storage units for the *specific items* to be stored in each one. Space shelves for the items they will hold. If part of a pantry is for 6-in. cans, I'll design shelves that are about 7-in. high, which leaves clearance for easy loading or access.

Sometimes the size of the shelves should be tailored, too. For example, extra-large plates may need an extra-deep shelf that will store them well. Similarly, size drawers carefully, by measuring the heights of each drawer's contents. Often, top drawers for utensils or silverware can be quite shallow inside, perhaps as little as 3 in. or 3½ in. If a lower drawer will hold baking supplies or small appliances, measure these items, add an inch for clearance, and design the drawer accordingly.

Drawers usually work best

Although drawer cabinets cost more than door cabinets, they are usually worth the premium. A door cabinet with two or three shelves is dark inside. You have to lean down to find and retrieve things, and items in back are blocked by what is in the front. It can take many awkward motions to retrieve what you need. Besides being inconvenient, door cabinets are sometimes inefficient; a lot of cabinet volume ends up being filled with air.

Drawers, particularly if they have good full-extension hardware, can be filled front to back. You can open the drawer, see everything easily, and

Storage specific to contents makes for easier retrieval, and better use of cabinet capacity. Photo on left by Charles Miller, ©The Taunton Press, Inc.

Most things store best in drawers.

select what you need with a minimal amount of fumbling. There is less leaning over, particularly for the top two or three drawers. I estimate that a well-designed bank of drawers can hold about 50 percent more than a door cabinet of similar size. Almost anything can be stored in drawers, including spices, knives, lids, large pots, small appliances, and also the trash can or compost bucket.

For all these reasons, the kitchens I design usually have a ton of drawers. When I can, I make them wide—up to 30 in. or even 36 in.—because it costs about the same to make a wide drawer as a narrow one.

The ORZ

It takes extra effort to reach high up, to stoop down low, or particularly to kneel down. Arthritis, poor vision, and other disabilities can make low or high storage particularly inconvenient or even altogether inaccessible. But there is a region that almost anyone of any height—including wheelchair users and children—can reach with ease. That is the area that begins at knee level, perhaps 20 in. up from the floor, and ends at 44 in. to 54 in. from the floor. Margaret Wylde, coauthor of *Building for a Lifetime* (The Taunton Press, 1994), calls this the *optimum reach zone,* or ORZ. This

IN DETAIL

If you decide to install conventional upper cabinets, consider lowering them. Uppers are typically located 18 in. to 20 in. above the counter, but positioning them at a 15-in. or 16-in. height makes the bottom shelf easier to see and to reach, and puts the next shelf up at a height that is convenient for more people.

TRADE SECRET

Open shelves in the margin above the counter make a kitchen more universally usable; items are easy to see and within reach for all users. Done well, it looks good, and it's usually less costly than enclosed cabinets.

The margin is often the most accessible storage location in the kitchen. Photo by Charles Miller, ©The Taunton Press, Inc.

area encompasses the top two drawers or base cabinet shelves, the space above the counter, and the first shelf of standard upper cabinets, if they are positioned relatively low on the wall. This is the prime storage area. Put the things you use the most in the ORZ.

Upper shelves and the margin

Kitchen designers often put upper cabinets above almost every counter. But in some situations uppers have drawbacks. For one thing, the top shelves are out of reach of many people. In addition, the cabinets can make the room seem smaller and the work areas visually cramped, particularly if the cabinets are dark. Sometimes upper cabinets obstruct one of the most useful storage places, the wall area right above the counter. I call this area "the margin." I often put open shelves on the margin, beginning right at the cabinet splash. If these are shallow, they don't interfere with the counter. Sometimes racks of various kinds make sense. Open storage of this type is handy, and everything is easy to see.

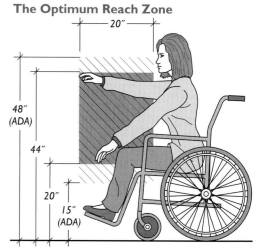

The Optimum Reach Zone

The ORZ—the area between 20 in. and 44 in. above the floor —is the area where most anyone can reach things easily. The larger zone, from 15 in. to 48 in., is the reach zone recommended by the Americans with Disabilities Act.

Trash, compost, and recycling

Your trash can is in constant use. I locate it as carefully as I do a major appliance. It should be central, near the sink, and handy to the mix center. It should be very easy to use without being in the way. If possible, it should be where people who aren't involved in cooking the meal can toss things out without disrupting the cook too much.

The margin just above the counter provides some of your most visible and convenient storage. Photo by Charles Miller, ©The Taunton Press, Inc.

Stainless steel items such as this compost bin can be purchased from restaurant-supply houses.

A big drawer for recycling.

The most common location— in the cabinet under the sink—is very inconvenient. You have to step back, open the door, and reach down and in each time you want to throw something away. I much prefer a pullout of some sort or a can with a foot pedal located to the side of the sink, where it won't be obstructed by someone working at the sink (see top right photo on p. 35).

If you compost your vegetable scraps (see top right photo on p. 35), a pullout for a stainless steel compost bin is very convenient. It should usually be located in a top drawer, right where you chop vegetables. A restaurant-style bin accessible through a cutout in the counter is another nice solution.

Recycling has become part of our everyday routines. And while different locales have different requirements, the main thing is to keep your recyclables contained and organized, and easy to remove when the time comes. The storage capacity should match the cycle of pickups or trips to the transfer station.

Sometimes an oversize drawer works well for recycling. I've made pullouts with one or two large bins inside. A simple shelf in a cabinet or pantry works perfectly for newspapers and maga-

zines. Another approach is to have modest storage space in the kitchen to use as you cook but larger bins outside in a shed or garage.

Planning for Universal Access

Consider accessibility or "universal" design as you plan your kitchen. The idea of universal design is that everything can and should be designed for all possible users, not just currently able-bodied adults. You or a family member might at some point become injured or disabled. An elderly parent might come to visit or live with you. Or, you might simply want disabled acquaintances to be comfortable in your house. By addressing these possibilities, your kitchen will be improved for all users, because many accessible features are really just good basic ergonomics. With good planning, a high level of accessibility can be accomplished with little extra cost by using standard materials and equipment in more ergonomically correct ways.

If you have lowered your upper cabinets to 15 in. or 16 in. above the counters, provided different counter heights, included many drawers,

PRO TIP

Check electronic controls for ease of use. Little black buttons with tiny markings make many electronic devices troublesome to use.

IN DETAIL

Usually ergonomic details that make a kitchen efficient and convenient also contribute to accessibility. Drawers on full-extension hardware are handier for all users but essential for a wheelchair user or for a person who has difficulty kneeling down or who has poor vision.

Good drawers on full-extension hardware are essential in universal design.

placed good storage in the margin, and made passageways generous (see chapter 1), you have already gone a long way towards designing an accessible kitchen. But other details also are important.

Work counters with knee spaces

Wheelchair users need a knee space under a food-preparation counter. Often I'll leave a counter that is at least 3 ft. wide open underneath, and set the counter there at 32 in. or 34 in. high. An additional knee space is needed at the sink, and the sink itself should ideally be a shallow model that is only 5 in. or 6 in. deep, rather than the typical 7 in. or 8 in. deep.

At one time, research kitchens always provided a place for the cook to work seated. It's less in fashion today, but if this idea suits the way you work, you will be making your kitchen more accessible at the same time.

Sometimes I include provisions in the kitchen that allow cabinets to be modified in the future for greater accessibility. For example, in the kitchen pictured on p. 25 the cabinet to the right of the stove can slide out to create a knee space, and the counter can be cut and lowered. Most people do not want a knee space under their sink when they remodel, but it may be essential if wheelchair accessibility is needed in the future. But details can be included to make later modification easier. For example, the finished floor can be run all the way back to the wall under sink cabinets.

Universal design doesn't have to look institutional. When accessible features are part of the design process from the beginning, the details just make the home look more spacious.

Controls

The term *controls* refers to switches, knobs, buttons, cabinet pulls, dials, faucet handles, and read-

Accessible features in this kitchen include a knee space under the sink, a work table with knee space below, multiple counter heights, lots of drawers, higher toe space under counters, and easily operated D-pulls on doors and drawers.

outs. Many controls are difficult for people with limited hand motion, low strength, or poor vision. Poorly designed controls are hard to see and turn, and they may not give the user clear feedback on the status of the equipment being used.

Good controls are obvious, easy to reach, and easy to grasp and move. The ideal is a control that can be operated easily with a closed fist; anyone will be able to use it. On cabinets, D-pulls are better than knobs of any kind. Lever handles are preferable for faucets, particularly single levers with nice long handles. Stoves vary greatly in how convenient their knobs are. Look for big, clear knobs, located at the front of the stove, which are easy to turn and have very definite markings. My experience is that these features, essential for disabled users, will be appreciated by other users as well.

Other accessible features

There are several other important features of an accessible kitchen. Doors should be wide, and they should have levers instead of knobs. I try to avoid thresholds or level changes whenever possible. If thresholds are necessary, as at exterior doors, make them low-profile, ½-in.-high accessible versions. If your renovation involves steps or a staircase, make them gradual (7-in. rise and 11-in. run is ideal) and provide easy-to-grasp handrails on both sides. Crank-operated casement windows are generally easier to operate than double-hung windows. Locate all of the electrical controls within easy reach, placing wall-mounted switches at 40 in. high (instead of the standard 48 in.) and outlets at around 24 in. (instead of around 18 in.).

With the exception of casement windows, these features cost little or no more than standard details. Besides reading up on these ideas (see Resources on p. 196), it's a good idea to have a designer familiar with accessibility issues review your plans.

Your Cabinet Elevations

The next step is to produce a series of elevation drawings. These drawings show appliance locations, cabinet configurations, and features like windows and doors. I find it helpful to make these drawings in a relatively large scale, so I can legibly represent small details and also easily show dimensions and make notes on the drawings. I use a scale of ½ in.=1 ft. If your floor plan so far is in ¼ in.=1 ft., you can get it blown up to ½-in. scale at a copy store that has a digital copier, which can easily make an accurate enlargement. If you are using stock cabinets, get a catalog showing stock cabinet sizes to help you fill in the details with commonly dimensioned elements. Even if you

D-pulls are easiest to grasp.

Kitchen Standard Dimensions

Most dimensions in the kitchen can be adjusted to your needs. But for many purposes the standard dimensions work well and can represent a good starting point for your design.

Counter height	36"
Cabinet depth	24"
Kickspace height	4"
Counter width	25
Counter thickness	1½"
Splash height	4" or more
Dishwasher width	24"
Single sink	22" x 25" wide
Double sink	22" x 33" wide
Overhead cabinets	12" deep from the wall
Cabinet widths	usually multiples of 3", starting with 9"

PRO TIP

Don't make your sink base any bigger than necessary; it is usually the least useful cabinet for storage. A 25-in. sink will fit easily in a 27-in. base.

TRADE SECRET

Many readers will be their own designers, with input from a variety of sources. But consider obtaining a little professional review of your ideas. A designer/builder, kitchen designer, or architect who does a lot of kitchen projects will almost certainly be able to make some valuable suggestions. Buying an hour or two of professional design time should be well worth it. Ask among your friends and building professionals for recommendations. Most important, find someone whose work you have seen, admired, and feel comfortable with.

Kitchen Plan

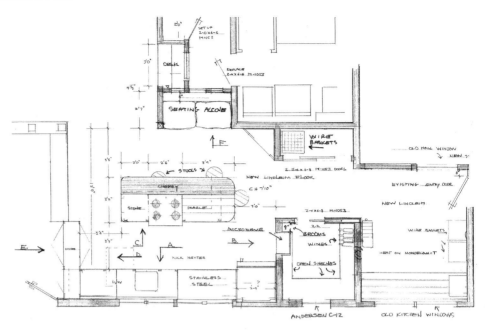

A large-scale plan makes it fairly easy to produce useful elevation drawings of your cabinets and other details. For easy reference, each elevation is given a letter designation, shown on the plan. Counter materials, appliance dimensions, and other key information should also be labeled.

end up with a different style or brand of cabinet, the sizes will still probably apply.

To make a ½-in. elevation, tape your ½-in. plan to the drawing board, oriented with the area you want to draw an elevation of at the top. If I'm going to draw an elevation of the sink wall (Elevation A), the sink wall goes at the top. Then place a sheet of tracing paper over the plan or just above the plan. In either case, you should be able to transfer the left-to-right dimensions of all the features to be drawn in elevation directly from the plan, with no measuring. Draw lines indicating the floor and ceiling in scale, and then transfer the wall locations from the plan. If there are windows, transfer their location, using light lines. Then make light reference lines showing counter height (and thickness), kickspace height, and the location of any overhead cabinets.

Next, draw in the appliances and other fixed elements, in this case the refrigerator and sink. The owners had scrounged a neat old stainless steel

sink with integral drainboard, so I drew in a 24-in. sink cabinet, or *sink base,* to match it.

Review how you have defined your work centers; that decision really guides what you do next. Here (see the bottom drawing on p. 29), the cleanup center includes the sink and extends to the right. The mix or food-prep center is the area to the left of the sink.

I like to place the dishwasher next. It usually goes beside the sink. Here, that would be in the cleanup area to the right side of the sink. I draw that in at the standard 24-in. size (see the drawing on the facing page).

After that, I usually locate the trash can. It's a crucial fixture, which has to be handy to the dishwashing operation and the mix center. Here I placed it to the left of the sink, which makes it handy to both areas.

Then fill in the remaining areas. In this case, because of the huge window, there is very little wall space available on Elevation A for overhead cabinets or shelves. In the cleanup center, we

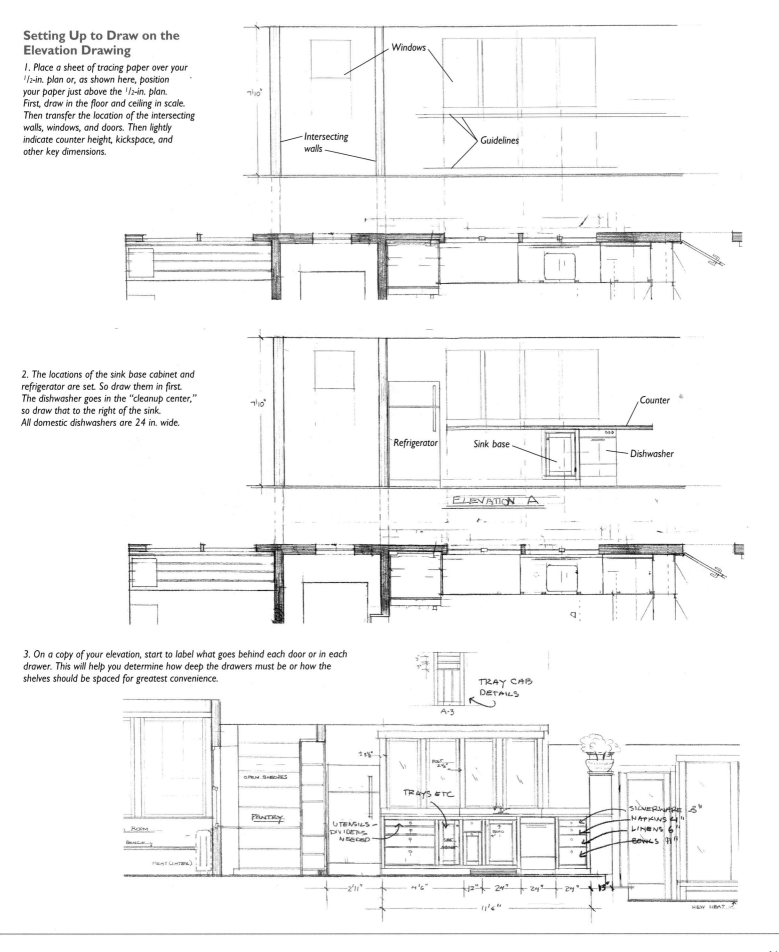

Setting Up to Draw on the Elevation Drawing

1. Place a sheet of tracing paper over your ¹/₂-in. plan or, as shown here, position your paper just above the ¹/₂-in. plan. First, draw in the floor and ceiling in scale. Then transfer the location of the intersecting walls, windows, and doors. Then lightly indicate counter height, kickspace, and other key dimensions.

Windows

Intersecting walls

Guidelines

2. The locations of the sink base cabinet and refrigerator are set. So draw them in first. The dishwasher goes in the "cleanup center," so draw that to the right of the sink. All domestic dishwashers are 24 in. wide.

Counter

Refrigerator

Sink base

Dishwasher

ELEVATION A

3. On a copy of your elevation, start to label what goes behind each door or in each drawer. This will help you determine how deep the drawers must be or how the shelves should be spaced for greatest convenience.

TRAY CAB DETAILS

A-3

OPEN SHELVES

PANTRY

ROOM

BENCH

HEAT (LATER)

UTENSILS DIVIDERS NEEDED

TRAYS ETC

SILVERWARE 3"
NAPKINS 4"
LINENS 6"
BOWLS 9"

2'11"   4'6"   12" 24" 24" 24" 15"

11'6"

NEW HEAT

41

IN DETAIL

Detail your design: Picture what stuff you will need when standing at each point on the plan. Visualize exactly how you will collect, scrape, wash, and put away dishes. Think about where you will be standing when you need your favorite carving knife. Picture where you will be typically when you need salt, oil, peanut butter, and so on. Make sure your design accommodates the way you will actually work.

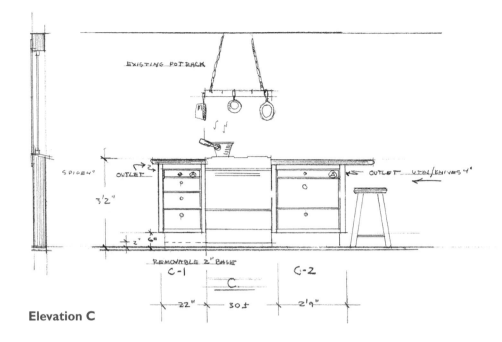

Elevation C

placed a set of drawers, primarily for dish storage, where they could be easily stocked directly from the dishwasher. On the mix-center side, we placed one door cabinet and some wide drawers—always my first choice.

Although this kitchen lacks upper cabinets, most kitchens have them. Most uppers are about 12 in. deep. Standard heights are 30 in., 36 in., and 42 in. Larger sizes of course can hold more, but I often prefer 30-in. uppers because they don't look so massive. Even smaller units, often used over sinks or stoves, are made in 12-in., 15-in., 18-in., and 24-in. heights.

The height above the counter is another important issue. Uppers are typically placed 18 in. above the counter, sometimes 20 in. For better access, I usually prefer to locate them only 16 in. or 15 in. up, which makes the contents easier to retrieve, particularly for shorter people. As you draw your overheads into your design, vary both size and position to see what will work best for you.

Consider these elevations a first draft. Tack them up and spend some time with them. To apply the ideas of "storage at point of first use"

and "one-motion storage," imagine performing basic cooking and cleaning tasks in the spaces they depict. Make a set of copies of your elevations (or maybe several sets), and label the contents of each shelf, drawer, or other storage area as specifically as possible, along with any critical dimensions.

For example, in Elevation A, the top drawer is stainlessware, the next napkins, the third linens, the bottom some very tall bowls. A little measuring showed us that we needed only 3 in. (minimum inside dimension) for stainless, about 4 in. for napkins, 6 in. for linens, and 11 in. at the bottom for the tall bowls. You can also identify any special details that might improve things. The top drawer on the left will be for utensils, so some dividers inside the drawers would be great. To its right will go trays, cookie sheets, etc., stored vertically. Since these items are at most 20 in. high, we still had room for a couple of narrow shelves above the tray bay. I made a little detail drawing showing this arrangement.

This level of detail may seem excessive. But I've found that this step helps in three important ways. First, I can see if there is enough storage overall. I want to be sure to include enough cabinets but not too much more. Second, I can make a lot of small adjustments to make storage more convenient and compact. Third, it gives me insight into how people will use the kitchen in practice, which may lead to revisions or refinements I otherwise would have missed. Also review your original design program. There may be points mentioned there that bear on the cabinetry.

After all this analysis, revise the elevations as needed. I find I usually make significant revisions at this stage. The elevations also should show elements other than cabinets that are important parts of the design. In this case, I drew details for the alcove seat, pantry shelving, and a home office, using the same kind of analysis used with the cabinetry.

After lighting, wiring, and other details have been thought through (see below), they can be included on the elevations where it would be helpful.

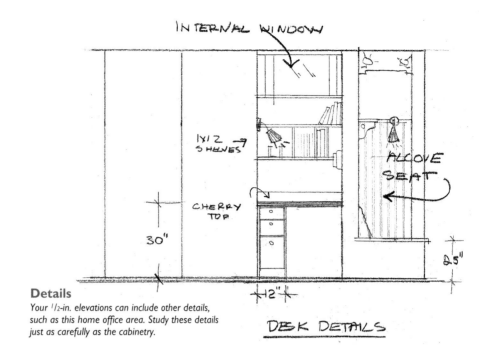

Details

Your ¹/₂-in. elevations can include other details, such as this home office area. Study these details just as carefully as the cabinetry.

Lighting and Wiring

Lighting and wiring your new kitchen will constitute a major part of your kitchen budget, unless the kitchen you are remodeling dates back only 10 to 15 years. Good lighting is crucial and deserves as careful thought as the layout and cabinetry. Also, modern electrical codes mandate a lot of heavy-duty circuitry in a kitchen, because the kitchen is where the electrical use is heaviest and (along with bathrooms) where electrical hazards are highest. All this can seem expensive, even if you are doing the work yourself, but the money will be well spent. Your kitchen will be more convenient and much safer than older, underwired kitchens subjected to modern demands.

Lighting is usually divided into two major categories. *Ambient,* or *general lighting,* means the fixtures that provide overall light for the major spaces of the home and for the passageways that lead to and through them. These are the lights you

Computer Drawing of Elevation

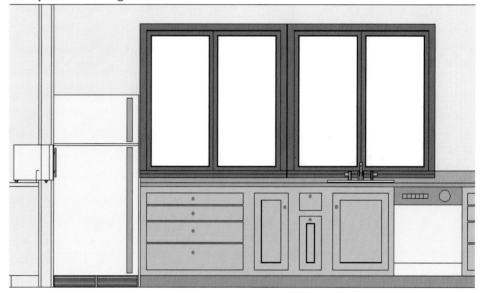

turn on and off as you move from one space to another. *Task lighting* refers to the fixtures that place more intense and focused light on work areas. Although certain types of fixtures tend to be used primarily for one or the other, it's *how* you use the fixture, *where* you place it, and how you *control* it that determines whether it is ambient lighting or task lighting. Let's look at ambient lighting first.

IN DETAIL

Switch location is crucial. You want to be able to turn on the light as you enter a space, so you don't ever have to stumble across it in the dark. You also want to be able to turn it off as you exit to conserve electricity. Therefore, ambient light fixtures are usually controlled by switches placed where you enter or leave the space that the fixture or group of fixtures serves. If there is more than one entrance to a space, there should be two three-way switches, one at each entry. With three entries, use two three-ways and one four-way switch.

Ambient lighting

Ambient lighting should provide enough general light so that people can move through the space comfortably and safely. It's particularly important that major passageways, halls, exits, and walkways be clearly lit. The ambient light should be bright enough so you can use the space, but doesn't have to be intense enough to read or work by. If there are doorways, the switches go on the handle side of the door. In many older homes, most ambient light is provided by ceiling-mounted globe fixtures of some sort. This is often still the most economical way to provide ambient lighting, particularly if you can use the existing wiring locations.

Recessed lights are increasingly used to provide general lighting. However, since they tend to focus a cone of light below the fixture, you may need several of them to brighten a space that could be lit with one or two ceiling fixtures.

You could just blast a space with enough ceiling lights or recessed lights to make the whole place bright. But it's better to tailor the lighting to the differences in how various areas are used. I like to use sconces in a stairwell, along a passage, or beside an entrance door. A sconce also works well to highlight a painting or other decorative feature. A hanging light or pendant of some kind—or more than one—makes a dining table cozy. Lamps controlled by switches can provide a milder, more intimate, and less harsh light than would be provided by ceiling lights or recessed fixtures. Lighting is a design tool, just like color, natural light, and various material choices. Use it thoughtfully to add variety and interest to your design.

Task lighting

Task lighting usually has to be brighter and more focused than ambient lighting. You want your counters, appliances, writing surfaces, and other work areas bright enough so you can see easily what you are doing. Locate the light source where no shadows will be cast on the work surface by upper cabinets, shelves, or equipment (hoods, for example) or by your own body as you use the counter. With my floor plan before me, I visualize myself working at each work station, and then try to imagine the possible places a light could go to illuminate my work.

This is easiest when a kitchen is relatively small or open and there are few upper cabinets or other projections. In that case, two or three wall or ceiling fixtures may be all that is needed to light the work surfaces. But often there will be upper cabinets that make such a solution unworkable.

As the drawing below shows, typically your primary task lighting will go right above the counter, far enough out from the wall so that the wall cabinets won't block the light. I usually center them 18 in. to 20 in. from the wall to

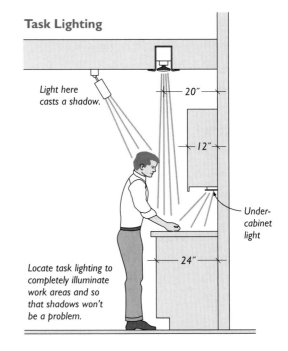

Task Lighting

Light here casts a shadow.

20″

12″

Under-cabinet light

24″

Locate task lighting to completely illuminate work areas and so that shadows won't be a problem.

minimize shadows. Often my first thought is to use track lighting because of its ease of installation and flexibility.

Sometimes recessed fixtures make more sense. Track lighting makes a visual statement; it becomes part of the décor. Also, track lighting could obstruct upper cabinet doors as they open.

Upper cabinets will block the light at the back of the counter. Under-cabinet fluorescent lights, as little as 1 in. thick, are often used to add light at the back of a counter. These can be concealed in a recess in the bottom of the cabinet. Note that fluorescent lights cannot have dimmer switches, but halogens can.

Pendants can provide lots of light where there are no obstructions above. Although we most often see them over tables or islands that are used as eating counters as well as work areas, they can be used in a variety of other ways. A beautiful hanging light can be a decorative feature and help define the kitchen space in a way recessed lights cannot.

There is no reason to limit yourself to a single type of fixture in the kitchen. On one recent project, we used track lighting over the sink counter, recessed lights over appliances, and two pendants over the peninsula. Go by what functions and looks best to you.

You usually perceive the need for task lighting as you start to do something at a counter, not as you enter the work area. For that reason, locate switches for task lighting right near the counters. Switches can be mounted right above the counter splash or in the splash itself. To conserve electricity, it's best to have at least two separate lighting circuits in the kitchen. You may not need to light all the counters all the time. The under-cabinet lights could be switched with the primary work lights above, but also can have their own switches.

Types of Lighting Fixtures

There are six basic types of lighting fixtures:

Ceiling-mounted fixtures are perhaps simplest and most common. They usually consist of a surface-mounted fixture that houses one, two, or three incandescent bulbs (or fluorescents), enclosed in a removable glass or plastic diffuser. Many older homes use these for almost everything. They are relatively inexpensive, and a few of them can cast light over a large space. In a renovation, the wiring for them will often be in place; only the fixture itself has to be changed.

Recessed lights have become very popular. They consist of a canlike housing, brackets to support the housing, a light socket and bulb inside, a reflector or diffuser to control the light pattern, and a trim ring to frame the fixture. All this gear except the trim ring and perhaps a diffuser is tucked up into the ceiling. Although more costly than ceiling fixtures, recessed lights are perhaps more elegant and definitely less obtrusive.

Track lights also are widely used. A lighting track is simply a long metal channel with conductors running the entire length, usually fed from a single ceiling box. Lighting heads can be installed anywhere along the track and aimed in any direction. A wide variety of lighting heads are available, including hanging fixtures. You can change and tune the lighting based on experience or as requirements change. Cost is often similar to recessed lighting; the fixtures cost more, but the wiring is much simpler.

Wall-mounted lights are available in several types. Some are similar to ceiling lights, made for wall installation. **Sconces** cast light along a wall or ceiling, providing a gentle, more decorative light. They also are decorative elements. Sometimes a **spotlight** can work well mounted on a wall, often using a **monopoint,** which is simply a socket to which any standard track-light head can be mounted.

Pendants are lights that hang from the ceiling (see the photos on p. 46).

Plug-in lamps of all kinds, including floor lamps, wall lamps, table lamps, and little spots, can be elements of your basic lighting plan. They can be controlled by their own built-in switches, but when a lamp of some sort is used a lot, it makes sense to switch the outlet that feeds the lamp. It's relatively easy to switch one half of a conventional double outlet (known as a *duplex receptacle*) for this purpose. Note, however, that a switched outlet can't have a dimmer.

IN DETAIL

Counter outlets often go between the backsplash and the upper cabinets, positioned low enough so that they can be seen easily. When windows or shelf units make a wall location impossible, outlets can be cut into the backsplash.

Although it's easier to wire an outlet into a wall, when necessary it can be mounted in the counter backsplash.

On a kitchen island, outlets can be recessed into the cabinet if there is room for a box.

Outlets and other wiring

Start by making a preliminary assessment of your existing wiring. If your existing kitchen was built recently (say within the last 20 years), the wiring may be almost up to code, and upgrading may be simple and economical. But older kitchens may have far too few circuits; these circuits also may be ungrounded or not of sufficient wire size.

If you have less than 100-amp service, this is probably a good time to update your entrance, though your existing service may suffice if some of the major appliances are gas. If you have an electric stove, electric water heater, and electric dryer, you may need to upgrade to 200-amp service. If your house still has an old-style fuse panel, I'd encourage you to replace it with a breaker box. You can usually keep an existing breaker panel, even if all the openings are full, by using tandem breakers, though breakers for an obsolete panel may no longer be available.

Pendant lights—with a dimmer switch—work well over a dining table or eating counter. Photo by Charles Miller, ©The Taunton Press, Inc.

Pendant lights also can work well over a counter, particularly where there are no upper cabinets that would be obstructed by them. Photo by Charles Miller, ©The Taunton Press, Inc.

A Comprehensive Wiring Diagram

The wiring diagram for our project house illustrates many of the options and dilemmas you are likely to encounter. There are several types of ambient lighting shown. One spotlight on the outside of the breezeway lights the pathway to the drive. A motion sensor can control it, or it can go on automatically after dark. All entries to the breezeway have exterior wall lights controlled by switches just inside the door. The breezeway ceiling lights can be operated from three different stations: mudroom, front entry, and garage, via four-way switches. The mudroom is lit by an ordinary floor lamp, controlled by two three-way switches. In the kitchen itself, two ceiling lights provide the ambient lighting. One is positioned to light up the coat closet, and the other is near the two steps down to the dining room. Both the home office and the seating alcove have nice, secondhand simple wall lights with glass shades, both operated by nearby switches. The task lighting (over the countertops) is conventional track.

For outlets, the stove and fridge have dedicated outlets; the dishwasher is hard-wired and switched. On both counters, the outlets were hard to locate. In the island, they had to be placed in the end of the cabinetry. I had to make sure there was room enough here for the electrical boxes. Surface-mounted "plugmold" could have been used instead. On the sink side, the window comes down very low to the counter, so the outlets had to be cut into the backsplash of the stainless steel counter (see the photos at left on p. 46).

Wiring Diagram

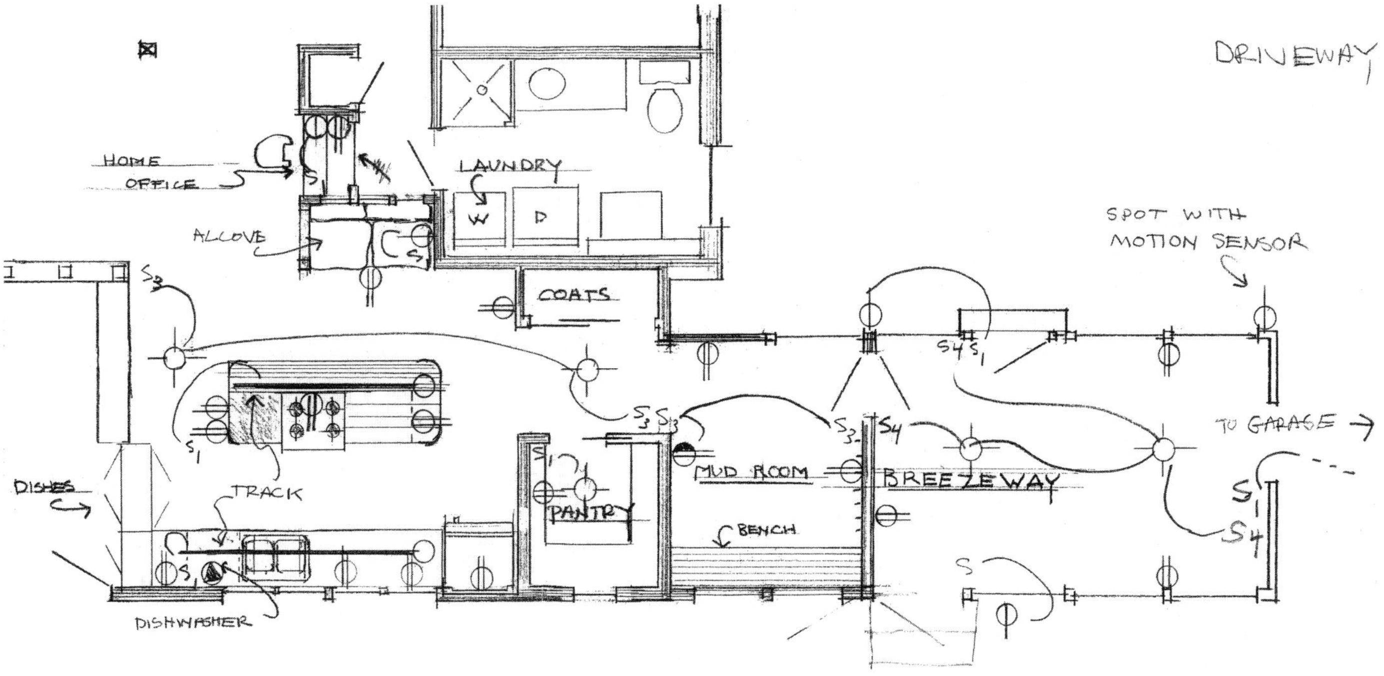

A wiring diagram shows lighting, outlets, and switch locations using standard symbols.

WHAT CAN GO WRONG

It's not unusual to renovate a kitchen or bathroom and then be unhappy with the water pressure available. Ideally, main water lines (called *headers*) are made with ¾-in. pipe, while ½-in. lines branch off the header to each outlet. The large line supplies enough water so that turning on one fixture doesn't rob others on the line of pressure. But in many homes, all the water-supply lines are ½ in. If you have a ½-in. header and low pressure, you might want to replace it.

requires new or extended water-supply lines, drains, and vents.

Vents are the pipes that go from the fixtures up and out the roof. They allow sewer gases to escape, keep the drains flowing smoothly, and admit air to the system so that water rushing down the drains doesn't siphon out the traps, which would allow sewer gases to flow into the house. A fixture can have its own vent, or its vent can join a common vent that serves several fixtures.

In this project, we chose to leave the sink near its old location, but because the old drain was sluggish, we replaced it with a new one of larger diameter.

A gas stove, cooktop, or oven will require a gas line for natural or bottled gas (propane). I've noticed that the regulations that govern stove installation change more frequently than other codes and vary by location. Often propane is run in flexible copper pipe, joined with flare fittings. Since copper is soft and easily damaged, it is always run exposed. Concealed lines are run in

ACCORDING TO CODE

Sinks in island counters present a special dilemma because a vent can't go directly up and out the roof near the sink trap. Instead of a conventional vent, codes sometimes permit you to simply increase the drain size to 2 in. or more, which admits some air into the system and keeps the trap from being siphoned out. An increasingly popular and probably more economical solution is to install an air-admittance valve right after the trap, a one-way valve that lets air into the line and prevents siphoning (Studor®, 800-447-4721; www.studor.com). These are now approved by most plumbing codes.

black iron pipe, which won't be damaged by an errant nail. Natural gas that is piped into urban areas is usually run in black iron pipe. Many (if not most) of the tasks and trades described in this book can be safely done by homeowners. The exception is working with gas. I discourage anyone from getting involved in gas work. Leave it to the pros.

Design considerations for heating and air conditioning

Many kitchen projects will require some modifications to the heating system, as walls are removed, space added, or cabinets installed where heating (and possibly air conditioning) is now located. The task at this stage of design is to arrive at possible solutions. Unless you are doing the work yourself, go over the details with a heating and air-conditioning contractor.

Most types of central heat and air conditioning can be modified to reflect your new layout. Hot-water baseboard convectors or radiators can usually be relocated without great cost if there is a workable way to reroute the pipes. Similarly, it's not too hard to relocate forced-air ductwork, again provided there is a route for the ducts to follow. Ducts or pipes should be routed through insulated spaces. I avoid putting either in outside walls.

Radiators, hydronic convectors, and hot-air-duct outlets are usually located on outside walls. That's where the heat loss is. Also, the warm air at the perimeter rises and displaces the cold air, creating a more even temperature in the room.

Your new cabinetry can make it difficult to place conventional radiators or convectors in hydronic heat systems. In that case, I use kick heaters, which are incorporated into one zone of the heating system. Instead of a long run of baseboard, a kick heater has several lengths of "fin tube" coiled together in a small box that fits under a cabinet. An electric fan blows warm air into the room.

In a similar way, heating and air-conditioning ducts can simply be run under the cabinet and exit through a register in the toekick.

The problem becomes more complex when you are adding to the size or heat load of the space or extending service a long way. Air ducts are less effective the longer they are, and there are limits to how much baseboard heat can be included effectively in one loop or zone of the system. You may have to add another zone to a hydronic system. This is the point where the advice of a heating contractor will be needed.

Instead of trying to figure out how to supply more heat, sometimes it makes sense to approach the problem from the other direction. Old houses often lose a lot of heat because of drafts, inadequate insulation, and poor windows. If you insulate the walls, install quality windows and doors, and seal up air-infiltration routes, you may reduce heat loss by a large margin. In fact, often you can add significant new space and increase the number of windows, yet still reduce the total heat load, because your new work is so much more energy efficient. Existing 2x4 exterior walls can be built out to make room for thicker 6-in. insulation. Such changes may be cheaper than upgrading your heating plant and will save heating costs every year.

Typical Drain and Venting Options

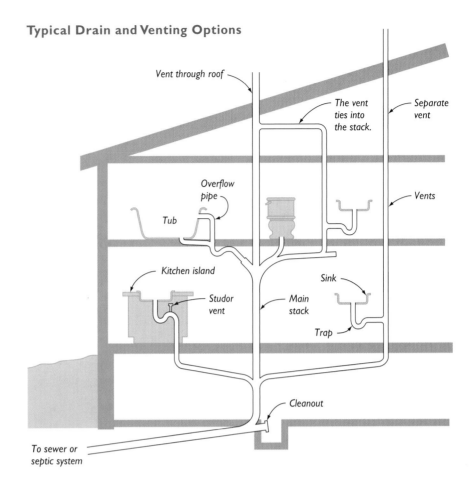

All fixtures must be vented somehow. In each configuration, pipe sizes and other details are regulated by code.

When walls are covered with cabinetry, an electrical hydronic or kick heater can be installed in the cabinet kickspace.

Cabinets and

CHAPTER THREE
Surfaces

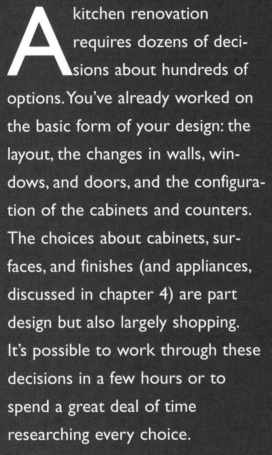

A kitchen renovation requires dozens of decisions about hundreds of options. You've already worked on the basic form of your design: the layout, the changes in walls, windows, and doors, and the configuration of the cabinets and counters. The choices about cabinets, surfaces, and finishes (and appliances, discussed in chapter 4) are part design but also largely shopping. It's possible to work through these decisions in a few hours or to spend a great deal of time researching every choice.

These choices have a huge impact on project cost. For example, with less costly cabinets and appliances, the kitchen pictured here at left might have cost 20 percent to 30 percent less, without sacrificing the basic design and function of the kitchen. Similarly, with a commercial range, custom cabinets, and solid-surface counters, it might have cost easily 40 percent to 75 percent more.

IN DETAIL

Factory-made cabinets are categorized in three ways:

- **Stock cabinets** are built ahead of time in standard sizes. They may be available on quite short notice, but your choices will be limited to what you see in the manufacturer's catalog.

- **Semicustom cabinets** are similar, but their makers will adapt their lines to your requirements. If you want one or two units with an unusual counter height or drawer size, they will make them for you.

- **Factory "custom"** cabinets are made specifically for you in the factory, based on one of their standard designs but to your order and sized to your specifications. In general, semicustom and factory custom cabinets cost more than cabinets from stock, and delivery can take as long as two to four months.

Choosing Cabinets

Choosing cabinets can be complicated. There are several major and many minor types of cabinets, and they vary greatly in style, quality, cost, and availability. They may be the most expensive element in your kitchen renovation, and it pays to spend some time finding out what the choices are.

Face-frame cabinets

Most cabinets used in the United States are *face-frame* cabinets, with trim boards—often made of hardwood—that cover the cabinet box (or *carcase*). The face frame trims out and conceals the plywood or particleboard edges of the box and provides a place to attach door hinges. It also helps to hold the cabinet box square. Doors and drawers are fitted to a face frame in several ways.

⅜-in. overlay cabinets: In ⅜-in. overlay cabinets, doors and drawer fronts are notched (or *rabbeted*) about ⅜ in. over the face frame. This is a forgiving design, as the rabbet covers the fit where the door or drawer front meets the face frame, making construction quick and easy. Many houses from the 1940s, 1950s, and 1960s have

Common since the 1950s, face-frame cabinets often have rabbeted ⅜-in. overlay doors and drawer fronts. The material here is butternut.

this design, sometimes with panel doors and sometimes with simple plywood doors.

Full-overlay cabinets: In this design, the full thickness of the door is placed on top of the face frame. Most commercial cabinets are made this way. It's a simple, flexible system that is easy to build and works well. Manufacturers offer this type of cabinet in a wide variety of woods, finishes, and door styles.

Typical Construction of Face-Frame Cabinets

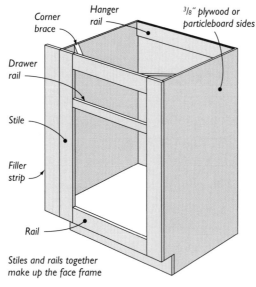

Corner brace
Hanger rail
³/₈" plywood or particleboard sides
Drawer rail
Stile
Filler strip
Rail

Stiles and rails together make up the face frame

Standard Cabinet Dimensions

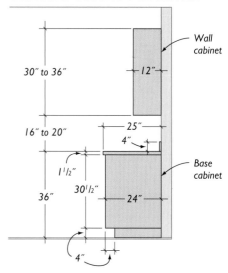

Wall cabinet
30" to 36"
12"
16" to 20"
25"
4"
1¹/₂"
Base cabinet
36"
30¹/₂"
24"
4"

In full-overlay face-frame cabinets, the entire thickness of the doors and drawer fronts sits on top of the face frame.

Flush face-frame (or inset) cabinets:

Here the door and drawer fronts are in the same plane as the face frame. This is a traditional, more elegant design that shows off the workmanship of the maker. It's also a less forgiving system; if a door is ⅛ in. too small, or ⅛ in. out of square, it's obvious. Flush face-frame cabinets are making a strong comeback in the kitchen market, particularly in more expensive grades of cabinets.

Cabinet Quality

Regardless of the type of cabinet, certain features make for a better, more durable cabinet.

Look at what the cabinet boxes are made of. Particleboard is strong, stable, and tough, and many good cabinets, particularly European-style cabinets, are made of it. But in my experience plywood is stronger; it's also less subject to water damage if, for example, you had a slow leak under the sink. Without ruling out particleboard, I'd prefer plywood.

Look carefully at drawer construction. Drawer boxes—the sides, back, and inner face—can be made of particleboard, softwoods (such as pine), or hardwoods (such as maple). There's a lot of stress on the corner joints of drawer boxes. Particleboard is a real liability here because it's difficult to make a really strong corner between two pieces of particleboard. Solid-wood joints, whether hardwood or softwood, are much stronger. Although many methods of joinery have been used on drawer corners, dovetails, the traditional joint for centuries, is still the best. Get dovetailed drawers if possible.

While you are at it, look at the drawer hardware. Most cabinets now use European-style hardware, which works well and is strong. Ask also about *full-extension* hardware for drawers, which is usually available as an upgrade. It provides complete access to items stored at the back of a drawer.

Also check finishes. On less expensive cabinets, poor sanding will show up as scratches that show through the finish. Ask vendors to describe the finishes on their products, and compare characteristics.

Although pricey features like dovetailed drawers and plywood carcases are nice, I think finding a door style, design features, and the accessories you like are just as important. Mid-range cabinets with particleboard carcases and no dovetails can be perfectly serviceable and long lasting.

Flush face-frame cabinets are very elegant style, harder to build, and usually a bit more costly.

PRO TIP

Uppers and base cabs don't have to match. Sometimes light uppers, perhaps with glass doors, can look great with dark-colored or painted base cabinets.

IN DETAIL

Of the several innovations introduced by European cabinetmakers to the American market, perhaps the best is the *cup hinge.* Mounted in a large hole on the inside of the door and directly to the cabinet side, they aren't visible from the outside of the cabinet. These hinges can be adjusted easily up/down, left/right, or in/out with a screwdriver, making cabinet installation and "tune-up" quick and easy.

IN DETAIL

At first, European cabinets looked totally different from American face-frame cabinets. Sleek and modern, they had little or no decoration. However, as both systems have evolved, European manufacturers have introduced more traditional and complex door styles and moldings, while face-frame cabinets can be had with European hardware and simple doors.

Frameless Cabinet Box Construction

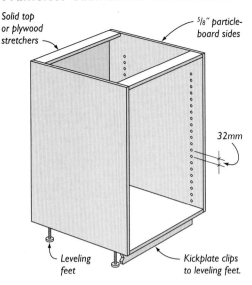

Solid top or plywood stretchers

⁵/₈″ particleboard sides

32mm

Leveling feet

Kickplate clips to leveling feet.

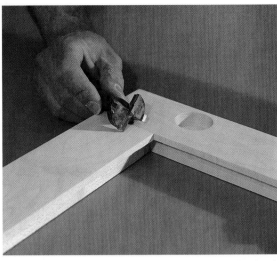

Cup hinges fit simply into a large hole in the back of the door. Photo ©Paul Levine.

Frameless cabinets

After World War II, European manufacturers, faced with a vast new market for cabinets, developed an innovative system that is now known as the *European, frameless,* or *32mm system.*

It's a simple, elegant design. The box, even on more expensive brands, is typically ⅝-in.-thick particleboard faced with melamine, wood veneers, or plastic laminate. There is no face frame. Instead, the particleboard is edged with a veneer to match the face finish. Inside, each cabinet side has a series of holes, 32mm on center. Drawer hardware, accessories, and shelf supports all are designed to fit these holes, making manufacturing, assembly, and installation quite simple. The doors and drawer fronts cover the edge of the box. When closed, these fronts are all you see (see the photo on p. 52).

Where standard cabinets normally have to be shimmed or trimmed at the bottom for a level installation, frameless cabinets are sometimes supported on and leveled with adjustable, threaded legs. The kickboard simply clips to these adjusting legs. Upper cabinets typically hang from a metal hanger, which also has a built-in provision for adjustment.

At one time, frameless cabinets were available only from extremely expensive European manufacturers. Today, many domestic manufacturers and cabinetmakers market their own versions of frameless cabinets in a range of prices and qualities. The differences between the face-frame and frameless cabinets now are largely matters of taste rather than price or quality.

Custom cabinets

While you can buy what are called *custom cabinets* from a home center or kitchen showroom, cabinets also can be individually made for you by a cabinetmaker or small shop. These shops are really the expression of the tastes, skills, and resources of their owners, so you'll have to do some research to find out what is available in your area.

Some custom shops make cabinets similar to those offered at kitchen showrooms. Others have developed their own variation of these common themes. Still others have invented their own styles, producing cabinets that look very different from commercial products. Finally, there are shops that work in a variety of styles and will build cabinets to almost any design you bring them.

Whichever is the case in your area, cabinetmaking shops offer services that don't usually

Custom cabinets come in all sorts of nonstandard designs. These cabinets, built from cherry and pine, are a hybrid, somewhere between face frame and frameless in style.

A custom cabinetmaker can make your cabinets in any size, shape, or color, and incorporate details not always found in stock lines. Although sometimes very expensive, these cost about the same as good-quality semicustom cabinets.

Custom cabs can use any materials. Here, beaded-douglas fir. Photo by Steve Culpepper, ©The Taunton Press, Inc.

come with factory-made products. First, since the shop is small and your project is important to them, you'll get a lot of personal attention. Often you will be dealing directly with the individual who will build and install your cabinets. Second, the specifications available to you should be more varied. It is relatively easy for a small shop to make your cabinets 2 in. higher, lower, or deeper than standard. Unusual drawer sizes, specially shaped units, open shelves, odd tray cabinets, or an unusual choice or combination of materials will be no problem; small shops deal with such requests every day—that's what makes it fun. Since every detail is designed for a particular kitchen, it won't necessarily cost extra for the odd-sized drawer or cabinet.

Another advantage of having your cabinets made (or making them yourself) is that they can

look much more integral and built-in than factory cabinets. There is less need for fillers, as cabinets are made to exact sizes. They can look seamless. This is particularly so of face-frame styles. With stock face-frame cabinets, you see a seam wherever cabinets meet. With custom cabinets, a large face frame can encompass an entire run of cabinets, creating a very different look (this advantage is also available from some larger cabinet

PRO TIP

Get references for kitchen vendors. Ask whether the cabinets came through complete, undamaged, on time, and as well built as the floor model.

TRADE SECRET

A cabinetmaker will never be able to make your cabinets for the price charged for low-end or middle-quality factory cabinets. But some custom cabinets will be price competitive with the higher-quality factory cabinets that are found in many kitchen showrooms. There are also factory-built cabinets that can be every bit as expensive as custom-made cabinets. On the other hand, some cabinetmakers' work can be extremely expensive. In general, the more you want special materials or nonstandard dimensions, the more likely it will be that the price quoted by a small cabinet shop will be competitive.

TRADE SECRET

Many kitchen designers use CAD programs that have the current catalogs of major cabinet manufacturers, appliance manufacturers, window companies, and other suppliers loaded into their databases. This makes it easy to compare and contrast various models and configurations as your kitchen is designed.

With custom cabinets, a run can be seamless, one large unit rather than separate boxes screwed together.

manufacturers). And you can also match existing cabinets, which in some circumstances can make your renovation much less costly.

CAD systems

I may be one of the last people designing kitchens using a pencil and paper. Now, most professional kitchen designers design on computers using increasingly powerful CAD systems. Designers can start with a floor plan (based either on their own or someone else's actual measurements), establish a few basic parameters (ceiling height, for example), and then begin placing design elements on the plan. Stoves, base cabinets, wall cabinets, pantries, and countertops can all be dropped into the plan, manipulated, and rearranged. The designer can specify the species or color of wood, the color of countertop, the wall color, even the view through the windows. It then becomes a simple matter to generate quite realistic, full-color, three-dimensional images of the kitchen, from any chosen angle. It's also quite easy to vary the layout, appliances, colors, and so on, and generate more perspective drawings, so you can compare the different versions.

Kitchen-design programs of varying power and flexibility for home use are increasingly available. In some cases, there are home versions of the more sophisticated programs professional designers use. If you use a program from the same vendor as the program your selected kitchen dealer has, you can work on your design as far as you are able and then deliver it to the designer on a disk or over the internet for more input. Conversely, you might be able to rework or fine-tune the design he or she provides you.

Even though CAD programs become more sophisticated and flexible every year, there are limits to their ability to create a kitchen plan that is right for you. Where I can draw cabinets and shelving in any configuration I can imagine, the computer has trouble representing nonstandard solutions. The options the programs present cover the majority of design choices people tend to make, but if you're looking for a solution that is off the beaten path, you're probably better off with pencil and paper.

Buying cabinets and design services

Many cabinet dealers, home centers, and large lumberyards have kitchen designers on staff and do not charge for their services. These designers may be on salary or receive a commission for the kitchens they sell. In either case, their success depends on the products they market, their displays, and their skill in presenting design ideas to clients.

Other vendors, including some major home-center chains, do charge a modest fee for design, which is deducted from the cost of cabinets if you end up buying from them. This fee may include

The kitchen as built.

Using **CAD**, the designer can show your kitchen as seen from any point on the plan and easily vary the design to show possible options. This is a **CAD** drawing for the kitchen shown at right. Design by Lawrie Morrison, Gallery of Cabinets.

coming to your home and measuring the site. There are many variations on each of these ways of charging for design services.

In addition to these sources, there also are *independent kitchen designers.* They may be happy to sell you cabinets, but they are are primarily interested in design. Independent kitchen designers could have formal training in architecture, home decorating, or kitchen design, or (like me) they might be builders or cabinetmakers with a special interest in the kitchen. The best of them emphasize how people work, ergonomics, and affordability, and pay particular attention to how their clients will actually work in a kitchen and how the kitchen relates to other activities in the home. Design work from an independent kitchen designer may cost you from $1,000 to $2,000.

I used to believe you would get good, unbiased design only if you paid for it by the hour, on the theory that when the designer works on commission, he or she has a financial motive in selling you as many expensive cabinets and counters as possible. Now, however, I think it is more important to seek out designers whose approach you

like, whom you are comfortable with, and can help you get the kind of cabinets and accessories you want. Look at the work of anyone you are considering hiring, and talk to recent clients. Talented people who put your interests first will be found using a wide variety of approaches. As you research your local cabinet market, ask people to describe their approaches to design and how design services are paid for, and settle on someone you find compatible.

A kitchen by independent designer Anne Remby of The Kitchen Works. Photo ©Matter Photography.

TRADE SECRET

IKEA® is a Swedish company that sells a wide variety of Scandinavian-style furniture and housewares. It also sells a line of European-style frameless cabinets of very good quality. The cost is low, particularly for a European cabinet, because everything it sells is "flat pack," or KD (for knocked down), and has to be assembled. While most European cabinets are prohibitively expensive, IKEA's are affordable and well designed.

TRADE SECRET

One of the added bonuses of European cabinetry is the improvements that have been made to drawer hardware. European designers developed a new type of coated steel drawer hardware that is cheap, easy to install, high capacity, and very reliable. This type of hardware is now commonly used in American cabinets of all types.

The most economical cabinets usually come from large home centers or lumberyards, though these organizations will also sell mid-range cabinets. Most kitchen showrooms sell primarily mid- to upper-price-range cabinets. There also are kitchen showrooms that specialize in a single high-end cabinet line, either domestic or imported, that can cost as much as the most expensive custom cabinets. Custom-built cabinets are usually comparable in price to high-quality stock or semicustom cabinets, though they can be considerably more. However, in all categories, the bottom line will depend on materials, drawer hardware, special features, and, above all, the total number of cabinets ordered. If the extent of the cabinetry is moderate, a higher-quality cabinet may not be an overriding factor in total project cost.

Building the cabinets yourself

Many homeowners who are not professional woodworkers have built their own kitchen cabinets. Though demanding, it's one of the most fun parts of building. In fact, if I had to choose, I'd hire out the carpentry, wiring, plumbing, and drywall, and save the cabinetmaking and perhaps the trim carpentry for myself. It's a very satisfying process; you can build just what you want, and you can invent your own unique details. Building your own cabinets is feasible if you are comfortable with woodworking tools, particularly table saws, routers, and hand tools, and can work to close tolerances of $\frac{1}{32}$ in. or less.

Cabinet joinery can be simple and can be done with the ordinary tools found in many basement or garage shops. While you would probably end up buying or making a few specialized items,

Cabinet Cost Comparison

The company I work with, Iron Bridge Woodworkers, built and installed the cherry cabinets shown in the photo on p. 96 for about $9,500, not including counters. In pine, the cost would have been about $500 less. The cabinets were unfinished, as the clients did all of the varnishing; this saved them about $1,300. All the drawer hardware was top-of-the-line Accuride, and the cabinet details were completely custom-tailored. Materials alone approached $2,000.

We could have used stock low-end unfinished pine face-frame cabinets. These would have cost about $3,000 uninstalled (figure another $1,000 or so for installation), but these would not have had full-extension hardware, and some of the cabinets would have only approximated the ideal configuration. The storage capacity of the cabinets would have been a bit lower, with a bit more space wasted on the face frames.

Semi-custom frameless cabinets, with standard hardware and hardwood fronts, priced out at about $5,500. With full-extension hardware like we used, the cost went up to about $6,500. Beautiful semi-custom face-frame cabinets with beaded inset doors started at about $7,000, but again, the full-extension hardware brought the actual uninstalled price up to about $8,000, not that far below our price. Of course, the cost for some of the up-market brands of factory-made custom or semi-custom cabinets could have been almost double that. The price we charged should be considered the low end for cabinets made by hand in a small shop.

Many great kitchens have been built with very modest budgets. A flair for design, good colors, and artful scrounging can bring very rewarding results. Simple unfinished pine cabinets costing less than $3,000 were used in this kitchen, for example, to create a thoughtful and effective design.

there are plenty of good books of instruction, as well as some useful videos (see Resources on p. 196). You would also need a big enough space to build and store the cabinets, as well as a well-ventilated place to do the finishing.

However, it is a major undertaking. It's common for a professional cabinetmaker to spend several weeks doing an entire kitchen, putting in 150 to 300 hours of work, including finishing and installation. It will take you much longer, perhaps two to three times as long. Of course, there are several strategies that you can use if you are determined to build your own cabinets. One is to *keep it simple,* always a good idea. Another is to build the cabinets ahead of time, so they can be "popped" in as soon as the space is prepared. Another strategy, which I've used in my own home, is to build the basic base cabinets, install them, then build the upper cabinets, doors, and drawers as time allows. Just don't install the cabinets unfinished, thinking that you'll do the varnishing or painting while the kitchen is in use; the cabinets will get dirty and damaged before the finishing is done.

What You'll Need to Build Cabinets Yourself

Space
- A place to store materials, including 4x8 sheets of plywood
- Shop space big enough for a table saw, a large bench, and tools, with good light and good wiring
- A clean, ventilated space for varnishing or painting. In warm weather, this can be the outdoors.
- A place to store assembled cabinets before installation

Power Tools
- Table saw with extension tables for handling large sheets
- Miter saw, sliding miter saw, or radial-arm saw
- Router and router bits
- Two cordless drills with a variety of bits and driver tips
- Portable circular saw with a sharp blade
- Jigsaw
- Belt sander and half-sheet orbital sander
- Shop vacuum

Hand Tools
- Hammers
- Level
- Framing square
- Speed square
- Scribes
- Screwdrivers
- Homemade jigs of various kinds
- Stud finder

BUILDING YOUR OWN CABINETS: SIMPLE BOXES

(See Resources on p. 196 for books and videos on building kitchen cabinets.)

The heart of cabinets you build yourself will be simple plywood boxes. The plywood can be cut with a table saw or even a circular saw using a plywood track to ensure straight cuts.

The boxes can be assembled with screws, dowels, even nails. I use a router to make a *rabbet joint,* and then glue and screw the boxes together with 2-in. drywall screws. I find it much easier to attach the drawer hardware before I assemble the box.

Instead of a traditional face frame (which can be made with a pocket-screw jig and applied with a biscuit joiner), I cover only the side edges of the cabinet box, using a rabbeted hardwood post.

A run of post-style cabinets.

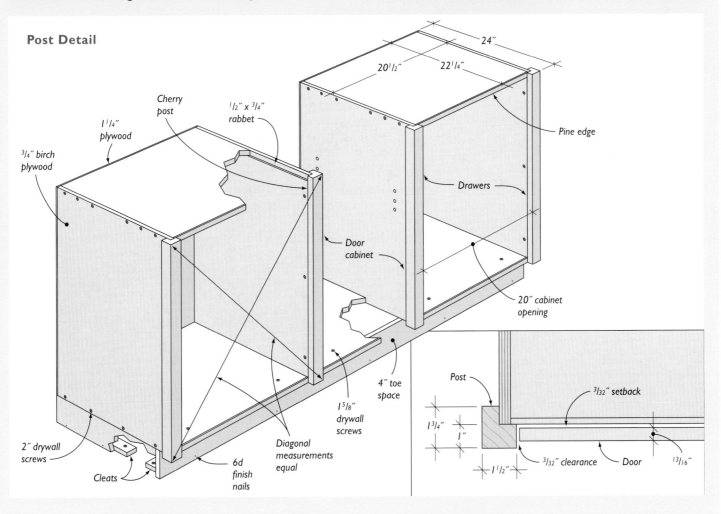

Post Detail

$1^1/4$" plywood

Cherry post

$1/2$" x $3/4$" rabbet

$3/4$" birch plywood

$20^1/2$"

$22^1/4$"

24"

Pine edge

Drawers

Door cabinet

20" cabinet opening

4" toe space

2" drywall screws

Cleats

6d finish nails

Diagonal measurements equal

$1^5/8$" drywall screws

Post

$1^3/4$"

1"

$1^1/2$"

$3/32$" clearance

$3/32$" setback

Door

$13/16$

BUILDING YOUR OWN CABINETS: SIMPLE DOORS AND DRAWERS

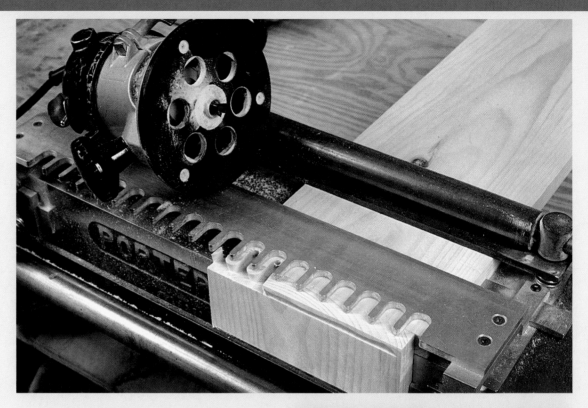

Dovetailed drawers can be made using a special router jig.

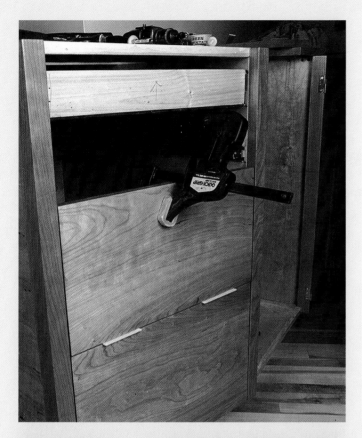

Simplified Drawer Construction

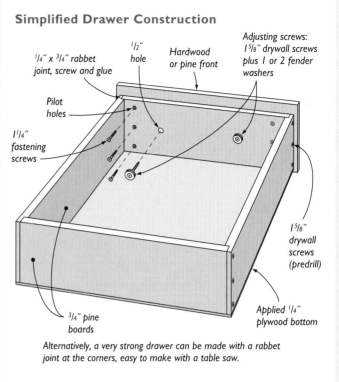

1/4" x 3/4" rabbet joint, screw and glue

1/2" hole

Hardwood or pine front

Adjusting screws: 1⁵/₈" drywall screws plus 1 or 2 fender washers

Pilot holes

1¹/₄" fastening screws

1⁵/₈" drywall screws (predrill)

3/4" pine boards

Applied 1/4" plywood bottom

Alternatively, a very strong drawer can be made with a rabbet joint at the corners, easy to make with a table saw.

A Flat-Panel Door

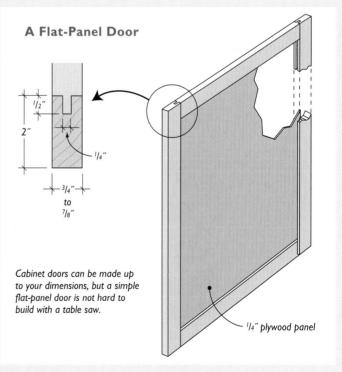

1/2"

2"

1/4"

3/4" to 7/8"

Cabinet doors can be made up to your dimensions, but a simple flat-panel door is not hard to build with a table saw.

1/4" plywood panel

After the drawer boxes are installed, a finish front can be adjusted for a perfect fit, then screwed in place.

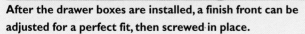

WHAT CAN GO WRONG

Though it's relatively durable, plastic laminate can be damaged by hot pans and can be scratched fairly easily. And once damaged, it can't be effectively repaired. Patterns that are mottled and textured hide the ravages of time better, while dark, shiny laminates show scratches more.

IN DETAIL

The finish you choose depends on how you plan to use your wood countertop. If you want to chop directly on it, use a mineral oil or pure tung oil finish. Butcher block usually comes with an acrylic finish that also can be chopped on. When needed, this acrylic finish can be renewed with tung oil. Bally®, a major manufacturer of butcher block (610-845-7511), also makes a product called Good Stuff®, available through its distributors, for this purpose. These chopping counters are tough and tolerate quite a bit of heat. In my experience, pots full of boiling water won't harm them, but I'm more careful with hot griddles.

Choosing Counters

Almost anything that can be fabricated into a flat surface has been used by someone for a kitchen counter. The ideal countertop would be water-resistant, stainproof, resistant to abrasion, easy to clean, and easy to repair. You'd also be able to cut on it without damaging it. Unfortunately, no single material offers all these properties. Therefore it sometimes make sense to have different types of counters in different work centers. Not that long ago, most counters were made with plastic laminates, such as Formica®, but in recent years much more expensive materials have become popular. Solid-surface counters (Corian® and Gibraltar® are common brands), granite, and stainless steel are beautiful and have some practical advantages, but they can add thousands to your project cost.

Plastic-laminate counters

Though perhaps not quite as fashionable as they used to be, well-detailed laminate counters can look great and last a long time at a very moderate cost. Modern laminates consist of several layers of kraft paper, which imparts the color and pattern, and a tough melamine top layer, all bonded together under heat and pressure. Plastic laminates are available in hundreds of colors and patterns.

The laminate used on countertops is about $\frac{1}{16}$ in. thick and is usually bonded to $\frac{3}{4}$-in.-thick high-density particleboard, built up at the edges to achieve the desired counter thickness. At one time, almost all laminate counters had laminate at the front edge and splash. Now a wood edge at the front and a wood or tile splash are common and, to me, more attractive.

You can make your own laminate counters, but counter shops or lumberyards can make up your counters for you at moderate cost, using your dimensions or full-scale templates. (See pp. 173–174 for information on how to make templates.)

Wood counters

Wood counters are still my favorite for many applications. Commercial butcher-block counters are widely available in maple or oak, while a cabinet shop can custom-build a plank top. We've made tops and insets in many hardwoods, including cherry, oak, ash, and beech. Softwoods

A plastic-laminate counter with a wood edge and tile splash. A well-detailed laminate counter can look great at low cost. It's also relatively easy to fabricate yourself. Photo by Steve Culpepper, ©The Taunton Press, Inc.

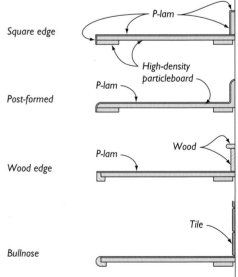

Plastic-Laminate Counter Options

Square edge

Post-formed

Wood edge

Bullnose

P-lam

High-density particleboard

P-lam

Wood

Tile

By varying the edge and splash details, you can achieve many different looks with laminate.

Wood Counter Details

Always finish both sides of wood counters to minimize warping. Also, make sure the end grain is varnished, even if the top will be oiled. This helps prevent end checks, the small cracks that sometimes appear at the end grain. Wood counters are stable in length (parallel to the grain) but expand and contract considerably in width (across the grain) in response to changes in humidity and moisture content. Therefore, to permit this movement, they have to be fastened down using oversize or slotted screw holes (use washers under the screw heads). Where a wood counter meets a more stable material, like a plastic laminate counter, it has to be fastened in such a way as to accommodate the difference. Tight joint fasteners (see the photo at left on p. 178) are a good solution.

Fastening Wood Counters

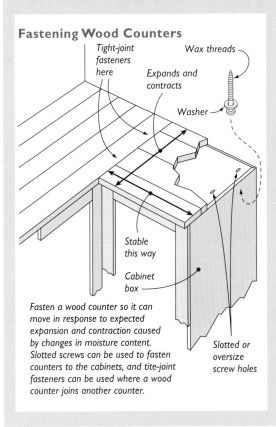

Fasten a wood counter so it can move in response to expected expansion and contraction caused by changes in moisture content. Slotted screws can be used to fasten counters to the cabinets, and tite-joint fasteners can be used where a wood counter joins another counter.

A custom cherry work counter with an oil finish.

Maple butcher block, sold with a nontoxic acrylic finish.

such as pine are not tough enough and are too porous.

These counters won't stay new looking. Instead, they'll develop a good, honest patina. Any oil finish is subject to staining, but food stains such as beet juice will usually go away on their own. On the other hand, iron pots, tin cans, or carbon-steel knives, if they're left on a wet counter, can leave a black iron stain that can be removed only by scraping down the wood. When the finish looks shabby to you, it can be scrubbed down or scraped, left to dry, then refinished.

PRO TIP

Don't use water-based finishes for counters or shelving that can get wet. In my experience, oil-based finishes age better, and are less subject to staining.

IN DETAIL

I've often applied tiles directly to a plywood substrate using ordinary tile mastic. But to ensure against cracks developing in the grout and possibly the tile, it's better to have a plywood base topped with a ½-in. cement backer board screwed to the plywood. Then use thinset mortar to attach the tiles to the cement board.

WHAT CAN GO WRONG

We've had mixed results with wood counters around sinks. They can be beautiful, particularly with an undermount sink and a beautiful drainboard carved into the wood. But no matter how well varnished the countertop is, water can get under the finish, which will eventually lead to black stains or worse. So we recommend against wood at the sink. If you do use it, though (as I have), wipe it dry after doing dishes, and every year touch up the finish and make sure the caulk between sink and counter is intact.

Counters that will not be chopped on can be finished with an oil-based satin polyurethane or traditional varnish. Such a counter will have to be treated with some care; it won't be as tough as a laminate or stone top, and hot pots shouldn't be placed on it. It can't take abrasive cleaners, either. But with proper care, a varnished wood countertop is relatively durable and will remain beautiful for years. Treat it like you would a wood floor, renewing the finish on it every few years. Sand the original finish lightly to get a good bond.

Tile counters

Ceramic tile has several virtues as a counter material. It's very durable, heatproof, and, if well installed, waterproof. I like to have a section of tile counter near a stove as a place to put hot dishes, and it can also work well at the sink.

For hygienic reasons, a glazed tile with low porosity makes the most sense. Also ask your vendor if a tile you are considering is tough enough for use as a counter. Many floor tiles work well. I'd advise using a smooth, relatively uniform tile for a flatter, easier-to-clean counter. Although some tiles are costly, many are affordable. Tile is also a relatively easy material to work with, particularly compared with solid-surface materials or stone.

But tile has some drawbacks. It's hard, which means that things dropped on it can break. The

+ SAFETY FIRST

Never cut meat—particularly poultry—on an oiled wood counter. Salmonella and other microorganisms can breed there and contaminate other raw foods that are processed on the counter. Always use a chopping board made for the purpose, which can then be thoroughly cleaned.

A tile counter with a wood edge.

A Good Way to Construct Tile Counters

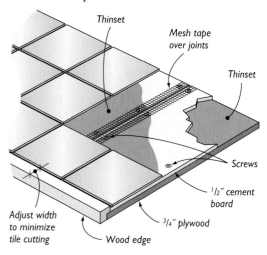

Thinset

Mesh tape over joints

Thinset

Screws

½" cement board

¾" plywood

Wood edge

Adjust width to minimize tile cutting

unevenness of the tiles themselves and the grout spaces make the counter less flat and smooth than most continuous materials, so cleanup is more troublesome. Also, the grout itself can stain or break down, though this last problem can be addressed by using the new epoxy grouts.

With the proper equipment, it's not too difficult to make your own tile counters. Sometimes I have made the substrate, and my customers have done the tiling. Careful layout is essential for a good-looking result and should minimize cutting.

Solid-surface counters

Solid-surface counters, such as Corian®, Gibraltar®, and Avonite®, are cast plastic: acrylic,

Cutting Tile

Different tiles are cut different ways. Thin, uniform ceramic tile can be cut with a small tile cutter that simply scores the face of the tile like a glass cutter. Then the tile is snapped apart over a fulcrum bar. Larger, thicker tiles probably need to be cut with a wet saw. Both of these tools can be rented. However, I like to avoid cutting tile whenever I can. Sometimes the dimensions of a counter can be adjusted to allow you to use the tiles full size. If you lay out the tile ahead of time and know the size of cuts you'll need, sometimes your tile vendor can cut some to size for you.

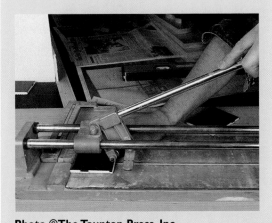

Photo ©The Taunton Press, Inc.

This Corian counter is bonded to a contrasting Corian sink. Many variations are possible with solid-surface materials. Photo courtesy of DuPont.

polyester, or a combination of the two. They are very expensive materials, but in some ways they make almost perfect countertops. They are the same substance all the way through, like wood, and can be machined almost like wood (they are worked with ordinary, carbide-tipped woodworking tools). A drainboard can be routed into the surface, and the edges can be decorated with various profiles. Pieces can be bonded invisibly. Sinks of the same material can be joined directly, seamlessly, and permanently to the counter. Scratches can be sanded out. These surfaces are also resistant to stains and heat and are

available in a variety of colors and patterns.

Solid-surface countertops are typically expensive, costing several times more than equivalent laminate countertops. In addition, while the materials aren't that difficult to work with, they are difficult to buy in sheet form unless you are a certified fabricator.

Stainless steel counters

Stainless steel is tough, heatproof, and impervious to water. It doesn't stain and is very easy to clean. It can be fabricated into almost any configuration, and sinks and backsplashes can readily be integrated into the counter. Although stainless steel counters are expensive, installation is a snap, which perhaps recoups some of the cost. After wood, it's my favorite top.

Stainless steel is fabricated in metal shops. The metal is bent on a huge, computer-operated folding machine, then welded at the joints. If you're planning a stainless steel counter, make a very detailed drawing because the cost will depend on the number of cuts, folds, and welds required.

PRO TIP

Stainless steel, though expensive, is versatile. Counters and sinks can be fabricated in any size and shape and permanently integrated together.

TRADE SECRET

Can you make your own solid-surface countertop? The short answer is no. Despite all of the advantages of the material, manufacturers will sell it only to certified fabricators. If you want a solid-surface countertop, you'll have to buy it through a dealer or from a certified fabricator.

Also, be sure to discuss the type of stainless, look at samples of the finishes available, and discuss those, too, with the supplier. Although stainless is stiff, it is usually installed over a full plywood substrate for support.

Stone and masonry counters

Granite has many virtues as a counter and is currently very popular. It's extremely durable, stain-resistant, and heatproof. It stays cold, which is great for rolling out pastry. It's also the most expensive of the currently common tops, unless you can scrounge a used piece and adapt your design to it. It also can be used as an insert in other counters.

Marble is softer and more porous than granite, but otherwise it has many of the same advantages. It just won't stay as pristine as a polished piece of granite. Slate also is sometimes used for counters.

Countertops made of granite, marble, or slate are usually made by local stone fabricators, who will have a large selection of samples for you to look at. The cost of the countertop will vary greatly depending on the stone chosen. Unless the counter is extremely simple, the fabricator will

Stainless steel is coming back into fashion. Photo ©Claudio Santini photographer.

come to your site after the cabinets are in place, make a full-scale template, fabricate the counter, and install it.

In addition to natural stone, there also is increasing interest in counters made of concrete. In fact, this is becoming a new kitchen specialty. These counters can be cast in place after the cabinets are built, which can be a mess, or built elsewhere, which may require sections to be joined

A stone top can be combined with a wood, stone, or tile backsplash. It looks great, protects the wall, and seals the space between counter and wall, which simplifies fitting and installing the countertop.

Improving Indoor Air Quality

For some, indoor air quality will be a major issue (see Resources on p. 196). Here are some basic tips.

- Begin by having adequate ventilation. Besides well-operating windows, install and use a range hood.

- Use water-based (rather than oil-based) paints, look for nontoxic finish materials, and leave things unfinished where it makes sense.

- Use unprocessed natural materials where you can. Many new, processed materials "offgas," or emit fumes of various kinds. For example, the adhesives in most particleboards and plywoods contain urea-formaldehyde.

- Some of the worst air-quality problems come from natural sources, such as molds, dust mites, and pollens. If your house has moisture problems, solve them, or your house will have mold. Unfinished wood harbors mold; if you are sensitive to mold, paint unfinished wood.

A used granite counter, at right, and a new piece of marble, left.

Concrete counters can be cast in place or fabricated off site and then installed, as was this example. Photo ©Richard Barnes.

on site. The materials are inexpensive, but fabrication is not. The finished counters can be surprisingly varied in color and texture. They also are tough and heatproof, though they're subject to staining and should be sealed.

The counters in the photo at left on p. 57 and in the top photo on p. 73 are a material known as Fireslate-2®, which is essentially the same material as the counters in your high-school chemistry lab. It's a proprietary product made with portland cement. It comes in black, gray, or a lovely green. It's hard and tough, but not nearly as hard as granite. For that reason, it's relatively easy to sand,

PRO TIP

A standard backsplash is 4 in. high, but it can be adjusted to match the width of tiles or to line up with the sills of windows above the counter.

TRADE SECRET

The cost of a counter will vary with the material, how complicated the counters are, and how the edges are detailed. A simple rectangle will be a lot cheaper than a counter of the same size with curves, an integral backsplash, an undermount sink, or other features that add labor. For comparative purposes, here are typical installed prices for simple counters of different popular materials.

Material	Cost/running ft.
Laminate	$ 47
Tile	$ 57
Fireslate-2®	$ 90
Wood	$ 93
Solid Surface	$ 175
Stainless Steel	$ 212
Granite	$ 250

Backsplashes

The design of the backsplash is often an afterthought, but actually the splash detailing can make a big difference. It protects the wall from moisture and stains, it seals the counter at the back, and makes cleanup easier. It also can present opportunities to add a little storage as well as make an aesthetic statement. It can do a lot particularly for a laminate counter, which can be a bit humdrum with the standard matching laminate edge and laminate splash. The same counter, with a wood edge and a wood or tile splash, can look quite smart. If there is a window over the counter, I like to carry the splash right up to the window sill, which then becomes a shelf. Another detail I like is a wood cap above the splash. The cap trims the splash and serves as a little shelf. At a window, it can be continuous with the window sill (see the photo on p. 66 and the bottom on p. 70).

The splash detail can make your counter installation much more straightforward or more troublesome. It's often easier to install a splash after the counter is in, particularly on long counters. I prefer to run a row of tiles behind a counter (caulking the joint between counter and splash later) than to make a long section of plastic laminate or wood, attach it to the counter, then install them together and fit them to the wall. Other times, I like to screw a wooden splash to the counter from below before installing the counter, then add a cap piece, which is fit or "scribed" to the wall to close off any gaps due to unevenness in the wall. In either case, the idea is to come up with a detail that closes the gap at the back and enables you to avoid handling long heavy counters more often than necessary.

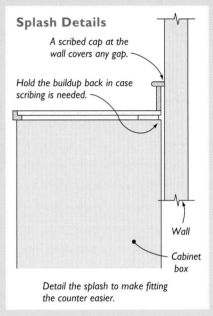

Splash Details

A scribed cap at the wall covers any gap.

Hold the buildup back in case scribing is needed.

Wall

Cabinet box

Detail the splash to make fitting the counter easier.

cut, and machine with ordinary tools. It also has to be sealed with a special sealer, then finished with tung oil. It's less costly than granite or solid-surface counters.

Flooring Options

A kitchen floor probably receives more use and abuse than any other surface in the home and must satisfy several somewhat contradictory requirements. Like a countertop, it should be unbothered by water and spills; its surface should be stainproof, abrasion-resistant, and easy to clean. At the same time, it should be easy on the feet, nonskid, and warm. No floor meets all of these criteria perfectly.

If you're renovating your kitchen, other criteria come into play. It's best if the new floor is flush with adjacent floors. A level change of up to 1 in. isn't typically a problem at a doorway because our feet are used to finding thresholds at doorways. But if the kitchen opens directly into a dining room or other space, a change in level should be avoided; it can be a tripping hazard. Since floorings vary in thickness, this consideration might influence what flooring you select.

Fireslate-2 is a durable material, the same as that used for the counters in your old high-school chemistry lab.

Visually, the floor is a major design element, the largest single surface of material in the project. It's a major source of color or pattern of colors. It can contrast or agree with the other materials you use, such as the cabinet wood. It can be a simple, unobtrusive pattern, or it can make a big statement. If it matches the rest of the house, it ties the spaces together or unifies the house; the kitchen, dining, and living spaces can seem like one large "great hall." If it differs, it can differentiate the kitchen from the rest of the house.

Save the floor you have

Perhaps the simplest choice is to keep the floor you have and extend it as needed. We have built many kitchens where we found ways to save the existing floor while making substantial renovations. Removing walls or moving cabinets will usually mean patching in at least some new flooring. So the first question is to determine if this is possible.

Traditional wood flooring is probably easiest to patch, extend, or refinish if it is in decent condi-

Environmental Concerns

Here are some tips that will help you renovate your kitchen in an environmentally friendly way.

- Minimize demolition, and make sure what you remove is disposed of safely, particularly if it is lead, asbestos, or other hazardous materials.
- Save what you can, and wherever practical, recycle. Refurbish cabinets that are still good, use existing furniture as part of your cabinet plan, and consider used sinks or stoves.
- If your existing floor can be repaired, repair it.
- Where possible, choose simple, locally produced, natural, relatively unprocessed materials. Look at its "embodied energy" (that is, the energy—and toxic wastes—generated in its manufacture, distribution, transport, and eventual disposal). Getting some air-dried pine from a local sawmill to your house will require much less fossil fuel and emissions than a similar board that has traveled across the country or across the sea.
- Make sure your house is energy efficient. Use good-quality windows and doors, upgrade your insulation levels as you renovate, and make sure your heating system is efficient and tuned.
- Buy a new refrigerator because new models use far less electricity than those made 10 or more years ago.
- Keep it simple. Building a small and simple kitchen uses fewer resources than does a huge or elaborate kitchen.

This kitchen features cabinets largely made without plywood or particleboard, recycled appliances, and natural finishes from Livos® in a superinsulated house.

TRADE SECRET

Salvaged building materials—including antique heart-pine flooring that was widely used in the 1920s—have become increasingly popular and are widely available through mail order.

IN DETAIL

In one recent project, most of the house was floored with beautiful #3 maple, which was about 20 years old. We removed the old vinyl flooring in the kitchen and mudroom and extended the maple flooring throughout. The crew was able to blend the new flooring with the old almost invisibly, giving the flooring a continuity that unifies the entire house.

tion to begin with. Sometimes old tongue-and-groove strip flooring, which is about 2¼ in. wide at the top face and tapers slightly toward the bottom face, has been sanded down so many times that spaces appear between the boards. If so, the floor is probably ready to be replaced. Sanding further may begin to reveal the tongues and grooves. Sometimes the floor will be badly stained where a stove has been sitting for a few decades. But a decent strip floor can often be patched almost invisibly, if you can find a source of matching wood. With a relatively recent floor—only 30 to 40 years old—it should be possible to buy new matching flooring. The older the floor, the more difficult this will be, as flooring sizes may have changed.

Old, wide pine floors, such as those found in old farmhouses, are usually easy to patch, although the new flooring will be lighter than the old, even after refinishing. It's still possible to get pine boards up to 24 in. wide from local sawmills, at least in the Northeast.

Since ceramic tile is so durable, an old tile floor may be in nearly perfect condition. But it may be difficult to find matching tiles for patching. First, though, check to see if there isn't a box of leftover tiles in the garage or basement. It's surprising how often there will be a stash somewhere left by a previous owner. Lacking that, you will have to find the best matching new tile. You may be able to lift tiles from one place to use somewhere else, but if they are well secured, it may be impossible to remove them intact. Often, though, you can count on the poor workmanship of previous renovators to make salvage possible.

It is much less likely that you will have an old resilient floor (either vinyl tile, linoleum, or "sheet goods") that is in good shape or that you want to save. But it isn't impossible. Again, you may have some extra tiles somewhere in your house, or the local tile company may have a box somewhere.

Some floor-tile designs haven't changed that much and are still available. If you opt to try to repair a resilient floor, I'd suggest having a pro look at it. He or she may be able to salvage a floor that a do-it-yourselfer cannot.

New hardwood floors

Hardwoods such as oak, maple, and birch and now even tropical species make great flooring. They are beautiful, tough, somewhat flexible, easy to work with, repairable, and refinishable. Traditional strip flooring most commonly comes in a 1x3 tongue-and-groove format and is usually *end-matched*, which means that the ends of the pieces (they come in random lengths) are tongue-and-groove also.

Strip flooring isn't difficult to install. It's simply blind-nailed through the tongue to the subfloor, with the groove of the next piece covering the nails. Until recently, this nailing has been done with flooring nailers driven by a rubber-tipped sledge. Whacking the nailer with the sledge drives the piece into position as it secures it. Today, pneumatic flooring nailers make this process much easier. They may be available from tool-rental places or from your flooring supplier, although many vendors still offer only the older-type machines. If you are able to find a pneumatic model, you also will need to rent a compressor. (for more on installing wood flooring, see pp. 152–153).

Wood-strip flooring is usually put down in straight rows throughout a whole room, but it also

Prefinished Flooring

Lately my partners and I have started using prefinished hardwood strip flooring. It's available in a variety of species, grades, and widths and at a price that is comparable to unfinished flooring plus finishing and even less. It is installed similarly to regular strip flooring but without the mess and delay of sanding and finishing. You don't even have to evacuate the room completely of furniture—just shift it over to one side at a time. This flooring isn't as smooth as a sanded floor because there is a slight "microbevel" at the boards' edges to minimize the joints between adjacent boards. But the finish, applied under factory conditions, is more uniform than you can typically achieve on site.

A floor of face-nailed wide pine boards is economical and charming, but it does not wear nearly as well as a hardwood floor. It has to be refinished more often. And even with carefully dried boards, expect some spaces to appear between boards.

Nailing strip flooring with a pneumatic flooring nailer.

can be put down in a herringbone or parquet pattern, and it can have ornate borders in contrasting species. Of course, these patterns require far more labor, and there is also more material waste.

Once the floor is laid, it will need to be sanded and finished. My preference is to use at least three coats of an oil-based polyurethane floor varnish. The water-based polyurethanes that I'm familiar with do not seem to be as durable as oil-based and not nearly as resistant to abrasion and staining, although there are good two-part water-based products used in commercial applications.

In addition to traditional solid-hardwood strip flooring, there are new types of flooring that feature thinner formats using veneers of more exotic woods. There also are wood-flooring systems that attach together with special clips that allow the floor to float over its subfloor, which is useful when a floor is being installed over a slab.

Softwood floors

While we think of softwood flooring as being less dense than hardwood flooring, the term *softwood* really refers to the fact that the tree from which the wood comes is coniferous rather than deciduous. A few softwoods—particularly heart pine—are as hard as some true hardwoods. Yellow pine is a widely used softwood of intermediate hardness. But most softwoods—like eastern white pine,

IN DETAIL

Sometimes it's possible to make small design adjustments to minimize or eliminate the need for floor patching. For example, the position of a cabinet or the depth of a kick space might be adjusted slightly to cover an open or bad place in the floor. You might add a built-in bookcase or use a thicker baseboard to cover a gap neatly. These measures might save you the labor and expense of a whole new floor.

TRADE SECRET

Why is hardwood flooring made from narrow boards? All boards swell and shrink as they absorb moisture in summer and dry out in winter. Narrow boards minimize the effects of this expansion and contraction. Where wide boards might leave big cracks after shrinkage, or even buckle under expansion, narrow-board flooring can have no noticeable spaces at any time, if the flooring was seasoned and installed properly.

A pine floor is inexpensive and attractive but subject to wear. Shrinkage gaps between boards are hard to avoid.

probably the most common softwood flooring—are much more subject to denting and wear than a hardwood floor.

Pine-board floors are a good low-cost alternative to hardwood strip flooring, as long as you are willing to live with their disadvantages. The wider boards (typically 1x8s or 1x10s, though even wider boards may be available from local sawmills in rural areas) install quickly either with nails or screws. A wide pine floor can't be blind-nailed like strip flooring; it has to be nailed through its face. But you can make a virtue of this by using cut nails, an old-fashioned nail with a square head that can be left exposed. It's also standard practice to screw down a pine floor and plug the counterbored screw holes with wood plugs.

But besides being prone to denting, the finish on a softwood floor won't stand up as long, par-

ticularly in high-traffic areas like at the sink. That means refinishing the floor perhaps every two years, requiring that people take their shoes off when they come in, or simply reclassifying the wear as patina to be enjoyed.

Also, because pine is less stable than oak or maple and because the boards are wider, these floors have a significant shrinkage problem. It's not unusual to see a pine floor with ¼-in.-wide cracks between the boards in the winter. It's essential to dry pine flooring carefully before installing it by "stickering" the wood, which means stacking it carefully in a heated space with narrow wood strips separating the rows to maximize airflow. With heat nearby and a fan blowing air on the wood, air-dried pine boards will become really dry in a few weeks' time. If your wood is quite dry and the boards are wide and you are installing your floor during the dry heating season, you may want to leave a coin's thickness of space every few courses to allow for summer expansion.

Resilient floors

Resilient floors include old-fashioned linoleum, square vinyl tiles, and what is referred to in the building business as "sheet goods," synthetic vinyl flooring that comes in large sheets in a great variety of patterns.

Resilient flooring has many advantages that help make it perhaps the most popular choice for kitchens. It's soft to walk on, usually costs far less installed than hardwood flooring, and can be installed quickly, with no sanding or finishing (although sealers or waxes are often used). And of course, it's available in an unbelievable variety of colors, qualities, and patterns. Most resilient flooring is $\frac{1}{16}$ in. to $\frac{1}{8}$ in. thick and can be installed right over an intact previous floor, or better, over a new plywood underlayment. If it's necessary to raise the floor level to bring it into alignment with the flooring in adjacent spaces, a thicker underlayment or an extra layer of plywood can be used.

While self-stick vinyl tiles are widely available, I don't think that they have the durability of thicker, higher-quality tiles applied with mastic. The most common tiles are 12 in. square, though there are other sizes. Such tiles are often installed by homeowners because they can be cut easily with a utility knife or linoleum knife and installed piece by piece. Even intricate shapes can be cut easily if the tile is heated with a heat gun or torch. It's less daunting than working with sheet goods, because if you make a mistake in fitting, you are out only one tile. Still, there are many tricks to doing a quality job, including starting your layout in a logical place.

Sheet goods, of course, are handled in large sheets. The usual practice is to make a pattern out

Some vinyl floorings, in both sheet and tile forms, were once made using asbestos fibers. If in doubt, have a sample tested.

Asbestos in Your Floor?

Until the mid-1980s, vinyl tile was known as VAT, or vinyl asbestos tile. Asbestos fiber was used as a reinforcing binder. Asbestos also was used in sheet vinyl. For many years, VAT was probably the most common flooring, particularly in public buildings, and there is a lot of it still out there. VAT floors that are intact are safe because the asbestos is encapsulated. But when the tiles age and fall apart, the asbestos that is released is hazardous, particularly if you are trying to repair an old VAT floor. The tiles you remove are hazardous waste. Increasingly, the practice is to avoid removing these tiles by flooring over them with another layer of underlayment and new nonasbestos flooring. If you suspect your old floor contains asbestos, you can have a sample tested. Your state environmental protection agency or health department should be able to tell you where to have this done. Also call your local building department about current regulations that may apply.

PRO TIP

Design your vinyl-tile floor on your floor plan. Draw in the grid of 9-in. or 12-in. squares, make photocopies, then use colored pencils to try out ideas.

TRADE SECRET

The quality of a resilient-floor installation depends on the quality of the underlayment installation. I like to use ¼-in. lauan underlayment because it has no voids in the inner layers and no knots on the top surface. We level and fill gaps or voids in the subfloor below, then nail the underlayment down with a grid of special underlayment nails every 4 in. to 6 in. in both directions. Leveling materials can be applied on top of the underlayment to smooth the surface for laying the resilient flooring.

IN DETAIL

If possible, select flooring materials that allow your new kitchen floor to be flush with adjacent spaces not separated by doorways. A height change up to perhaps 1 in. isn't a big problem if there is a doorway; people are used to level changes marked by doors. But a threshold in the middle of a space is a tripping hazard that should be avoided.

A classic pattern in vinyl tile. Photo ©davidduncanlivingston.com.

Vinyl tiles in a neutral pattern. Photo ©The Taunton Press, Inc.

Typical Floor Cross Sections

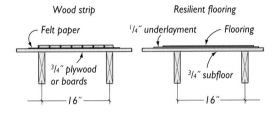

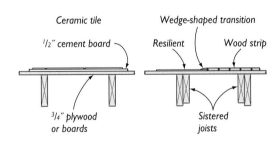

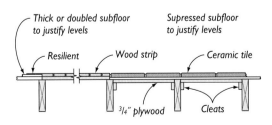

Wood flooring usually goes over a subfloor of ³/₄-in. plywood or boards. Resilient floors usually go over special thick-plywood underlayment made for the purpose. Ceramic tile goes over a reinforced cement board. Sometimes you can alter the detailing to make different areas of flooring flush.

of kraft paper, then cut the flooring to match the pattern. If the room has a simple shape, and particularly if the edges will be covered by cabinets or baseboards, this isn't a difficult project. For a really large or complex floor, though, you might want to have a pro do this for you.

Laminate flooring

Plastic-laminate floorings are increasingly popular. Like plastic-laminate countertops, they are a composite with several layers: In this case the base is particleboard, about ⅜ in. thick. To that is bonded a layer of plastic with a printed design, usually from a photo of wood flooring or ceramic tile. A tough, transparent top layer provides the finish. The result is a floor that looks more or less like wood or tile and is fairly inexpensive to install. It goes down in panels about 1 ft. by 3 ft., joined by tongue-and-groove joints.

Laminate flooring isn't nailed or glued down. A thin, slick foam pad is laid down over any smooth, flat subfloor, or over the existing flooring. The pieces are fastened to each other and simply rest on the foam pad. Some laminate floorings are

The new laminate floorings are easy to install and provide an alternative to resilient floorings.

glued together, using special band clamps to force the panels together. The newer versions, though, use a modified tongue-and-groove joint that allows the flooring panels to interlock easily with no glue. This *click-together* flooring is very easy to install (see pp.154–155, for more details).

Ceramic-tile floors

Ceramic tile and natural stone (like slate, for example) are popular flooring materials and for good reason. They are very durable and probably age better than any other type of flooring. I've seen stone and tile floors in good shape that were hundreds of years old. There are, of course, many

Flooring Costs

Installed flooring costs (includes underlayment, if needed):

- Softwood boards $3 to $6/sq.ft.
- Vinyl (tiles or sheet) $3.50 to $7.50/sq. ft.
- Plastic laminate $5 to $6/sq. ft.
- Wood laminate $6 to $8/sq. ft.
- Hardwood tongue-and-groove $7 to $14/sq. ft.
- Ceramic tile $10 to $18/sq. ft.

Heat From Your Floor: Two Alternatives

In solar design, dark-colored masonry floors are often placed in south-facing spaces where they will receive direct sunlight. The floor's mass absorbs and stores the sun's heat, and when the sun goes down, the heat is slowly radiated back into the room. It's the simplest solar storage system. If your kitchen has ample south-facing windows, a tile floor could make sense in exactly this way, particularly if the house is well insulated.

In-floor radiant heat has become increasingly popular. A network of special tubing is looped either within or underneath the floor, and hot water from your boiler circulates through it, turning the entire floor into a warm, gentle radiator. This is an extremely comfortable and efficient heating system that completely replaces baseboard convectors or radiators. Although this system can be done with a floor of any construction, it makes the most sense with tile set on a concrete slab perhaps 2 in. thick, into which the tubing is cast.

Photo by Charles Miller, ©The Taunton Press, Inc.

IN DETAIL

Most flooring vendors can help you figure out which adhesives, grouts, additives, and finishes you will need. In many cases, they will also have avail-able for rent the wet saws and other tools that you may need.

TRADE SECRET

The most common drywall thickness is ½ in., but ⅜-in.-thick drywall is a little more flexible and can be handy for patching. Where fire protection is an issue, use ⅝-in.-thick fire-rated drywall; in certain applica-tions it's required by code.

TRADE SECRET

Moisture-resistant drywall, sometimes called green board or MR drywall, is intended to be used in high-moisture areas such as above counters or on bathroom walls or ceilings. It isn't waterproof, however, and should never be used where it might come in direct contact with water, nor should it be used as a tile sub-strate in wet areas.

Large Mexican quarry tiles, installed by the owner, continue through the entry and hallway to tie the spaces together. They also help store solar gain from the ample south windows.

This slate floor was set over cement board, like ceramic tiles. So that it would be flush with the brick hearth, the joists under the hearth were notched.

kinds of ceramic and stone tiles in many price ranges, but in general, a tile floor will cost more than a resilient floor.

On the negative side, tile is hard under foot. Some people find it more fatiguing to work on a ceramic floor than on wood or resilient flooring, and dropped dishes will certainly break. Also, tile can feel cold, particularly if it is over an unheated basement or uninsulated slab, because the material quickly conducts your body heat away. Also, tile is relatively expensive.

If you're thinking about tile flooring, make sure the floor system can take the extra weight. If the subfloor is too thin or the joists too widely spaced or undersized, the floor system will deflect and cause cracks in the tiles or at grout lines. If the floor feels at all springy when you jump on it, consult a builder or flooring contractor for an assessment. (See pp. 123–127 for ways to beef up floor framing.)

Walls and Ceilings

Beyond selecting a color, most people give hardly a moment's thought to the ceiling and wall treatment in most kitchen projects. But the materials, textures, and colors of these surfaces, and sometimes the structure of the ceiling, can go a long way toward establishing a style for your new kitchen, particu-larly if you want to set it off from the rest of the house. Although you may end up with the obvious choice—a painted drywall wall or ceiling—it may be worth looking at some alternatives.

Many kitchens are so fully packed with cabinetry that the walls are barely visible. While that some-times is necessary, it can make the kitchen feel dark and too much like a kitchen display. Don't neglect the appeal of a bit of open wall to look at, a place to hang a picture or post a calendar.

Installing long sheets of drywall minimizes the number of joints. The 1x3 strapping on the ceiling joists allows the ceiling to be leveled or flattened, if it is uneven, and to establish 16-in. centers. Photo by Charles Miller, ©The Taunton Press, Inc.

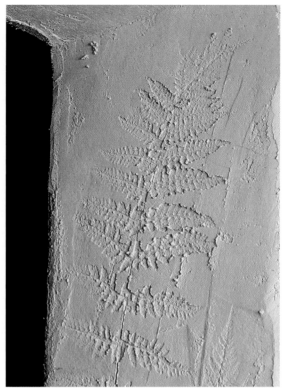

To get the fern design on this plastered wall, designer Kerrin McCadden imbedded ferns in the wet plaster, and pulled them out at just the right moment.

Gypsum drywall

Drywall—often referred to generically by the brand name Sheetrock®—consists of gypsum (a naturally occurring mineral) faced with paper. Drywall sheets are 4 ft. wide and come in lengths from 8 ft. to 16 ft. The long edges are tapered, which allows the plastering of the joints to be virtually invisible. (For more information on drywall, see pp. 143–150.)

Drywall is by far the least expensive wall and ceiling finish. It goes up fast and can be cut and finished with simple, inexpensive tools. It takes paint and wallpaper well, and it's easily repairable. The most dramatic day on a building project is the day the drywall goes up. Done by pros, the speed seems miraculous, completely transforming a building in a matter of hours.

Skimcoat plaster

If your house is old enough, you may have plaster and lath walls instead of drywall. Plaster used to be applied about ⅜ in. thick over a base of wood lath, the spaces between the laths providing purchase for the plaster. If you have this type of wall, there is a good chance you will be using drywall to patch it.

Today, most plaster is applied in thin layers over a special water-resistant ½-in.-thick drywall known as *blueboard*. There are different systems, but typically the joints are taped with a mesh joint tape and the joint coated with a quick-drying joint compound such as Durabond 90®. A "scratch" or brown coat is applied to the whole wall, then a final coat of a finer plaster. Sometimes the process is accomplished with a single coat. A single layer of brown coat can leave a nice textured or rough plaster wall.

TRADE SECRET

Homeowners often successfully hang and tape their own drywall, but here are three arguments against it: First, a professional's joints will be flat and invisible, while yours are likely to be uneven and show through the paint. Second, a professional can do in a single day what it might take you weeks to do (this can make a big difference when your family is without a kitchen). Third, drywall is the bargain among subcontract specialties. You won't save that much doing your own work compared with the time spent. Concentrate on tile or carpentry, where you can probably realize some significant savings, and leave the drywall to the pros, unless the amount needed is quite small.

IN DETAIL

Traditional beaded wainscoting is available quite inexpensively in common knotty pine and clear pine, as well as in more expensive woods like clear Douglas fir. It also is available in a plywood sheet-goods version that actually looks quite realistic.

Beaded wainscoting is easy to install and adds an informal and practical element to a kitchen.

Different ceiling elements add variety. Here are exposed timbers, a nice hood.

A good plasterer can achieve an amazingly smooth finish that is harder and more durable than the usual paper surface of drywall. It has a distinctive effect, reflecting light differently, even under a coat of paint. While it is unlikely that you'll be able to achieve this kind of result if you haven't worked with plaster before, textured plaster walls are well within the capabilities of most homeowners.

Paneling walls and wall trim

Traditionally, many kitchens had *wainscoting*, 30-in.- to 36-in.-high wood paneling covering the lower half of a wall and trimmed with a chair-rail molding. Above that is plaster. The idea is that the paneling could take some rough use, and the chair rail protects the wall from being banged up by chairs being leaned against it. Apart from these practical benefits, I just love the way wainscoting looks: It's intimate, homey, and old-fashioned, all the things I'm drawn to.

Applying drywall to all surfaces isn't the only possibility. Here, simple wood paneling is painted differently on the walls and ceiling. The ceiling slopes, and a skylight lets in lots of light. Although the cabinets and fixtures are simple and economical, the kitchen looks great. Photo ©Richard Stringer.

While boards used for paneling and wainscot can be beaded, they also can be flat, and they're available in different widths and configurations for different looks. Many kinds of paneling can be used on walls, or even on ceilings, including recycled barn boards, rough shiplap boards, and various molded patterns. You can choose a painted finish, though wainscot and paneling also can be varnished.

Ceiling variation

Most houses have ceilings that are 8 ft. high, and almost all ceilings in a house are treated the same way: with a coat of white paint. A variation in ceiling height, design, color, and treatment can add a lot of life to a house design. A high ceiling, for example, might make sense for a big public space and a lower one for a smaller or more intimate space. Along with the floor, a ceiling can help establish the feeling of a kitchen and distinguish it from the rest of the house.

One option is to use paneling on the ceiling. Another is simply to paint the ceiling a different color than the walls. A ceiling also can be set off with indirect lighting. In some cases, you can leave ceiling joists exposed, finishing them or leaving them rough.

CHAPTER FOUR
Fixtures

1 Large Appliances, page 86

2 Sinks and Faucets, page 90

3 Accessories, page 92

Appliance manufacturers are constantly changing their products. Some relatively recent innovations, like microwave ovens, self-cleaning stoves, and frost-free refrigerators, are now standard. Although some changes are strictly cosmetic, a few are quite significant. New appliances are quieter and much more energy efficient. Dishwashers use less water, and refrigerators use so much less electricity that it no longer makes sense to keep an older model that may work perfectly well.

At the same time, old appliances—or new appliances that look like old appliances—have become very popular. Old soapstone sinks and wood/gas stoves that 20 years ago were happily tossed into the dumpster are now so highly prized and highly priced that a whole new market in restoring and selling them has emerged. New appliances in retro styles come with top-end price tags. While there are more choices, it means more homework.

IN DETAIL

In addition to the recommended clearances in the manufacturer's specifications, several other considerations should influence where you put your stove. It should never go up against a wall at the side; leave at least 6 in. clearance here. The side of the stove should not be exposed where people walk by. Also don't locate a stove right at an inside corner, where two runs of cabinets meet.

Large Appliances

Not so long ago, my customers tended to buy basic appliances: 30-in. self-cleaning stoves for $600 to $800, simple faucets that cost $50 to $100, double-bowl sinks for $100. These items functioned perfectly, so why spend more? When they did choose more expensive options—a cast-iron sink, perhaps, a down-draft stove, or a separate cooktop with wall ovens—often as not they made these choices for visual reasons. The more costly stove or sink might not work all that much better, but it had *style.* Even more expensive appliances existed, particularly in obscure, commercial, or European brands, but few people were aware of them, and even fewer still were tempted: Why spend $400 for a faucet that did essentially the same thing as the $75 model?

Today, though, more of my customers are choosing the more expensive options: the $250 to $400 faucet, the $400 sink, the $3,000 stove. One of the big reasons is that domestic manufacturers are now making some elegant products with appealing features, and they are very widely available at appliance stores, home centers, and on the Web. Fortunately for consumers, the features once found exclusively on these expensive products are increasingly appearing on standard and

The owners make maple syrup on this stove, making the powerful burners and the big hood a necessity.

economical models. For example, my $500 stove has sealed burners, a power burner, ergonomic controls, and simple black-glass styling.

Be practical as you make decisions about your kitchen appliances. Look at your actual uses and the features you need, and check out the energy-consumption and noise ratings on the appliances you are selecting. Examine the controls, making sure they are easy to grip and turn and also easy to grasp mentally. A lot of the newer models are controlled by electronic keypads. If you're not inclined to master these, you might look for simpler models with old-fashioned buttons and knobs.

Perhaps most important, find out how difficult it will be to get the appliance serviced. Expensive appliances are sometimes more trouble-prone, particularly a new model or one with a lot of electronics. Parts may be costly or difficult to obtain. Check out who can service your new

Safe Locations for a Stove

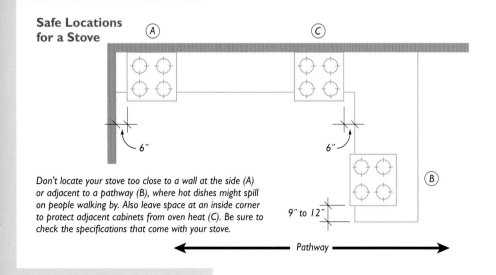

Don't locate your stove too close to a wall at the side (A) or adjacent to a pathway (B), where hot dishes might spill on people walking by. Also leave space at an inside corner to protect adjacent cabinets from oven heat (C). Be sure to check the specifications that come with your stove.

6″

6″

9″ to 12″

Pathway

A freestanding KitchenAid® stove. It has a 6-in. back, a continuous burner surface, and power burners of 14,000 and 12,500 Btu. The burner controls are big and easy to grasp. The oven control is an electronic touch pad.

appliances locally, and look for solid warranties. Make sure your purchase won't turn sour when service becomes necessary.

Stoves

The standard domestic stove is 30 in. wide with a 36-in. counter height, and is designed to go with standard 25-in.-deep counters. Within these limits, dimensions vary. Some stick out farther at the front; some have much higher backs. Also, some fit tight to the wall at the back, while others are designed to have a gap for airflow.

The 30-in. size is standard for good reasons: It has a big oven and plenty of room on the burners. If you are considering a wider stove, make sure it won't rob you of essential counter space. In many kitchens, a 36-in. or even wider stove will leave you with too little work surface. In really small kitchens, a 20-in. or 24-in. stove may make sense. In Europe, in fact, where space is at a premium,

24 in. (60 cm) is an accepted standard for stoves (some of these small—but expensive—European stoves are available for the American market). For most, a 30-in. stove should be completely adequate, unless there is a compelling reason to go larger or smaller.

Freestanding stoves simply sit on the floor and have backsplashes that extend 4 in. to 12 in. up at the back. *Slide-in* stoves also sit directly on the

Alternatives to the Standard Stove

Used stoves are making a comeback. Some are beautiful, and they may offer practical advantages, too. Being simple and heavily built, they may be rugged and trouble-free, and if you're lucky, they may be cheap or even free. But if you are considering using an antique stove, make sure it meets modern safety standards. Although charming and beautifully made, some early pilotless gas stoves, lit only with a match, don't comply with modern building codes. Your gas company will not install them. There are a few companies that specialize in restoring old stoves or making them meet newer regulations, but this work may cost you more than a new stove.

A beautiful old gas/wood stove. But it took a lot of work to get it working safely.

While commercial restaurant stoves have become popular, they often don't work well in a domestic kitchen. For one thing, they are very deep from front to back, up to 36 in., so they take up a lot of room. And although the amazingly powerful 20,000-Btu burners are fun to use—they will boil water in a minute—that kind of heat creates problems. Many restaurant stoves are not designed to be installed next to wooden cabinets (though they're often installed this way anyway, with some sort of heat shield on the sides in the hopes of avoiding a fire hazard). Now many manufacturers are making "professional residential" stoves. They are styled like commercial stoves and have burners almost as large—up to 16,000 Btu—so they work well for wok cooking and boiling up large pots of water, but they can be built into a run of cabinets like a conventional stove. Available from manufacturers such as Viking®, Garland®, Thermador®, Wolfe®, and DCS®, these stoves cost from $2,000 to $9,000.

IN DETAIL

My partners and I have built many kitchens without dishwashers and continue to do so, particularly with rural sites that are "off the grid." When there is no dishwasher, we build a draining dish rack that we call a "wonder no-dry," located over the sink. Dishes get hand-washed, then stored in the no-dry where they can drip-dry. Since the dishes are handled only once, it is about as quick as using a dishwasher for everyday dishes for a small family.

Occasionally, customers who have wanted to dispense with the dishwasher change their minds a few years later. To make adding a dishwasher simple, I try to place a 24-in. cabinet next to the sink. If I get that call, the cabinet can come out easily to make room for the standard 24-in. dishwasher.

floor, but usually have lips on either side to cover the gaps where they meet the counters. Since it's intended to sit between cabinets, a slide-in may not have a finished side, and typically there will be no splash or back. For that reason, slide-ins usually make sense for island or peninsula installations, or where a tile backsplash will cover and protect the wall. Less common are *drop-ins,* which have lips and no backsplashes, like slide-ins, but do not sit on the floor. Instead, they're built into the cabinetry. There may even be room for a drawer below a drop-in, and the cabinet kickspace will run right through. Slide-in and drop-in stoves are generally more expensive than freestanding stoves.

Regardless of the type of stove you choose, you'll want to make sure that it has small and large burners, so it can simmer delicately as well as heat quickly. Also, see if the stove has sealed burners and other features that make it easy to clean.

Refrigerators

To my eye, few refrigerators are elegant. They're blocky and massive, with most of them sticking out beyond the counter by 4 in. to 8 in. Don't buy a bigger refrigerator than you need, particularly if the layout is at all tight or limited. If you can do with a 27-in.- or 30-in.-wide unit, a 36-in. model will simply reduce the amount of counter and cabinet space you can develop. The smaller the fridge, the bigger and more spacious the room will seem.

There are other approaches to making this appliance less imposing. Companies such as Sub-Zero® and Conserv® make 24-in.-deep units that can be blended into your cabinetry. Another idea is to make a niche in the wall behind the refrigerator so that the unit doesn't have to project quite as far into the room. In some cases, you can recess the unit completely into a wall. If you do this, you have to make sure there is sufficient air circulation around the fridge.

Recessing the refrigerator partway into the wall keeps the face flush with the adjoining cabinet faces, making the refrigerator less obtrusive.

There are three common types of refrigerators. The conventional style has the freezer on top, usually with its own door. The main disadvantage is that the lower shelves are awkward to reach. The second type, with the freezer on the bottom, is more convenient because all areas of the fridge are at a comfortable height. The freezer, of course, is less convenient, unless the model mounts the freezer as a drawer. As a rule, hinges and doors are designed to be reversible to accommodate your

Considerations for Locating a Refrigerator

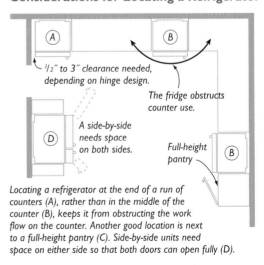

Locating a refrigerator at the end of a run of counters (A), rather than in the middle of the counter (B), keeps it from obstructing the work flow on the counter. Another good location is next to a full-height pantry (C). Side-by-side units need space on either side so that both doors can open fully (D).

Refrigerator Door-Hinge Geometry

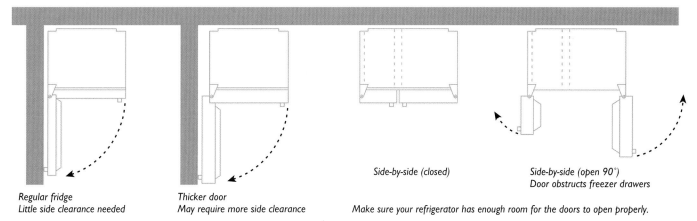

Side-by-side (closed)

Side-by-side (open 90°)
Door obstructs freezer drawers

Regular fridge
Little side clearance needed

Thicker door
May require more side clearance

Make sure your refrigerator has enough room for the doors to open properly.

kitchen layout. Side-by-side models—with the freezer on one side and the fridge on the other—have narrow doors that make this style quite useful when the fridge is in a narrow walkway. The limitation is that the shelves, being narrow, won't handle as large items as conventional units. In addition to these common styles, there are built-in units that blend in with the cabinets and smaller under-counter models.

Normally, a refrigerator is positioned by itself or at the end of a stretch of counter, up against a wall or pantry unit. As a rule, putting a refrigerator in the middle of a run of cabinets makes the counter very awkward to use.

For many years, most refrigerator doors operated much the same way. Special hinges located the pivot point of the hinge at the outer corner of the door. That meant that the space for a refrigerator had to be only a little wider than the unit in order to open its doors 90 degrees. A 30-in. fridge might need only a 30½-in. space. This is still true for many models.

Today, however, it's important to study the hinge geometry carefully, particularly if you are considering a corner location for your fridge. The spec sheets that come with the fridge may help, but there is no substitute for studying the unit carefully in the showroom, with tape measure in

hand and seeing what happens when you open the door and try to remove things from the fridge.

Many units now have thicker doors to increase door storage. If the fridge is between cabinets and a wall, as is often the case, the opening might have to be 1 in. or 2 in. wider than the unit, or the door won't open enough to access the interior. Always study the door with your layout in mind. If your layout allows the door to open only 90 degrees or so, open the door that amount and make sure the drawers will pull out properly.

Side-by-side units present an additional problem. With the doors open only 90 degrees or so, the doors and their bins may almost completely block the narrow interior. Side-by-sides are really designed for a position that allows the doors to swing all the way back.

Dishwashers

The standard dishwasher is designed to fit in a space 24 in. wide, 24 in. deep, and 34½ in. high (the usual space found below a 36-in.-high counter). Since floors are seldom flat and level, dishwashers have adjustable feet that allow some latitude, perhaps from 33¾ in. to 35½ in. If you have a low, nonstandard counter height, you may find that European models, such as Bosch® or Miele®, will fit where a domestic model will not.

TRADE SECRET

You can occasionally find old stainless steel or enameled cast-iron sinks that are in great shape. Sometimes they have integral drain boards and other attractive features that are no longer common.

IN DETAIL

If your kitchen has room for only a small sink, try to find a space-efficient one. Many stock 25-in. sinks have relatively wide margins at the fronts and sides and big decks at the back. But some models use their limited dimensions more efficiently. For example, Franke® sinks, (www.frankeksd.com, 800-626-5771) have very narrow margins at the fronts and sides, and avoid much of the decks at the backs by tucking the faucets in the corners, giving the sinks greater capacity. They also have another nice feature worth seeking in any sink you check out: The drains are located near the back of the bowls. That opens up extra space in the cabinet below for shelving or other storage.

Normally, a dishwasher goes in the cabinet next to the sink because all of its plumbing is attached to the sink plumbing. The water supply, with its own shutoff, will T off of the supply to the sink, and the dishwasher drain will join the sink drain right under the sink or drain into a garbage disposal.

Position the dishwasher carefully in relationship to the sink, as well as to the spot where you will pile dirty dishes and the place where those dishes will get stored after cleaning. It should be possible to stand at the sink, rinse off dirty dishes, and load the dishwasher without taking any steps. Similarly, it should be possible to unload the dishes and put them away with a minimum of steps. I advise my clients to look for quiet models, particularly if their kitchens are open to family-gathering areas.

Sinks and Faucets

Not long ago, almost all of the sinks put into new kitchens were either 22-in. by 25-in. single-bowl or 22-in. by 33-in. double-bowl models. Designed to drop into counters from above, these sinks are supported by lips that sit on top of counters. Stainless steel models have clips that secure sinks from below, while heavy enameled cast-iron sinks stay in place by their own weight (assisted by beds of flexible caulk). Stainless steel sinks are available in a wide range of prices, starting at around $60 for a simple model to perhaps $250 for a good-quality double-bowl sink; cast-iron sinks cost more. While these sinks are affordable, functional, and easy to install, they have one major drawback: The lips at the edges make cleaning off the counter awkward.

Because they make cleanup so easy, under-mount sinks have become popular. Undermount sinks are usually more expensive, and installation is definitely more difficult because the sink requires a precisely cut and finished hole in the counter.

An undermount sink makes cleanup easier because no lip obstructs sweeping water and debris into the sink. Sink installation is more difficult because the sink hole has to be precise and well finished; there is no sink lip to conceal it.

A granite counter with an undermount, solid-surface sink.

An old sink, designed to surface-mount, worked fine undermounted in this Fireslate-2 counter. The sink is simply screwed to the bottom of the counter with sheet metal screws and sealed with silicone caulk.

However, I think this is one luxury well worth considering.

Undermount sinks can be made of the same material as solid-surface counters (such as Corian) and seamlessly bonded to the countertop. This one-piece system is probably the most durable, convenient, and easiest to clean (see the photo on p. 69). I've also undermounted solid-surface sinks in other materials, such as granite.

Most types of sinks are now made in models designed to undermount. I've also found that conventional, drop-in sinks can be undermounted if sealed well to the countertop.

Sizing the sink

Whether you are using a high-end custom sink or a basic model, several design issues arise. First is the size of the sink. Large sinks are usually desirable, but sometimes a big sink can be a mistake. If a kitchen is small, the extra 8 in. that a double sink requires can make the difference between an adequate food-preparation counter and a cramped one. If your layout is tight, try both sizes in your layout drawings before you decide. Consider that depending on how you work, one big basin can be more useful than two small ones, while taking up less room.

Many designers recommend having two separate sinks: one for cleanup and another smaller one, located near the mix center or main work counter, for washing vegetables, adding water to recipes, etc. If you have a big, spread-out kitchen, this can make sense. In a compact kitchen, the cost is probably not justified, and the second sink may displace needed counter space.

Consider counter height at the sink. While sinks are typically installed in standard 36-in.-high counters, normally you are working down inside the sink, particularly if you are washing dishes. The effective working height is actually more like

A paddle-type double-handled faucet is easier to operate than one with small knobs. The tall spout is handy for filling large pots. Photo by Charles Miller, ©The Taunton Press, Inc.

PRO **TIP**

Although you can buy sinks, faucets, and appliances yourself, if you buy them through your builder or subcontractor, they are responsible if a unit is defective.

IN DETAIL

If you have a powerful commercial-grade stove, want better hood performance, or do not plan to have cabinetry above your stove, you will need a high-capacity (and more expensive) hood. Several companies, including Thermador, Miele, Viking, and Broan/Nutone®, make high-capacity hoods that can pull from 600 cubic feet per minute (CFM) to 1,200 CFM, using either an internal blower or a quieter external one.

TRADE SECRET

Hood design and installation is rather technical. If you are putting in a simple standard hood, it's fine simply to follow the directions that come with it. But if you are getting into a more complex or expensive system, avail yourself of the help offered by the technical departments of most hood manufacturers. If you can produce a cross-section drawing, in scale, that accurately describes the situation you are working with, they can advise you how best to use their products.

32 in., which requires leaning over awkwardly. If you have experienced back strain with your current sink, consider raising the counter. Sink depth factors into this as well. People often choose 7-in. or 8-in.-deep sinks (rather than the more typical 6 in.) because they hold more and offer more options. But a deep sink exaggerates the working-height problem. A deep sink may be an asset, but make sure it will really work for you.

In accessible design, there should be knee space below the sink, which generally requires a shallow sink. Although special accessible sinks are made (and can be fabricated), I've found that the simplest way to accomplish this is to use a basic, low-end stainless steel sink, which will usually be 5 in. deep to 6 in. deep.

Faucets

The choice of faucet is almost as important a decision as picking a sink. I feel the single-lever faucet, developed by Al Moen in the late 1940s, is one of the most important innovations in kitchen equipment. Although almost any faucet can do the job, a single-lever faucet with a large lever is a huge convenience. Turning the faucet on and off is one of the most frequent movements in the kitchen, even more so if you wash dishes by hand. A single lever streamlines these movements, making temperature and volume adjustments particularly easy.

A big lever is convenient in another way. I can operate my faucet with any part of my hand, but often I can also operate it with whatever is in my hand at the time. If I'm holding a small saucepan, I can hook it under the lever and turn the water on, or tap the lever down to close the flow. For these reasons, accessible design usually calls for lever faucets. If you still prefer double handles, paddles or levers will operate more easily than knobs.

Not all lever-handle faucets are created equal. Paddle designs vary, and a big, long, flat paddle is preferable. Also, look for faucets with a distinct, easy-to-regulate action: Moving the lever up and down changes the volume, while moving the lever side to side changes the temperature, for instance. That system makes sense and allows the water to be shut off without losing the temperature setting.

A spray, either incorporated into the spout or separate, is of course handy for rinsing pots and pans or for washing vegetables. Although a standard spout will work fine for most purposes, the high-clearance type is great for filling large pots.

Accessories

Hoods, small appliances, and other such accessories deserve as much care in selection as large appliances. They can have a large impact on the appearance of your kitchen. Small appliances can use up valuable counter space if not chosen carefully.

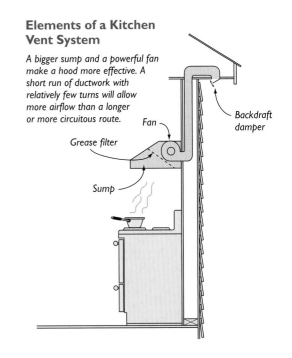

Elements of a Kitchen Vent System

A bigger sump and a powerful fan make a hood more effective. A short run of ductwork with relatively few turns will allow more airflow than a longer or more circuitous route.

Backdraft damper

Fan

Grease filter

Sump

Vents and hoods

A range hood is supposed to remove moisture, heat, food odors, combustion gases, and cooking grease. The conventional wisdom is that vented hoods are a necessity for maintaining indoor air quality, temperature control, and a pleasing, odor-free environment.

But hoods have drawbacks. They are noisy. They are often bulky, taking up a lot of visual space in the kitchen. Sometimes much of the grease from cooking falls onto the stovetop before it can get extracted by a hood. And a hood can be expensive. If you do relatively little frying, particularly of meat, have good general ventilation, and haven't felt the need for a hood in the past, you might consider doing without.

However, if you cook a lot of meat or greasy foods, are sensitive to smells, or have health issues involving air quality, I advise installing a hood or other ventilation system. Hoods tend to make sense in larger households or if you cook often for large groups. If you have a gas stove and a tight house, extracting combustion gases could be important. If you have a commercial stove with large, powerful burners, a hood really is essential.

A hood/venting system has several key components. The body of the hood is most effective if it fully covers the stove, is not too high above the burners, and has a deep cavity or *sump* to gather the air. The more powerful the fan, the more air it will move, while a backdraft damper will keep outside air from being blown back into the house (quite important in a cold climate). The duct works best if it is short and has a minimal number of turns. Most hoods specify how long the duct can be, given the number of turns there are.

With kitchen venting there is often no perfect solution. The features that make a design effective at extracting air can also create problems. A large, deep sump can make the hood look bulky and awkward, particularly in a small or narrow space;

For maximum effectiveness, a hood should largely cover the stove and be mounted not too far above the burners. New hood models have large sump areas but are detailed to minimize the visual bulk of the unit. Photo ©Richard Stringer.

A Miele hood. These are among the most elegant hoods out there, but they are fairly expensive, from about $1,300 to more than $2,000. Photo courtesy Miele, Inc.

PRO TIP

Ducted to a custom hood or to a wall vent above the stove, a commercial, roof-mounted extractor fan is quiet, economical, and effective.

IN DETAIL

Locate the microwave at a convenient height for your family. Generally, a height of about 4 ft. 6 in. is convenient for a standing person and reachable by both kids and adults. If wheelchair accessibility is important in your kitchen, the microwave can be installed below the counter.

IN DETAIL

If you drink coffee or tea, you may want to create a small work center for what is often one of the first rituals of the day. I have a little coffee grinder that stays plugged in on the counter, and on a small shelf above it is a special container for the beans, a box of filters, the plastic Melita® filter holder, and a coffee measure. My little setup makes preparing the coffee as much of a pleasure as drinking it. Whatever gear your morning ritual requires, include it in the plan.

Newer models of hoods, such as this Allure® hood made by Broan/Nutone®, are quieter and easier to clean than older models. Photo courtesy Broan/Nutone®.

the hood can actually make the room seem smaller. A more powerful fan will also tend to be noisier.

There are some standard approaches to mitigating these problems. You can use a smaller hood if you are willing to increase the power of the fan. Hood noise can be reduced by using better fans or by moving the fan out of the hood itself. Fans can be located in the duct or even on the outside of the exterior wall. A lot of hood noise also can be due to rattles or vibration in the duct, and it's possible to quiet a system by padding or tightening the duct or hood.

When the design calls for upper cabinets along the stove wall, the standard solution—a 30-in. hood mounted over the range and ducted to the outside—does a reasonable job. Broan/Nutone's new Allure range hood is available in several versions, and is quite a bit quieter and easier to clean than the old models. These hoods pull 200 CFM to 250 CFM of air, which is what the National Kitchen and Bath Association (NKBA) recom-

mends for a standard stove. The other standard solution, a microwave oven with an integral hood, also makes sense where the wall has cabinets.

Manufacturers are making ever more diminutive and graceful models. Miele makes several models of slim, elegant hoods, costing $1,200 to $2,000. Perhaps the most popular system is to eliminate the hood in favor of a downdraft system, such as those found on Jenn-Aire® stoves. A variation on this is a retracting vent, made by Thermador and Broan/Nutone, that rises up along the back of the stovetop when needed. Another solution is a tiny low-profile hood that disappears into the cabinetry above the stovetop when not in use, made by European companies such as Gaggenau® and recently introduced into the Broan/Nutone line.

Small appliances

Be sure to include locations for small appliances on your kitchen plan. If you can't find good places for them in your drawings, you won't be able to find them when you move in. Different small appliances present different problems.

Microwave ovens: There are still a few people who don't use them, but most kitchens now have a microwave. I have been in many kitchens

+ SAFETY FIRST

Typically there will be one or two spots in a kitchen where small appliances will be used the most. Provide extra GFCI-protected outlets at these locations. You may find that a clock, radio, coffee pot, or your big mixer will stay plugged in. Provide enough outlets so that other devices can be used without unplugging them. Locate these outlets so that the cords will be out of the way of work surfaces, knives, and stove burners.

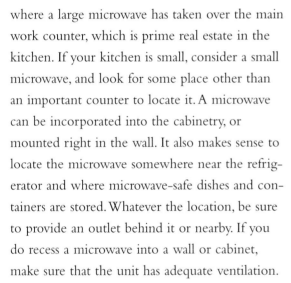

It's best to incorporate the microwave into the cabinetry, rather than sacrifice needed counter space.

An appliance garage offers countertop-level storage for the many gadgets and gizmos that are used in the kitchen. Photo ©Bruce Greenlaw.

where a large microwave has taken over the main work counter, which is prime real estate in the kitchen. If your kitchen is small, consider a small microwave, and look for some place other than an important counter to locate it. A microwave can be incorporated into the cabinetry, or mounted right in the wall. It also makes sense to locate the microwave somewhere near the refrigerator and where microwave-safe dishes and containers are stored. Whatever the location, be sure to provide an outlet behind it or nearby. If you do recess a microwave into a wall or cabinet, make sure that the unit has adequate ventilation.

Toasters and toaster ovens: These are usually left out on a counter. If possible, find a spot that will not interfere with your food-preparation counter. Some toaster ovens can be mounted on the underside of a wall cabinet using the manufacturer's hardware. Again, draw in its location on your plans, and provide outlets nearby. Sometimes it makes sense to place a toaster by the kitchen table rather than on a work counter.

Blenders and food processors: Although large and bulky, a blender or food processor is not typically heavy or difficult or move. I measure them carefully and provide a deep drawer for their storage.

Large, powerful commercial mixers: These have become popular for good reason, but they are very heavy. Most people will not want to lug one into and out of a drawer. If you use a commercial mixer frequently, find a place where it can be stored right on the counter. An ideal location would be near but not on your main food-preparation counter. An inside corner works well; the mixer can be slid forward when needed.

Sometimes a small *appliance garage* is provided for a mixer or other small appliances. This is essentially a little cabinet that encloses the storage area on the counter. A *tambour* (roll-away) door works best here because a hinged door won't open if there is anything on the counter in front of it. The appliance garage works well, but it does limit how you can use the counter, especially as your needs or equipment change.

Your Final

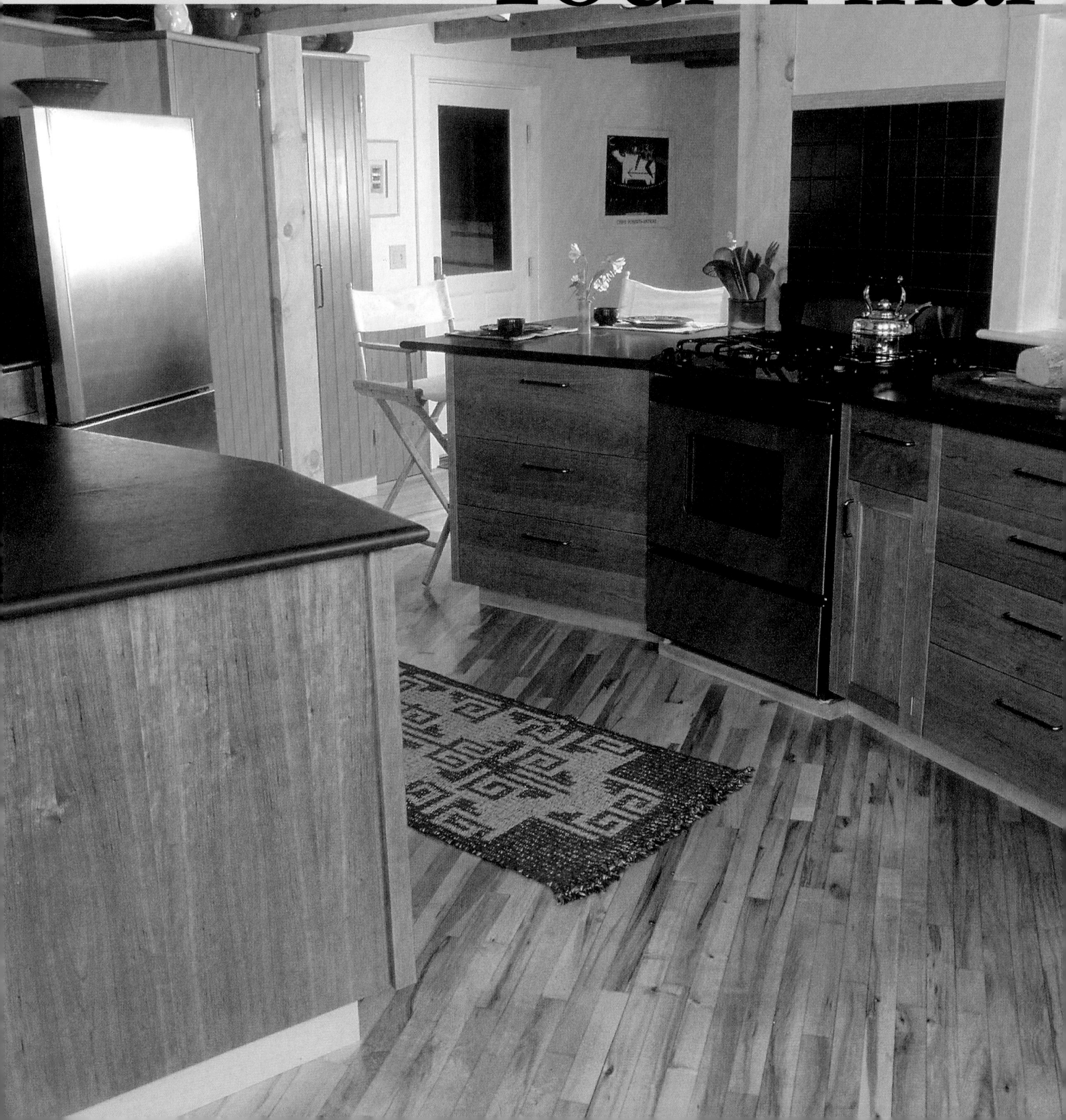

CHAPTER FIVE
Plans

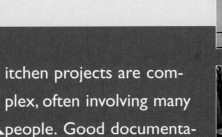

Kitchen projects are complex, often involving many people. Good documentation saves confusion and time.

For most kitchen projects, your necessary documents will include your revised floor plan and kitchen elevations, cabinet and countertop orders, spec sheets for appliances, your electrical plan, and, if needed, a window-and-door schedule.

An estimate is important and one of the more difficult items to prepare. If you are working with a general contractor, he or she will be responsible for the estimate. But if you are acting as G.C., you will have to do this yourself and budget as best you can.

You'll need a schedule that shows when each phase of the project will be done, when products must be ordered, and when business arrangements must be made to keep the project on track. Finally, you'll need permits and permit applications, plus bids, estimates, and contracts from people you hire.

PRO TIP

Make sure the lines on your drawings will be clear when copied. Make walls darkest and thickest, cabinets a bit thinner, and dimension lines thin, yet still clear.

IN DETAIL

It's easy to forget something important as you complete your design. Make sure you have found a convenient place (in the most appropriate work center) for these things:

- Knives
- Spices
- Cookbooks
- Paper towels
- Cloth towels
- Pot holders, hot mitts
- Plastic wrap, aluminum foil, etc.
- Trays, cookie sheets, etc.
- Most frequently used ingredients
- Phone, phone books, message materials
- Small appliances, where they won't obstruct food prep
- Recycling

Completing the Design

By now you should have a good floor plan (chapter 1), which shows a comprehensive layout with coherent work centers that meet your needs. You also will have elevations, which show the basic cabinetry plan and appliance locations, plus a preliminary lighting plan (chapter 2). You will have decided basically what *type* of cabinets you want and what finish materials the new kitchen will have (chapter 3). And you will have selected appliances and obtained spec sheets for each one (chapter 4). Review this material one more time, making sure the design confirms and supports your original design program. Make sure you've found a home for everything, particularly those things you use frequently. The sidebar at left lists some of the items that are easy to forget. Make any necessary revisions.

Fine-tuning your cabinet design

Before you order cabinets or start to build them, there are some further steps needed to make your design *complete* and *buildable*. The project that was our design example in chapters 1 and 2 can serve to illustrate what these steps are. The drawings on pp. 40–41 show where the project stood at this point.

Open-shelf units are often among the items designed last. This one has some narrow shelves for items of varying heights, plus 11-in.-wide shelves for plates, bowls, and cups. These wider shelves are slotted, designed to drain into the sink.

Typically at this stage there will be elements of the cabinetry that aren't fully thought out, particularly shelf units, pantries, and other components to be built on site. Draw these up now. There also are crucial dimensional issues that are easy to overlook. Errors or oversights here can make your cabinet installation much more difficult. Make sure you have enough room for the appliances, particularly the refrigerator. Double-check all your dimensions, especially as they relate to appli-

Factors That Influence the Space Available for Cabinets, and Your Cabinet Order

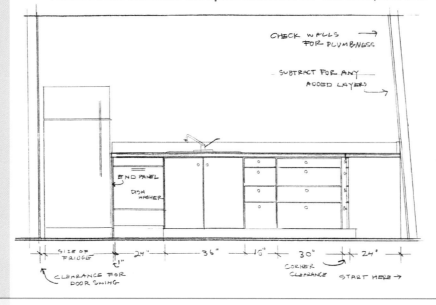

Out-of-plumb walls, new wall coverings, and needed corner clearances can influence the space available for cabinets—and your cabinet order. Stock cabinets are sized in 3-in. increments.

ances and fixed walls, to ensure that your cabinets will fit as built.

Use a level to check your walls, particularly where the cabinets will be installed between walls on both ends of a run. The out-of-plumb wall on the right in the drawing on the facing page is exaggerated, but it's not uncommon in some older houses for a wall to be off by an inch or two. In that case, there may be less space available for cabinets than a simple measurement at floor or ceiling level indicates.

Perhaps the trickiest issue is *corner clearances,* which involves the many ways the cabinets or appliances can interfere with each other at inside corners. The simplest example is the way doors and drawers open at a corner. If you had European-style cabinets meeting right at a corner, a drawer opening on one side might actually bump against the cabinet pulls on the other side; they wouldn't open fully. A cabinet door might open fully, or it might not.

To provide clearance, you'd add filler strips wide enough to make certain everything will open with room to spare. The size of the cabinet hardware you select is obviously a factor: Some handles project about 1 in.; others may stick out as much as 2 in.

Face-frame cabinets have a margin around doors and drawers, which may be as little as 1 in. or as much as 2 in., thereby creating an automatic clearance at the corner. Sometimes this will be sufficient without any added filler, but frequently filler will be needed, even with face-frame cabinets. There are several other reasons to add filler:

- Handles, doors, and knobs of appliances can project more than 2 in. beyond the front plane of the cabinetry. (Study appliance spec sheets carefully and, if possible, floor models, as well.)
- Houses aren't perfect, walls are out of square or plumb, and sometimes it's hard before demolition to predict exactly how long a run of cabi-

Corner Clearances
Make sure corner clearances allow doors and drawers to open properly.

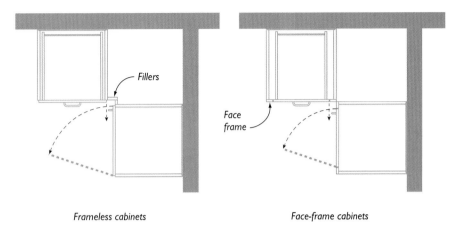

Frameless cabinets

Face-frame cabinets

nets will be, after old layers on the wall are removed and new ones added. An extra 1 in. to 3 in. of filler at an unobtrusive spot allows room for error of this kind.

- Stock domestic cabinets come in 3-in. increments in width, usually starting at 9 in. Sometimes fillers are added to make the total come out right without requiring custom units to be built.
- Fillers provide a convenient way to make a square, straight cabinet side conform to an uneven or out-of-plumb wall or other uneven surface, such as a brick wall.

There were several cabinet details to resolve in our design example. A number of storage units were fully designed. We knew that the 13-in. cabinet projecting out at the right in Elevation A (see plans in chapter 2) held dishes, but no details had been worked out. The idea was to be able to put the clean dishes in from the kitchen side and get them out from the sunroom side, where meals were served, which was two steps down. Shelves had to be at convenient heights on both sides. Additionally, we didn't want to block too much of the light, so the cabinet shouldn't be too high or bulky. Elevations D and E (on p. 100) show the solution we developed.

PRO TIP

To minimize confusion and delays during construction, plan everything well in advance and document your decisions in ways that others can understand.

WHAT CAN GO WRONG

Lead times will vary a lot with seasons, the economy, and other factors. here are some general guidelines:

■ Try to find your general contractor as much as a year ahead because good builders are often booked up.

■ Subcontractors such as drywallers or electricians might schedule work one to five months ahead.

■ Stock cabinets and laminate counters can be ordered a few weeks ahead, but "semicustom" or factory "custom" cabinets will often have a three- to six-month lead time.

■ If you are hiring a cabinetmaker, you may need six months or more in advance.

■ Most appliances can be obtained within a week or two, but more obscure items may take longer. (You don't want appliances delivered until the last minute if you can avoid it.)

■ Most flooring can be obtained within one to two weeks.

■ Most doors are available in about a week.

■ Some windows will be stocked by large suppliers, but they must be ordered and can take from one to about eight weeks to arrive.

Elevations D and E

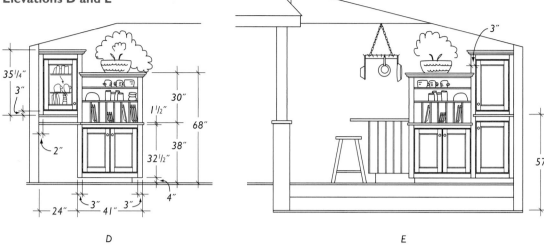

D

E

This custom unit for dishes was to be loaded from the kitchen side, then unloaded from opposite side, two steps lower.

We looked at several other storage details. One was the microwave, to be recessed into the wall. We decided after experimenting that it would work best 3 ft. 11 in. from the floor. We also looked more closely at the likely contents of the walk-in pantry. All of the pantry's shelving would be built on site out of plywood or pine, which would be much cheaper than trying to identify stock cabinets that might fit. Special areas, with dimensions, were set aside for canned goods, cereal boxes, recycling, wine bottles, brooms, and such.

Although I'm emphasizing function as I discuss these final revisions, this is also a chance to make your kitchen more beautiful. I've found that it often pays to ponder and even belabor your elevations at this point. I like to adjust dimensions, proportions, and details to try to achieve a harmonious and unified composition. I make things line up in different ways and try to create a little language of proportions and details that ties things together.

Your cabinet order

Your cabinet elevations should now show the basic dimensions of all the elements of each wall of cabinetry and appliance, including end panels (left of the dishwasher in Elevation A shown on p. 41), appliance clearances, and fillers needed to create corner clearances.

You can simply take your plan and elevations, with dimensions, to one or more cabinet dealers and ask them to put together a cabinet order based on your design. Every manufacturer sells its products in a variety of styles. You select a cabinet type, a door style, and a finish, and the salesperson takes it from there. You also could price out different product lines and price your kitchen at other vendors for comparison as well.

You also can get catalogs of the cabinet lines that interest you and put together the basic order yourself. One advantage of this approach is that you could determine which accessories and specialty cabinets are available from different sources. One company might provide more of the things you want as stock items.

Cabinet catalogs are usually easy to understand and provide relatively simple designations for the

Open shelves can be made on site and are endlessly variable. These are low, compact, and painted white to contrast with the base cabinets. They line up with the fridge at the top, for a more orderly composition. Photo by Sam Clark.

various products. A wall cabinet 30 in. wide by 42 in. high with hinges on the right might be designated simply W 30 42 R. A 24-in.-wide drawer base could be DB24. Standard cabinet widths are in 3-in. increments starting at 9 in. You can get a 21-in.-wide unit stock, but a 20-in.-wide one might be special order. Depending on brand, there will be a great variety of cabinets, including different drawer combinations, cabinets with pullouts, lazy Susans, cabinets made for inside corners, open shelf units, and so on. It's also important to be sure to order all the odds and ends, such as fillers, end panels if needed, and trim to cover the kickspace with finish material.

European manufacturers will have many of the same elements but will sometimes be marketed in metric dimensions. They may also use different systems for creating the kickspace—either threaded adjusting feet or continuous kickspaces built on site by the carpenters (see chapter 8 on cabinet installation).

If you do put your order together yourself, still have it checked by the vendor. Vendors do this every day and are sure to notice missing items; they're also likely to suggest useful alternatives.

Vendors can give you exact quotes on cabinet costs. Find out what the lead time is so you can order your chosen cabinet in time. You may find that some brands have such long delays that you can't use them on your schedule.

Ordering your countertop

Chapter 3 discusses the various types of counters and some of their advantages and disadvantages. The Trade Secret on p. 72 offers a cost comparison. Here it might make sense to divide counters more by how they can be *obtained*. Solid-surface, stainless steel, stone, and Fireslate-2 can't readily be made up by you or your contractor. They come from specialists. Most companies that market cabinets and counters can sell you solid-surface counters, made either by themselves or other suppliers they buy from. You can also buy stone or stainless steel tops from many cabinet suppliers, but you might consider going to the source: a sheet-metal shop for stainless steel or a company that markets and finishes granite for granite tops. These expensive tops represent a growing segment of the market, and it probably pays to comparison shop. Take a copy of your

TRADE SECRET

For stainless steel, solid-surface, or stone counters, be sure to find out when you have to order the counter to get it on time. Even if final measurements will be taken later, vendors can schedule a time slot for you and have the needed materials on hand.

IN DETAIL

Many doors are now ordered prehung, with the door already on its hinges (swinging the right way) and the hardware installed. For installation in an existing frame or for other special circumstances, doors can also be ordered *door only*, with or without the holes for standard hardware. Most door manufacturer and millwork catalogs offer a large variety of styles and types. As a rule, interior doors are 1⅜-in. thick and exterior doors 1¾-in. thick. In renovation work, doors are typically ordered and hung uncased (cased doors are installed much like windows) because the trim is usually made on site to match the existing house trim.

floor plan, showing material, counter shape, and approximate dimensions, to the various vendors and ask for prices. While there, ask about the options available. In solid surface, this will include colors, edge profiles, and special features such as built-in drainboards. With stainless, discuss the thickness and finish of the material they recommend. The term granite only begins to describe a counter, as different kinds of granite vary so much in color, pattern, and price. See what is available.

If you buy a wood top, and have to trim off ⅛ in., you can do it with your saw when the need becomes apparent. But these hard materials are expensive partly because they are difficult to work with, particularly using tools from the home shop. There is very little room for error. For that reason, it has become common practice to build them from full-scale templates, made on site *after* the cabinets are installed. That way, any changes in the theoretical dimensions shown on your drawings can be adjusted for. The vendor would estimate the project based on your drawing, obtain the materials, and set aside the time needed to make the counters. As soon as the cabinets are in place, have the counter fabricator come in and make the template to your design. Then, any mistakes are his responsibility. When that is impractical because of distance, I've made the templates myself and sent them by UPS® to the fabrication shop. Chapter 8 provides more detailed information on templating methods. If necessary, you can make temporary plywood counters so you can use your kitchen while the final counters are being manufactured.

Wood tops are typically obtained in one of two ways. Lumberyards and home centers sell conventional butcher block, usually in maple and oak, in a variety of stock sizes. They will cut them to size for you, or you can cut the final shape on site. Other hardwood tops are made to order by cabinet shops. Although not impossible, it's not practical to do this in most home shops because

The cooktop is flanked with recycled materials: a used piece of granite, cut down and refinished by a local granite shop, and butcher block, salvaged from the old cabinetry and refinished. We made up the long cherry section of the countertop in our shop.

of the jointer, planer, and numerous large bar clamps used.

The most practical counters for home fabrication are tile and plastic laminate. The substrate required in each case can be made in the home shop using ordinary tools, and the tile or laminate can also be cut and attached with simple equipment (see chapter 7). It often makes good economic sense to make your own tile counters, as tilework is an expensive trade. While there could be some savings making laminate tops, they are quite inexpensive to buy custom-made through home centers, lumberyards, or kitchen shops. You may not save much doing laminate tops yourself. If you do have them made up and the shapes are complex, templating may be a good idea. Pick the pattern (there are hundreds of colors and patterns available), get it priced, but then make the templates after the cabinets are in.

If you are having a builder, cabinet company, or cabinetmaker do your kitchen, work with them to determine the best way to obtain counters and to compare costs, availability, and scheduling issues.

Our templates showed size, shape, and location of special features such as outlets integrated into the splash.

In the kitchen shown on the facing page, we used many of these approaches. The sink with its drainboards was recycled. On either side of it were custom stainless sinks that we had made up after the main sink was in, using templates that showed every dimension, including details such as the holes for the outlets.

The island was really three counters combined. We took a butcher block from the old cabinets and resanded the top to use to the right of the stove. We glued up a long cherry slab and glued it to the old butcher block. The granite section was a recycled piece of stone, cut to size and resurfaced.

Ordering windows and doors

Chapter 1 discusses design considerations for windows and doors, including where they should be located, sizes, and other issues.

By now, your plans should indicate what size doors you need, which way they swing, and whether they have any glazing. Your plans should also show where windows go, their approximate sizes, and the style of window: double-hung, casement (hinged at the sides), awning (hinged at the top), slider, or fixed. If you haven't done so, show window and door locations on the plans by giving dimensions to the centerline of each unit, which is the easiest way to locate windows and doors during construction. Now, if there are more than one or two units needed, make a list that enumerates what you need. This is your *window and door schedule.*

The schedule lists each window and door and keys it to your floor plan. I usually number the windows and letter the doors, and mark them on the plan inside little circles to keep these designations distinct from the many other labels on the drawing. The schedule next gives the basic type of unit (double casement or wood slider, for example) and the size. For windows, I list the rough opening, which is the framing opening the unit requires. For doors, I list the size of the door itself and also the rough opening. The horizontal dimension comes first. A 3-ft.-wide door would be written 3'-0" x 6'-8", or more simply 3-0 x 6-8.

Unless you know which manufacturer's products you are using, these dimensions will be approximate at this stage, as dimensions vary with the manufacturer. I leave a blank column for different vendors to indicate which manufacturers' products they are specifying, and another column for the prices they are offering. Usually vendors will give you a quote on the whole order, so I leave a spot at the bottom for the total.

Doors are made of wood, steel, or fiberglass, in many styles and quantities (see the sidebar on p. 14). They come *set up* (prehung) or *door only.* You can order them bored for standard door hardware or do that yourself. If set up, you have to specify the jamb width, which should match the wall thickness, usually from the finish wall on one side to the finish wall on the other side, plus $\frac{1}{16}$ in. (see the drawing on p. 104).

Patio doors today have many configurations. For any of these, you'll have to indicate the size, the inte-

IN DETAIL

If you are taking out part of a wall, particularly a bearing wall, or adding a window or door in a bearing wall, a beam or header will be needed to support the weight above. Such beams must be strong and well supported and must meet building codes. Work with an architect or builder to determine how to do this correctly and safely. For more information, see the sidebar on p. 123.

For this pantry, we chose a traditional-looking wood four-panel pine door. It's economical, and it fits the style of the old house. We ordered the door only, rather than prehung. We ordered heavy-duty pocket-door hardware, with 125-lb. capacity, and built the door setup on site, though it can be ordered as a kit.

rior material (typically wood, vinyl, or aluminum), and the exterior material (also typically wood, vinyl, or aluminum). Often the interior is wood but the exterior *clad* in a more weather-defying material. If you are ordering exterior *sliding* doors, also specify which side *operates* (opens). For hinged patio doors, show whether the door swings in or out and which side operates. For a pair of French doors (both sides open), specify in-swing or out-swing and which is the *active* door (the one that opens first).

Windows are even more complicated. They come in wood, vinyl, or wood that is vinyl- or aluminum-clad (the outside is sheathed to minimize weather damage, but the inside is wood). Glass can be single (in which case you add some sort of storm panel), insulated (two layers of glass), Low-E (coated with a surface to keep the heat

from reradiating out of the house), and Low-E, Argon-filled (argon transmits less heat than air). Some brands, such as Andersen® (www.andersen-windows.com), are sold with only minimal trim on the outside, while others can be ordered with old-fashioned wide wood casings. Some companies sell only stock sizes (of which there will be many), while others, such as Marvin® (www.marvin.com), in addition to stock sizes, will make windows to almost any size or configuration. All these variables are reflected in price. Finally, some brands are somewhat better in quality and hence more expensive.

With all this complexity, the best plan is to take your schedule, along with copies of your floor plan, to local home centers, lumberyards, and window dealers. Sit down with the window-and-door specialist, and give him copies of the window-and-door schedule and the plan. Tell the specialist what style you are looking for, what your price range is, when you need the windows, and other relevant information. While there, pick up catalogs, which list products, available sizes, specs, and also detailed drawings of the window design that may come in handy. The plan helps a vendor understand what you are doing and also designates which way doors are hinged. Then the vendor can fill out the schedule with the products he thinks will best work for you.

When you have answers back from all potential vendors, and you've made your decision, carefully check everything, then update your window-and-

Determining Door Jamb Width

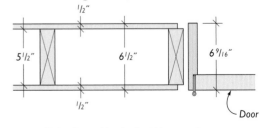

Order doors with a jamb width to match your wall thickness, (not including trim) plus 1/16 in.

door schedule with the particulars of the brand or brands of doors and windows selected. Finally, make any necessary adjustments to your drawings. In the case of doors, which are usually set directly on the subfloor (the layer of rough flooring under the finish floor), the centerline and rough opening are all you need.

For windows, you must also designate the height of the rough opening above the floor or subfloor level. Your window catalog will have clear cross sections that show the relationship of the glass area, the window sill, the trim, and other elements of the window to the rough opening. For example, in an Andersen casement window, the interior sill is about 1⅜ in. up from the bottom of the rough opening, and the glass starts about 2½ in. down from the top of the rough opening. Based on such data, figure out the heights that will work for you, and then mark your plans accordingly.

Window-and-Door Schedule (floor plan below)

WINDOWS

Unit #	Description	Quan.	R.O.	Mfg.	Model	Price	Total
1	Casement, flat casing	2	4-0 x 4-0				
2	Casement	1	2-0 x 2-0				
3	Double-hung	2	2-6 x 4-6	Recycled			
4	Double-hung	1	2-6 x 4-0	Recycled			

DOORS

Unit #	Description	Quan.	Door size	R.O.	Mfg.	Model	Price	Total
A	Wood panel	1	2-0 x 6-8					
B	Wood panel, pocket, door plus hardware	1	2-8 x 6-8					
C	Wood panel, sliding, door only	2	2-6 x 6-8					
D	Steel full glass, insulated	1	3-0 x 6-8					
E	Storm, full glass	1	3-0 x 6-8					
							Grand total:	

Sample Floor Plan

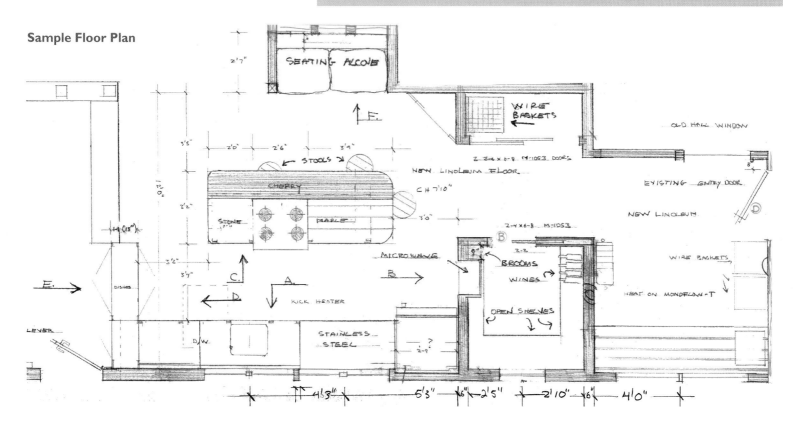

In this floor plan the windows are numbered and the doors lettered. These labels key the units in the window-and-door schedule. The position of each opening is indicated by a dimension to centerline.

TRADE SECRET

Even if you plan on doing most of your own work, you might consider hiring a general contractor briefly as a cost consultant. For the cost of a few hours of labor, an experienced builder may be able to help you figure out rough project costs, make other valuable suggestions, and perhaps along the way suggest electricians, plumbers, or other subs you may want to work with.

IN DETAIL

Possible subcontractors you might consider hiring on your project:
- Carpenter
- Electrician
- Plumber
- HVAC installer
- Tilesetter
- Cabinetmaker
- Flooring contractor
- Drywall installer
- Painter/finisher
- Trash collector

Hiring, Permitting, and Estimating

If you are hiring out most or all of the work on your kitchen, you might well hire a general contractor (or GC), who hires subcontractors, orders everything, schedules all the work, handles permitting (see p.109), and puts together a bid or estimate of the total cost for you. The GC has a lot of responsibility and significant business overhead for equipment, insurance, licensing, and many other real costs. You will be paying not only for the labor of the GC and his or her crew but also for the overhead the GC carries.

But many people opt to be their own GC, particularly if they are doing a substantial amount of the work themselves. If you choose that route, you may save some of the money the GC charges, but you will also take on the responsibilities and hassles the GC routinely handles.

Hiring a general contractor

If you will hire a contractor, begin interviewing candidates when you have basic plans in hand. The clearer your plans are, the better prospective builders will be able to give you good advice and good cost information. The more complete your plans are, the better you'll be able to compare estimates from different builders.

Usually I suggest looking for small companies for a kitchen project. You will get personal attention, and the overhead will be lower. In general, word of mouth is a good way to find builders. Look for those that your friends and acquaintances have hired and recommend strongly. Most builders have a style in what they do, so look for those whose work looks good to you. Set up meetings in your home with the builders who seem most appropriate.

Go over your ideas, goals, and drawings carefully with each builder. I think a good builder will

Custom features and nonstandard conditions will make your project take longer. The angled walls in this kitchen probably added 50 percent to installation time.

respect your ideas but also have useful suggestions for improvements, including ideas about choices that might save money. As you talk, you are looking for someone who likes your ideas and whose ideas you like. You are looking for someone who is comfortable to talk to. In addition to judging personal compatibility, though, ask some more specific questions.

Ask each builder when he can do the job and how long it will take. Ask for a careful explanation of how he charges for his services. Some builders work by the hour and add a percentage to cover business overhead (cost plus). Others prefer to give you a set price (bid) for the entire project. The first approach has the advantage of greater flexibility to adjust your project as it evolves; the second, greater certainty about cost. If you like the builder, ask for a written estimate or bid. This should be as specific as possible. Otherwise, you'll have no way of comparing it to other bids. Also ask potential builders for a schedule. And make sure the builder is fully insured.

While the estimates and rates of pay are important, I suggest hiring based on reputation, references, compatibility, and quality of work, rather than on price alone.

Acting as your own GC

If you are acting as general contractor, you will handle scheduling, arranging, purchasing, coordinating, estimating, and the resultant telephoning the GC typically takes care of. I hope this book gives you enough information to do this with some confidence. Of course, the larger or more complex the project, the more difficult this role is and the more people there are to coordinate.

Use the same method to locate a good electrician, plumber, or other tradesperson as you would to find a GC. Ask around, look at people's work up close, and talk to former customers. Look for someone who is interested in your project and has good ideas to share and who will show up on time.

Once you have estimates back from subs, you can begin the daunting task of putting together an estimate or project budget. By now you should have many key costs: subcontracts, cabinets, appliances, and windows and doors.

For planning purposes, assume the subcontracting work will run 10 percent over budget, often for extras or changes you ask for. The hard part will be estimating the projects you will do yourself. You'll have to do what the GC would do: visualize every step of the project, taking note of any materials you will need, including fasteners, caulks, finishes, and special tools you may need, and roughly gauging the labor required for each step. Add 20 percent to material costs to cover waste and unanticipated needs. Don't forget to figure in your own time. Add 25 percent to your labor tally to cover gophering, setup time, planning time, cleanup time, and errors. "Categories for an Estimate" at right gives some examples.

Categories for an Estimate

- Design costs (include any drawing materials and any kitchen designers you hire).
- Meet with subs and get estimates as needed.
- Permits: Call the building department in your town to find out what they cost.
- Move out of kitchen. Temporary kitchen and separation of work area from family area.
- Tool purchase.
- Demolition (including trucking, dumpster rental, special materials handling, i.e., lead or asbestos).
- Temporary bearing wall support/removal.
- Cleanup (every day; major cleanup on weekends).
- Structural repairs, if needed.
- Framing (partitions, beams, window and door headers; rough openings for windows and doors; Shimming, strapping, or other preparations needed to provide relatively flat wall surfaces and sufficient nailing for gypsum wallboard).
- Installing windows and doors (including interior and exterior trim, patching in siding).
- Rough wiring (include repairs of defective wiring uncovered during demolition, such as connections not made in boxes, boxes with too many wires in them, damaged or frayed wiring, etc.; includes installation of any recessed lights, phone lines, speaker wires, etc.).
- Rough plumbing (include replacing defective work found in the walls; make sure the system is vented).
- Rough plumbing or ductwork for any new heat.
- Rough inspection, if required.
- Insulation and vapor barrier.
- New drywall, drywall or plaster patching (including painting, if possible).
- Underlayment, flooring, and floor patching (could include sanding and first and second coat of a wood floor).
- Installation of cabinets and counters.
- Finish plumbing and wiring, hook up appliances, and install light fixtures.
- Finish carpentry: window casings and other interior trim and built-ins.
- Tile work.
- Odds and ends.
- Last coat of varnish on the floor, if wood.
- Final inspection and certificate of occupancy.

IN DETAIL

There will normally be two inspections: rough and finish. The rough inspection takes place when any structural work is complete, but before the walls are insulated or closed in with drywall. That way the inspector can see what you have done, and you can fix anything relatively easily. Sometimes the electrical and plumbing inspectors will come along with the building inspector, or you may have to make separate appointments. By the way, don't call them at the last minute. Give them up to a week's notice of when you need your inspection.

The finish inspection is done when the project is virtually done: walls are covered, cabinets in, plumbing all set, wiring completed. This is often cursory. When this is done, the inspector signs the card and issues a certificate of occupancy, after which technically you can move back in.

Calculating Project Costs

Project	Unit	Labor (hours)	Materials	Subcontract Cost (labor @ $30/hr.)
Wall framing, by owner	linear ft.	2–6	$3–$4	
Wall framing, by pro			$3–$4	$30–$90
Window/door by owner	each			
Create R.O.		8	$25	
Install unit		4	$200–$600	
Patch siding		6	$10–$50	
Interior trim		5	$24	
Window/Door by pro	each	12–16		$260–$700
Wiring by owner	per box	¾	$5–$8	
Wiring by pro				$50
Drywall by owner	sheet			
Hang only		1	$10	
Tape only		1	$1	
Drywall by pro	sq. ft.			$.75–$2
Laying plywood by owner	sheet	1	$7–$26	
Laying plywood by pro		½		$7–$26
Painting by owner	per room	4–10	$100	
Painting by pro				$400–$600
Insulating by owner	100 sq. ft.	1	$40	
Insulating by pro				$70
Hardwood floor by owner	100 sq. ft.	6–12	$400–$1,000	
Hardwood floor by pro			$400–$1,000	$800–$1,400
Cabinet installation by owner	linear ft.	2		
Cabinet installation by pro				$30
Counter installation by owner	each	3–8		
Counter installation by pro				$90–$140

Once you have your subcontractors, time estimates and your own estimates for other work, you can put that together with your own calendar and produce a schedule for the project. Consider the categories and stages itemized in "Categories for an Estimate" on p. 107. A careful reading of the construction chapters to come may be needed to get a complete sense of what is involved in the various procedures. It's good practice to allow some slack between each phase of the project. If ideally the electrician can finish Wednesday, have the drywaller come the following Monday. That will leave a little room for problems or extra work you ask for at the last minute. It's better to allow extra time than to have the drywaller trying to work while the electrician is still on site. It also allows you time to do the thorough cleanup that will make the drywaller's work more efficient and pleasant.

Your schedule should show not only when tasks should occur but also when materials must be ordered to be available when needed.

Permitting

If you are hiring a GC, he can handle all the permitting. In fact, that is one of the chief advantages of bringing in a GC; he knows the ropes of the local permitting process.

If you are the GC, you will have to understand and take on the permitting process yourself. Remember, the responsibility for following local regulations ultimately falls on you, whether you know what they are or not.

Most kitchen renovations require at least one permit, but jurisdictions vary in how they interpret this. If your project is small enough—just resurfacing and replacing things—local practice may not require a permit at all. But some jurisdictions are very strict. Ask building professionals you know or call your town building department and tell them how extensive your project is.

The overall building permit covers design, planning, zoning, and structural issues. Typically the general contractor *pulls the permit*, but most localities allow homeowners to do this. Bring two sets of your plans to the building department when you apply. It's a good idea to call ahead and make an appointment with an inspector, who will review your plans and who in some cases may ask for an architectural or engineering review. I've found that neat, professional-looking drawings are a big plus. If these drawings anticipate the points most likely to be raised, you're less likely to be asked for changes or engineering. The official will usually stamp the drawings, give one set back, and issue the permit, which you then post where it can be seen from the street. You will also be charged a fee, based on a small percentage of the total project cost.

There will also likely be separate electrical and plumbing permits. If you are hiring subs for these tasks, they will handle their own permitting and the resultant inspections. However, to avoid con-

Code? Which Code?

There are a variety of building codes in use in the United States. Each state, and often each town, decides which ones to enforce. In Vermont as a whole, the basic structure of the building is covered by National Building Code (BOCA 1996), a widely used code that covers structural issues and good building practice. Egress and other fire-safety issues are covered by the NFPA Life Safety Code, while wiring is governed by the National Electrical Code (1999). Plumbing is regulated by the 1990 BOCA plumbing code. However, single-family detached homes aren't regulated by the state, but town by town. While some towns—particularly the larger ones—use these codes, many leave single-family homes largely unregulated. In most states, though, all building is subject to codes.

Basic codes may be supplemented by other rules. Vermont now has an energy code, which applies to new construction. Before long, green building codes may be introduced to deal with air quality and environmental issues. There also are accessibility codes, such as UFAS (Uniform Federal Accessibility Standards). Although very useful as a reference, they don't apply to single homes.

Your local building officials and experienced local builders and subcontractors can usually help you figure out what you must do to keep your project up to code. Some states, such as Massachusetts, publish a separate volume that includes just those rules that apply to one- and two-family houses.

struction delays, you will want to coordinate these inspections. You can't move on to the drywall phase until structural, electrical, and plumbing rough-in inspections are complete.

Normally, you have to be a licensed plumber or electrician to pull a plumbing or electrical permit. However, many jurisdictions make exceptions for do-it-yourselfers, as long as the work is up to code and fully inspected. If you want to do such work yourself and your town allows it, find out from your building department what the procedure is. Sometimes unlicensed people seek to do their own work under a permit obtained by a licensed professional. The pro would then supervise your work before the inspector comes in. I advise against this, unless your skills are very good and the pro a very good friend.

PRO TIP

Make enough copies of plans and elevations so that each subcontractor can have a set. Revise them as changes are made, and mark the date.

IN DETAIL

A good way to cut costs without significantly compromising your kitchen's layout is to buy a less expensive grade of cabinet. We could have saved approximately $3,000 on this project by installing perfectly functional, stock frameless cabinets with hardwood fronts. Using plain white fronts probably would have saved another $1,000. It still would have been a really nice kitchen.

Shelving projects can be made in your home shop with basic tools. This saves money and allows you to add variety to the design, while tailoring shelving to specific needs.

Strategies for trimming the budget

Often the estimated cost is way over the budget established when you made your design program. Perhaps the project can go ahead as planned anyway. But just as often, the budget limit is real, and savings must be made. This is a point where it makes sense to revisit the design program to consider what is most important.

I think the most important aspects of a kitchen design, or of any major renovation, are the light, the circulation through the space, the overall layout, and an intelligent, thoughtful consideration of the details of work sequences and storage. I have seen many huge, expensive kitchens that really didn't function well and that weren't pleasant to be in. I have also seen many economical kitchens that were beautiful and a joy to cook in. It is often possible to make very large cuts in cost with very little loss in functionality. In short, if you must cut, don't cut the basic design elements: layout and light.

Instead, take a look at the features in your design for which there are less costly alternatives. Consider replacing expensive granite or solid-surface counters with a more economical laminate counter. Laminate is available in an incredible variety of colors and textures and with good detailing can look great. If you are attracted to the granite for its advantage in rolling out pastry, consider incorporating a smaller granite-topped section in your baking center.

Although drawer cabinets cost more than door cabinets, I wouldn't compromise here. On the other hand, you could do without full-extension hardware (which costs perhaps $20 per set) and instead use regular hardware (at $5 per set).

One way to realize some big savings is to substitute open shelves for overhead cabinets or, in some cases, for base cabinets. Done artfully and kept tidy, the simplest open shelves can look nice and function as well (or in some ways even better) than cabinets.

And you might consider a less expensive material for your cabinetry. With good design, pine or even painted plywood cabinets will work exactly the same as solid cherry ones. I'd much rather have a really well-thought-out kitchen, with lots of drawers in just the right places, made out of pine boards, than an inferior layout with raised-panel oak.

Staying on budget in a kitchen renovation doesn't mean you have to compromise on the space, the layout, or the light. Here, inexpensive cabinets that were finished on site helped control costs.

Some budgetary decisions don't have to be final. A number of expensive items can easily be cut now and added later when more money is available:

- Leave the spaces for the fancy appliances you want but use your old ones or inexpensive new ones. That will save thousands of dollars, and it will be easy to install the new ones later.

- Postpone the floor. With a little advance planning, you can probably do the floor last, without compromising any of the completed renovation. For example, if your ideal new floor would add another ¾ in. to the existing floor, add another ¾ in. to the counter height so that everything will come out right in the end.

- Buy your lighting fixtures later. With the exception of recessed lights, most (if not all) fixtures mount to the same type of electrical box. An inexpensive porcelain lampholder with a globe-light bulb will do the job for now and look okay; you can install the track lighting later.

These three simple steps might save you, or at least postpone your spending, $5,000 to $10,000.

Job Documentation

Here are the drawings and documents that might be included in your final plan. If your project is small, you probably won't need nearly all of these.

Drawings:
- Revised floor plan, annotated to show finish materials such as flooring and counters; also shows key dimensions such as window and door locations
- Elevations of cabinet walls in ½" scale, with dimensions and storage plan
- Detail drawings of cabinets if you are building them
- Electrical plan
- Other detail drawings as needed

Design documents:
- List of cabinets (if factory made)
- List of appliances (w/sizes, spec sheets)
- Window and door schedule
- Schedule or list of light fixtures
- Lists of materials for any projects you will carry out yourself

- Calculations or specs for any structural work, such as headers, beams, new floor framing, etc., including sources for these calculations, and the load assumptions you used

Business documents:
- Any written estimates or bids you have received, which might include plumbing, wiring, counters, tilework, flooring, etc.
- A schedule of the project to the extent possible
- Permit applications and permits
- Copies of codes or other documents that regulate what you can do

Demolition and

CHAPTER SIX
Rough-In

Builders often divide a renovation project into three major phases: demolition, rough-in, and finish. The goal of demolition is to remove all the old building elements that should come out, without damaging adjacent elements that aren't being remodeled. It also may include the careful removal of doors, windows, or flooring for reuse. It works best to do the demolition at the beginning, all at once, if possible. Then make everything nice and clean again, and set up for rough-in.

The rough-in stage includes new framing, floor patching, subfloors, preparation for drywalling, and any wiring and plumbing that will be inside the walls. This work will be covered up later; it has to be strong and functional, but it doesn't have to be pretty.

The third stage, the finish, includes all the elements you see: drywall, flooring, cabinets, trim, and the visible parts of electrical and plumbing. Finish work is covered in chapters 7 and 8.

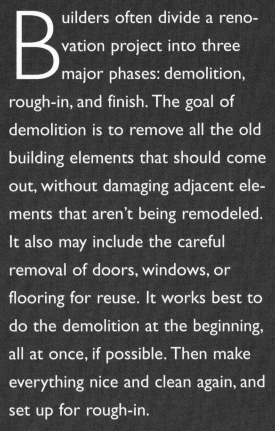

113

PRO TIP

During demo, clean up as you go along. It's safer and saves time in the end. Pull nails out of pieces to be saved before someone can get hurt by them.

IN DETAIL

Here's a list of tools and materials for demolition:

- Sledgehammers, heavy framing hammers
- Reciprocating saw
- Various pry bars, crow bars, and wrecking bars, including a "cat's paw"
- Leather gloves
- Step ladders
- Sheets of plastic or tarps to put down for floor protection
- Heavy-duty or (better yet) feed bags for debris
- Cardboard boxes (the liquor store has plenty)
- Flat, square-edged shovel
- Shovel for scooping up debris

IN DETAIL

Curtain off all of your furniture, artwork, and valuables behind plastic. Dust will get everywhere it can and soil or damage anything in the work area. The materials to be torn out in your project may be relatively benign: wood, drywall, and sheet foam insulation. With old horse-hair plaster, fiberglass, or loose insulation, the dust can be really awful, and it spreads quickly if the work area isn't carefully sealed off.

There are many steps in the journey from before to after. Working methodically makes the trip much easier.

Demolition

You might think that demolition is easier than building and therefore more the province of an amateur. But demolition is an art in itself. It has its own tools, methods, and tricks for working quickly without destroying the parts you want to save along with the parts you want to remove. As with finish work and cabinetry, it deserves careful thought. Set up carefully; plan well; rent, borrow, or buy the tools you need; and get help when needed.

Protecting your house

Demolition is a messy business, so do what you can to protect the house from the effects of the work. Most important is isolating the work area. You can just staple up plastic or tarps, but you can buy special barriers with zipper doors as shown in the photo below (the Zipper, by C and S Mfg. Co., 1-888-362-8269).

The plastic isolates the construction area from the rest of the house. The zipper door goes up like a piece of tape, then the opening is simply sliced out with a utility knife.

Make the work area as large and wide open as possible. There will be many tools and toolboxes, plus materials of all sorts. Table saws and chopsaws will need to be set up, along with their extension tables. It also helps if there is covered storage and a work area outside.

There is disagreement among builders about how best to protect good floors in the work area. Many builders carefully tape red building paper down over the floor, while others feel that covering the floor with paper doesn't work. In my experience, grit finds its way under the paper and slowly gets ground into the finish without anyone noticing that this is happening. The alternative approach is to leave the floor open, but sweep and vacuum it often. It's also important (whether using paper or not) to avoid dropping heavy objects onto the floor. When I do decide to cover a floor, I prefer to use old carpet, or perhaps sheets of ¼-in. plywood or paneling, to offer the floor more protection.

If a lot of exterior work is going on, it sometimes makes sense to cover plants that would otherwise be trampled. On some projects, the plants have been valuable enough that we've gone to the trouble of temporarily transplanting them.

Pets often get in trouble on building sites. Dogs and cats can get disoriented when the house is turned into a noisy building site, with a changing cast of strangers around. Cats will sometimes disappear into newly opened wall cavities and not come out. Dogs will run off in fright or—perhaps even worse—insist on hovering literally underfoot whenever heavy loads are being carried into the house, which is dangerous to workers and to the dog. A dog unaccustomed to pickup trucks going in and out constantly can get run over. We even had a horse do a somersault on one job. Protect the dog from the job, and the workers from the dog.

Safety and debris control

Safety precautions are particularly important during demolition. Besides having the right safety gear—such as dust masks, heavy gloves, and hard shoes—it's important to work carefully and safely, and that includes how you handle the debris you're generating.

There are three common ways to handle debris:

- Rent a dumpster.
- Hire a small hauler, a person with a truck who will take it to the dump for you.
- Take it to the landfill yourself in a trailer or pickup—keeping the load well secured and covered while in transit.

Whatever the system, locate the trailer, dumpster, or dump pile to minimize handling, usually near the door or under a convenient window. The fewer times things are handled, and the shorter the distance they are carried by hand, the better.

+ SAFETY FIRST

A list of safety equipment essential for demolition and most construction work:
- Shoes with hard tops and hard soles
- Safety glasses or goggles
- Earplugs or earmuffs
- Dust masks for ordinary dust
- Respirators for working with finishes or solvents
- GFCI outlet or add-on GFCI for running tools, particularly for use in wet areas or when taking down walls where your saw might hit a wire
- Tools in good repair
- Good light source
- Tough leather gloves for carrying rough stuff
- First-aid kit
- Fire extinguisher

TRADE SECRET

Professional builders have to get a lot done in a day, and they use a host of methods to do that. Advance planning is one of the most important. When I'm running a complex project, I sit quietly at home early each morning and visualize the day: what each person involved will do, when they will do it, and what supplies and tools they will need to do it well. This clarifies the phone calls I need to make and the tools and materials I need to be sure are available. And during the day I keep track of the materials, phone calls, and decisions that I have to attend to for the next day.

IN DETAIL

Separate trash from treasure. Designate a distinct area for storing moldings, trim, and other items being saved for reuse. On one project, the owner wanted us to reuse the old door casing on which his children's heights had been marked over the years. The crew thought the casing looked like junk, and pitched it in the dumpster several times. If possible, make a place for such items to be stashed safely and out of the weather.

Unfinished wood scraps can go into the woodstove, if they aren't reusable. Painted wood, pressure-treated wood, and plywood scraps go to the landfill. Sometimes it helps to sort things a bit as they get torn out. For example, when I tear down old plaster walls, I strip off the plaster first and box it up, then bundle up the wood lath separately. It's easier to handle that way rather than when it gets torn off in one tangled mass.

In renovations, many builders will gut the walls and ceilings down to the frame. But my inclination is to save surfaces and materials that can be reused or covered, an approach that can save time, reduce exposure to dust, and limit the impact (and the charges) at your landfill. If a wall is shot, I'm always tempted to drywall over it rather than tear it out, if possible. I'll patch a wall that others might redo. On the other hand, sometimes it is more cost-effective to gut it out and start over. Unfortunately, there is no definitive answer as to which approach is better, as it depends on the circumstances.

Remove the drawers and doors first. The cordless drill has become as indispensable to builders as the hammer. With a magnetic bitholder and the proper tip, it makes short work of unscrewing the doors.

Cutting the caulking allows the sink to be removed more easily.

Basic demolition strategies and techniques

Although not the only way, it's usually best to demolish in the reverse order of construction: cabinets first, then trim, then wall surfaces, then clean out insulation, then remove the framing if needed. This order is safer, cleaner, and requires less physical force.

In the project shown on these pages, we started with the old butternut cabinets. A good starting point is to detach the doors and drawers. They come out easily, and removing them makes room for the next steps.

Once the sink is disconnected from the plumbing underneath, it can come out. Stainless steel sinks will have little retaining clips. You may be able to unscrew them from below, but they might be rusted together, in which case, the sink can stay attached to the counter for now. In the photos here, the heavy cast-iron sink is held down simply by caulk, which can be cut away with a utility knife. Then the sink is pried loose from the countertop.

Counters can be attached to the cabinetry in different ways. Masonry or stone counters will be held down simply with dabs of caulk or by their own weight. If caulked, they can be devilishly difficult to remove intact. Fortunately, most old kitchens have laminate, tile, or wood counters that are screwed in place from below. With a good light, you can look inside the cabinets, find the screws, and back them out.

In the top left photo on p. 118, the countertop had been built in place, with the plywood core of the counter screwed to the cabinet from above before the laminate was applied. This makes the screws inaccessible, so the crew used a reciprocating saw to snip as many of these screws as possible. With the fastenings weakened, the counter could be pried up and broken free. This method of snipping the nails or screws is used a lot in

Disconnecting the Sink

You could have your plumber disconnect your sink, but it isn't difficult to do yourself. First, use a large pipe wrench or tongue-and-groove pliers (Channellock® is probably the best-known brand, 800-724-3018) to unscrew the drain fittings and disassemble the drain line. Plug the exposed drain with a rag to keep construction debris from getting into and clogging it up.

There should be shutoffs for the water-supply lines. If so, shut off the water firmly (double-checking by turning the faucet on), then unscrew or cut the water lines. For all these operations, use the gentlest force that will do the job; you don't want to damage the remaining plumbing. If you can't unscrew the water lines, cut them with a tubing cutter, or use a hacksaw or reciprocating saw with a sharp metal-cutting blade.

The shutoffs may not have been touched for 20 years, and some will drip a bit. If a little tightening doesn't fix it, and the drip is significant, you could end up doing more plumbing now than you wish to. Some older kitchens will have no shutoffs at all under the sink. If so, unless there are shutoffs farther back on the lines, you will have to turn off the water main, cut the pipes, and cap them off close to the floor or wall.

About Lead

Many older homes, and almost all homes painted before about 1930, contain lead paint. Lead is most likely to be found on trim paint and painted exterior wood. Lead from paint is toxic, particularly if it is flaking, sanded, or otherwise gets broken down into fine particles and distributed into the air. If in doubt, you can purchase a lead test kit and easily test samples for lead. In many areas, you can dispose of wood elements that may contain lead along with other construction debris. Be sure to check what the rules are in your locality. If you are removing any suspect wood outdoors, or scraping in preparation for painting, put down tarps to contain the lead. You don't want lead to get into your garden.

For more on lead safety, see the HUD publication *Lead Paint Safety: A Field Guide for Painting, Home Maintenance, and Renovation Work,* which you can download at http://www.hud.gov/lea/leahome.html, or contact HUD at:

Office of Lead Hazard Control
U.S. Department of Housing and Urban Development (HUD)
451 Seventh St. SW, Room P-3206
Washington DC 20410
Phone: 202-755-1785

TRADE SECRET

If you're trying to save trim that has finish nails in it, don't pound the nails back out. The wood will split or splinter around the nail hole in the face of the board. Instead, draw the nail out from the back with nippers, Vise-Grip® pliers, or Channellock pliers.

It often helps to snip nails or screws to free up elements such as this counter. Sometimes another pair of hands helps in prying things apart in order to see where the screws are to saw through them.

demolition when you are trying to avoid destroying what you remove.

Once the countertop has been removed, disassemble or remove the cabinetry. We wanted to save the cabinets where we could but without putting a lot of extra work into it. These weren't stock cabinets, though, but instead were built in place and part of the house. Some of the cabinetry had to be cut apart carefully to remove the components intact.

Removing the trim is next. If you want to save trim, remove it carefully with small, thin flat-bars. You might also snip nails with a reciprocating saw equipped with a metal blade.

If you take your old cabinets apart carefully, you may be able to use some of them in the garage or basement.

Cutting the cabinet free allows it to be removed in one piece instead of being destroyed.

A small bar works great for removing trim without damaging it.

Floor demolition

Old vinyl flooring, whether sheet or tiles, is usually dried out, and (if you're lucky) only partially glued down. If so, it can be removed easily. Here vinyl flooring was not firmly glued and came up in large pieces (see the top left photo on p. 120). The particleboard underlayment, on the other hand, was nailed down with dozens of nails. The crew used nail pullers (Cat's Paw® is one brand) to dig in and extract enough of the nails so that the sheets could be pried up and removed.

The approach to removing other flooring is similar. Gather a nice collection of demo tools, and experiment to find the most efficient way. You may find that ceramic tile pops up with a little encouragement from a thin flat bar driven under each tile. If the tiles are really well bedded in mastic or thinset mortar, it may take more force.

Special situations may call for more careful means. If you were trying to remove a hardwood floor in a kitchen while saving it in contiguous spaces, you would have to make a clean, accurate cut along the dividing line before tearing up the kitchen floor. Use a straightedge to guide the saw while making such a cut, and set the depth of cut

WHAT CAN GO WRONG

If you talk to an old-time carpenter, chances are good you'll have to speak up. That's why hearing protection is a good idea. There are two main styles: earmuff style and smaller soft-foam earplugs, which go in the outer ear. Both work, though not if they're hanging on a hook or stuffed in a pocket. You should use hearing protection whenever you (or someone nearby) is using a power tool. It's particularly important to use protection when using the noisier tools, such as a reciprocating saw or a pneumatic nail gun.

The right tool for the job: A flat shovel often works well on vinyl flooring. After removing most of the nails with a nail puller, the plywood underlayment can be pried up. Experiment to find the most effective pry bar.

Remove select pieces of hardwood flooring in order to weave in new flooring for an invisible joint.

to just the thickness of the hardwood. The photo above shows the opposite case. Here the vinyl floor was removed from the kitchen, and the clients wanted to have the adjacent hardwood continued seamlessly into the remodeled kitchen. The carpenters drove nail pullers into each board to be removed, then hammered on the nail puller until the board slid out, dragging its nails with it. After the board had moved about 3 in., it could be hammered out directly.

Opening the walls

Removing the wall surfaces and insulation, if any, comes next. Many house have thin plywood or other sheet paneling. This is fastened with tiny nails, sometimes also with panel adhesive, and is usually easy to pull off in large sheets. It's hard to get gypsum wallboard off in large pieces; it just breaks up. But once weakened with a saw or the claw of a hammer, it can be ripped off without much trouble by hand.

The next step will be to remove insulation from exterior walls wherever you will be making changes, such as by adding a window or door. This will typically be fiberglass, but in some houses you might find cellulose, rock wool, or other materials. Some of these substances are really nasty to work with. Use gloves, dust masks, and eye protection, and wear a long-sleeve shirt—old fiberglass insulation is itchy, irritating stuff. I like to work with insulation in the cool of the day or at the end of the day so I can get to a shower quickly. If the fiberglass insulation is clean and intact, it can be rolled up and used again. But sometimes moisture has gotten to the fiberglass or animals have made a home in it. Bag the insulation quickly, and do a thorough vacuuming immediately.

Removing walls

It's fairly easy to remove nonbearing partitions, a closet near the front door, for instance. One good strategy is to weaken something quickly to make it easier to remove. With the drywall removed on one side of the closet, it's a simple matter to saw through the nails in a few places to weaken the wall and then hammer it apart. Another approach is to saw the studs in two somewhere in the middle

Paneling is typically secured with small nails, sometimes also with panel adhesive, and disattaches easily.

Although not difficult to remove, drywall generally comes off in small pieces rather than whole sheets.

+ SAFETY FIRST

Watch out for hidden electrical wires and gas or water lines. You don't want to find a live circuit with the blade of your reciprocating saw. Outlets and switches will give a clue as to where wires will be, but they won't be a guarantee. First make an exploratory hole in a wall with your hammer and look carefully for wires or other surprises inside. If you can't tell where wires are running in a wall you're working on, turn off that circuit at the panel and run your tools from a different wall.

IN DETAIL

Sometimes you must remove circuits, wires, or light fixtures that are part of walls you are taking out. You may be able to detach electrical boxes from the framing and remove the wall, leaving the wiring intact. A better approach is to turn off the circuit at the fuse or breaker panel, pull out the wires, and then use wire nuts and tape to insulate the end of the feed line, which provides some protection should the circuit be turned on by mistake.

to make the wall weak. A third option is to use a sledge to bash the bottom of the wall out—but that can damage the floor more than the other methods.

Bearing walls are another matter. In most houses, the roof rafters and floor joists are parallel. The outer walls perpendicular to the rafters and joists normally support the roof and the floors and are therefore *bearing walls*. Usually the major walls in the middle of the house, perpendicular to the joists, hold up the middle of the floor and are also bearing walls. In the basement, you will often see a big beam—known as a *girder*—that lines up (or nearly lines up) with central bearing walls above. You cannot remove sections of these bearing walls without putting a beam of some sort back. The walls parallel to the joists and rafters are usually non-bearing, unless there are other partitions directly above them upstairs.

Strict engineering rules govern the size of beams or headers required when a bearing wall is removed. While installing the beam, the load above must be supported by temporary partitions

Sawing through the nails weakens this nonbearing wall to make it easier to remove.

or posts. If you are taking out even a small section of a bearing wall, you should consult with an experienced builder who can help you figure out the beam size needed, the correct detailing, the temporary support, and also advise about the simplest and safest way to get the job done.

Working with Plaster and Lath Walls

Older homes with plaster and wood lath walls are trickier to work on than those with drywall, and the dust is terrible. I like to line up a row of cardboard boxes at the base of a wall to be stripped. Then I use the claw of my hammer or a flat bar to strip off the plaster only, letting it drop into the boxes. If the plaster isn't loose enough to strip, I drive the claw deep into the wall, and pry up a few pieces of lath just enough to loosen the plaster. After the plaster is off, I use a wrecking bar to strip the lath, which I then bundle up with string.

It's tricky to remove part of a wall without tearing up the plaster on the section you'd like to save. To prevent this, use a level to draw the line separating the plaster you want to save from the plaster to come out. Use a sharp utility knife to cut through the plaster here. Don't try using a reciprocating saw to cut through the lath. Such saws cut on the pull stroke, which will effectively tear all the plaster free of the lath. Instead, use an electric jigsaw, with its base pressed firmly against the plaster. Although the jigsaw also cuts on the pull stroke, the base will minimize damage.

Identifying Bearing Walls

Before tearing out any walls, make sure you understand which walls are simple partitions and which are bearing walls supporting floors or roofs above. Sections of bearing walls have to be replaced with a beam of sufficient strength to support the load above. The beam, in turn, requires supporting posts that are big enough to carry the weight (or load) and the posts have to sit on something solid. The load has to be transferred all the way down to the foundation or to a new footing.

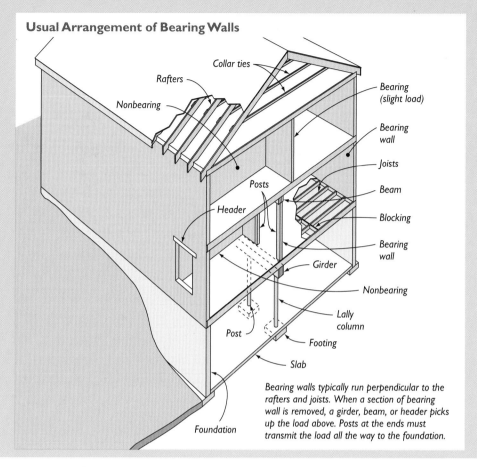

Usual Arrangement of Bearing Walls

Collar ties
Rafters
Nonbearing
Bearing (slight load)
Bearing wall
Joists
Posts
Beam
Header
Blocking
Bearing wall
Girder
Nonbearing
Lally column
Post
Footing
Slab
Foundation

Bearing walls typically run perpendicular to the rafters and joists. When a section of bearing wall is removed, a girder, beam, or header picks up the load above. Posts at the ends must transmit the load all the way to the foundation.

Framing

Framing is one of the more enjoyable parts of carpentry, certainly more so than demolition. The smell of sawdust is a lot more rewarding than the dust and dirt associated with demolition, and since the process usually goes quickly with tangible results, framing is gratifying. As you begin, take a few minutes to set up well. Tidy the workspace, and set up a safe, comfortable cutting station. Many builders have a dedicated saw stand with extension tables, but you can use a plank set up on sawhorses or even the lumber pile, if it is secure and set at a comfortable height.

Interior walls

Framing up nonbearing interior partitions usually goes rather quickly. Often the easiest place to start is to cut the bottom and top plates to the total wall length, then mark stud locations on 16-in. centers on both plates. The 16-in. interval begins at the edge of the first stud, then goes to

IN DETAIL

Traditionally, both interior and exterior walls were framed on 16-in. centers. Some builders still prefer this standard. But there are strong arguments for building on 24-in. centers. In most cases, it saves wood, saves time, and is plenty strong enough to support all loads. In exterior walls, it's more energy efficient because there is more room for insulation (exterior walls will typically be framed with 2x6s in place of 2x4s to make room for thicker insulation).

The argument for 16-in. centers in interior partitions is that the narrow spacing gives better support for the drywall. While true, my experience is that 24-in. spacing is fine if the drywall is run horizontally; drywall is stiffer when installed perpendicular to framing. Though codes support 24-in. o.c. wall framing, a few local officials still insist on 16-in. o.c. Your drawings should always indicate framing intervals and sizes so that the issue can be discussed with officials if needed.

Typical Framing of Window or Door Header

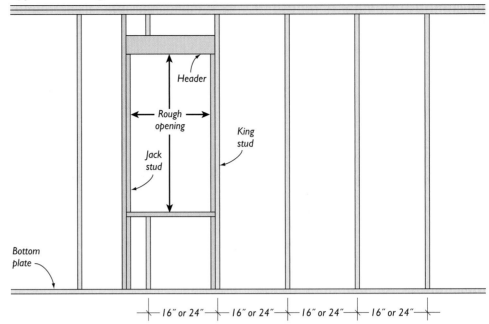

the centers of the rest, so that drywall goes up in full sheets as much as possible and so there is nailing support at the vertical joints. The plates provide nailing for the wallboard top and bottom. Additional studs might be needed at inside corners to support electrical boxes, or horizontally (called blocking) to support cabinets. Window and door openings get double studs at each side. This adds strength and stiffness to the wall, provides a good place to nail trim boards, and also keeps wall switches (which are attached to the studs) out of the way of the trim around windows or doors.

Although it sometimes makes sense to build a stud wall in place, the usual method is to arrange the pieces on the floor and nail them together with 16d common nails at each joint. If you pre-build walls, make them about ½ in. less in height than the actual vertical space. That way, you can tip it up into place without it binding. Once the wall is in position, use shims to fill the gap.

The photos on the facing page show a small closet partition is assembled on sawhorses, using screws. It's about ½ in. less than the actual space it

must fit. After being tipped into place, it's attached to the wall at the top. A plumb bob (or a 4-ft. level) is used to make it exactly plumb, then the bottom is secured with screws.

After the full-length partition is nailed or screwed into place, the remaining sections of the wall can be installed to complete the framing.

Exterior walls are built like interior walls and have many of the same elements. Ideally the walls are thicker, perhaps made of 2x6s, to make room for more insulation. Over the frame goes ½-in. plywood or oriented strand board (OSB) sheathing, which seals the wall, braces it diagonally, and provides a nailing surface for the siding. On older houses, the existing sheathing may be ordinary boards instead of plywood. House wrap or building paper typically covers the sheathing as a draft barrier. The window frames go over the sheathing and house wrap, and the siding normally butts up against the window trim. At the top, a folded metal flashing keeps rainwater from getting into the wall.

This closet partition is assembled with 3-in. screws and a cordless drill (top photo). After the top is secured in the right place (above left photo), it's plumbed and secured at the bottom (above right and top right photos). With the first section installed, the remaining pieces, around the closet door, can be quickly pieced in (right).

Sagging floors and other repairs

When you open walls and ceilings, you may find that some repairs are needed. If the floor sags visibly or is springy when walked on, you may want to strengthen it. It's possible that a building official may require you to do so if the joist size and spacing departs dramatically from code (see In Detail on p. 126). One way is to add a beam or partition in the basement to support the floor in mid-span. You might also *sister* the joists, which means simply nailing additional joist material to the existing joists, in as long lengths as possible (they have to be nearly full length). This increases the number of joists doing the structural work.

You may also find rotten framing in your walls or floors. Continuous roof or plumbing leaks will in time cause wood to rot and attract carpenter ants or other wood-burrowing insects that will further deteriorate your framing. Moisture from the earth can also rot your framing, and framing actually in contact with the ground will rot unless the earth is unusually dry. Framing in a

PRO TIP

Sight along an exposed floor. Every floor sags to some extent, but if the deflection is more than ½ in., reinforcement may be needed.

TRADE SECRET

I've found 2½-in. or 3-in. screws to be very handy in renovation work. Sometimes the material you are trying to fasten to is marginal, unstable, or weak, and hammering won't work. With screws, you can secure a partition to the wood lath of an adjacent wall, where nails would just break the plaster. Sometimes they're useful when there is no room to swing a hammer or for an assembly that might need to be adjusted or dismantled.

IN DETAIL

Exact spans for floor joists depend on the load, the species and strength of the wood you are using, and your local code. These are typical spans to help you assess if your floor needs structural work.

Size	Max. span 24" oc	Max. span 16" oc
2x4	4'11"	6'0"
2X6	7'9"	9'6"
2X8	10'3"	12'6"
2x10	13'1"	16'0"
2x12	15'11"	19'6"

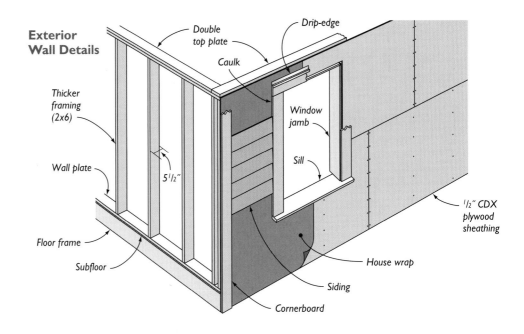

Exterior Wall Details — Double top plate, Drip-edge, Caulk, Thicker framing (2x6), Window jamb, Wall plate, 5½", Sill, Floor frame, Subfloor, Cornerboard, Siding, House wrap, ½" CDX plywood sheathing

constantly wet, humid basement will also rot eventually. If there are any suspect conditions, take a knife or screwdriver and probe for "punky" wood. If your probe penetrates the framing significantly, repairs may be in order. This may be a point to get some professional advice, particularly if the damage is extensive.

Of course, the first task is to remove the source of moisture, if possible. Find the leak and fix it. If the moisture is from the earth, there may be ways it can be limited or controlled, such as arranging for adequate drainage, improving ventilation to the basement, or covering a dirt floor with plastic or a properly sealed concrete slab. If moisture is an ongoing problem, repairs should be made with pressure-treated wood.

Safe Cutting

- Always take a minute to set up and think through every cutting operation.
- Set blade depth just a bit more than the wood thickness, perhaps ¼ in.
- Make sure the piece you are cutting is stable and will not move as you cut.
- Use clamps to secure smaller pieces.
- Use a solid stance and a firm grip.
- Use a sharp blade, designed to cut the material at hand.
- Start the saw motor before contacting the wood.
- Allow the scrap, or waste, to fall freely.
- With a portable circular saw, always make sure the blade guard returns to the closed position. before setting down the saw. Learn to listen for the click of the guard closing.
- Listen to the sounds the saw makes—a smooth sound usually indicates that cutting is okay. If the saw is struggling, you may be doing something wrong.
- If you are new to using portable circular saws, get a lesson or two from an experienced carpenter, who can demonstrate good practice and watch you make a few cuts.

Installing Windows and Doors

Modern windows and doors often come with detailed instructions, and do-it-yourselfers can install them successfully. But there are so many little tricks and techniques, plus specialized tools, that it makes sense to work with a skilled finish carpenter the first time, if possible. This is especially true if you are working with old windows or doors that may have to be repaired before they can go in.

Installing windows

Windows are usually installed from the outside. The rough opening the window goes into is a bit larger than the window unit itself to allow for adjustment. The exterior trim or nailing flange is nailed directly to the exterior sheathing, closing off the ¼-in. to 1-in. gap between the unit and the framing.

Most wood windows have either a 3-in.- to 6-in.-wide trim board (called a *flat casing*) or a narrower molded casing known as *brickmold*. Some windows—particularly vinyl- or aluminum-clad windows—do not have a conventional exterior casing, but instead have a metal or plastic nailing flange that attaches and supports the window, spanning the gap between the window and the framing. This flange can be covered with either applied trim or siding.

There are basically two approaches to removing siding around the new window. You can remove a lot of siding around the opening, and patch it all back in once the window is fully installed. Alternatively, you can try to cut the siding away precisely so the window, with its trim, slides seamlessly into place. In the sidebar on pp. 127-128, we were able to use a combination approach that minimized siding patching while making the installation fairly simple.

After sawing out the rough opening with the reciprocating saw and cutting back the siding, the window can be installed from the outside. If the window isn't too heavy, I like to install it with the sash in place and in the closed position. This holds the window unit square. If the window is large, it's a good idea to remove the sash to reduce weight.

Installation is usually a two-person job, one inside and one out. First, hoist the unit into position in the rough opening, resting it on the framing at the bottom and nudging it left and right to center it approximately in the rough opening. While the person outside holds onto the window and keeps it from falling out of the opening, the person inside checks the bottom with a level. Usually one corner or another has to be shimmed to level the unit. Once level, the casing or nailing flange can be secured to the wall with one fastener at the bottom on each side.

When the bottom is level, check the sides with the level. If the unit really is square (not always the case), the sides will be plumb. If not, the person working from the inside can gently pry the unit over at the top with a small flat bar until it is, at which point the person on the outside installs two more screws or nails at the top to secure the window in place.

✚ SAFETY FIRST

Take a few minutes to set up carefully for window installation. Put all the tools and fasteners that you'll need either in your tool belt or within close reach. If you're working above ground level, make sure that you have appropriate ladders or staging to safely work on the window. If the window is heavy, recruit help.

FRAMING FOR A WINDOW TO MINIMIZE PATCHING

The drawing on p. 124 shows the standard framing for window rough openings. The header size for a bearing wall would be determined by your local building code. Typically providing all this framing requires tearing apart the whole wall, with many drywall patches to follow. But sometimes it's possible to provide the correct framing with less disruption. First I carefully cut the existing drywall to the dimensions of the new rough opening, checking carefully for wires in the wall. The odd block in the middle of photo 1 is what's left of the stud I had to cut away for the opening; the stick attached to it is a little story pole that helped me get the height of the window correct in relation to exterior trim.

Just below and above the rough opening are horizontal slots. These are saw kerfs I cut with a circular saw and my reciprocating saw through the existing drywall. This enabled me to remove part of that central stud at the right heights so I could add the sill at the bottom and the double 2x6 header at the top. With the fiberglass removed, I could reach inside to add the needed framing. No drywall patching was needed because even the thin slots were covered by window trim.

1. Frame the opening first, drill a hole at each corner, then use the framing as a guide to cut away the wall with a reciprocating saw.

2. Installing a heavy window is easier with two people. The siding has been cut away so the window can go directly against the sheathing.

3. Center the window in the opening, and level it with shim shingles.

4. Secure the window at the bottom first, then check for squareness before adding the rest of the fasteners.

5. I removed shingles beyond where the nailing flange would lie but short of where the window trim would go. This way, I could use the trim to mark exactly where the remaining shingles had to be cut.

6. I cut the shingles away with a utility knife and patched back the unstained cedar shingles, carefully selecting used shingles (saved from the removed section of the wall) that matched adjacent ones in color.

Windows aren't always made perfectly, and neither are levels. The test is to go inside, replace the sash if it has been removed, take some more readings with the level, and then operate the window a few times, observing the cracks bottom and side. With a double-hung window, look at the joint where the top and bottom sashes meet. If the cracks and seams are straight and parallel, fasten the window permanently. If not, loosen the top fasteners, adjust the window from side to side, then refasten. You may not be able to achieve perfection, particularly with less expensive windows; just make sure the window operates properly.

With wood casings, the siding butts up to the casing. At the top, a flashing is inserted to keep water from running in. Aluminum head flashings are made to match most sizes of casings. With a nailing flange, the siding typically laps over the flange, and the flange itself serves as the flashing at the top. In the sidebar on pp. 128–129, we added traditional trim, and after

Some modern windows have nailing flanges in place of wood trim. Wood trim, including a sill, can be added to give the unit a traditional appearance.

TRADE SECRET

When you are installing a window, don't completely nail your fasteners until you're sure that the window is level, plumb, and square. Check the window instructions, but with wood trim I use 8d galvanized box nails (box nails are thinner than common nails)—and don't drive them in all the way. With a nailing flange, I use ⅝-in. galvanized drywall screws, at least until I have the window unit exactly where I want it.

IN DETAIL

A window's casing or nailing flange is usually caulked to the sheathing. Although some instructions call for putting caulk behind the casing before hefting it into place, I prefer to caulk after the window has been installed; it makes adjustment easier and less messy.

patching the shingles back, the window looked like it had always been there.

Installing interior doors

Start by figuring out the relationship of the door to the finish floor level. The side jambs of most interior doors typically come overlong at the bottom, so they can be trimmed as circumstances require. If the door frame will sit on the subfloor, you'll have to figure out how much of the side jambs to trim off so that there will be a nice ¼-in. clearance between floor and door, to allow the door to swing unobstructed. If the floor is out of level or if there will be a carpet, the gap will need to be larger.

Next, check the floor for level. If it's out of level, you may need to trim the two jambs differently. If the hinge side is ½ in. lower, it's jamb should be ½ in. longer. Using a handsaw or small circular saw, cut the door jambs to length at the bottom. Next, check the sides of the rough opening with the level. If the hinge side is dead level, great. You can use it to align the door in the opening. If not, you will have to shim the jambs to plumb them.

Put the door frame in place, making sure the jamb is flush or just proud of the wall on both sides. Sometimes I hang the door frame with the door on its hinges. But with a heavy door it may be easier to install the jambs tentatively without the door, hang the door, then finish nailing off the jambs when you are sure the fit is right. With either method, the goal is to make the jambs straight and plumb and the cracks between the door and the jambs uniform and straight. Pairs of shingles, as shown, are slid between the jamb and framing to adjust the door until it is correct. You can use large 10d (3-in.) finish nails to nail the jamb to the framing. I often use 3-in. drywall screws instead if the jambs will be painted. Start

with a minimum number of fasteners to get things in the right place. When everything seems good and the door opens and closes smoothly, add more pairs of shims and more nails. It's very important to have the door well supported at the hinges and near the knob and strike.

Testing Your Level

Not all carpenters' levels actually read level; most are just a bit off. But if your levels are accurate, window and door work and cabinet installation will be a lot easier. You can quickly test any level for accuracy by placing it on any flat, nearly horizontal surface (a table saw or a kitchen counter works fine). Read the level, and note exactly where the bubble lies. Then switch the level end for end, and set it down again in the same spot. Look again at the same vial. If you get the identical reading, the vial is accurate. Most levels have two vials for checking horizontal surfaces, so check the other vial the same way. If you get one accurate vial, consider yourself lucky and mark the good vial so you can always find it.

Then find a flat, vertical surface (a straight door jamb is perfect). Read the vial the same way, rotate it 180 degrees (same end up), and read it again. Most levels have four vials for reading plumb, so you have a good chance that one of them will actually be accurate. If so, mark it.

If your level isn't right, go to the store, pick out a few of the better brands, and check them in the store until you find one that will give good readings. Once you've found an accurate level, store it carefully, check it frequently, and don't drop it.

Before tipping the door into place, check and trim the bottom of the side jambs, if necessary, to yield a ¼-in. gap below the door swinging over the finish floor. Then check the rough-opening sides for plumb.

Put the door in place, shim it plumb, make sure it swings well, and nail it off. Be sure the hinges and strike are well supported with shims.

PRO **TIP**

An exterior door will last longer and work better if it's protected from rainwater by a porch roof, a generous eaves, or at least a gutter.

TRADE SECRET

Most wood doors and windows come primed, but it is still very important to get paint on wood window edges and exteriors quickly, before moisture enters, causing the wood to swell and, possibly, the unit to warp.

IN DETAIL

The standard size for a door jamb is either 4⁹⁄₁₆ in. (for a 2x4 wall) or 6⁹⁄₁₆ in. (for a 2x6 wall). This allows room for the wall framing, ½ in. of drywall or sheathing on either side of door, and ¹⁄₁₆ in. extra. For interior doors, you can also purchase split jambs, which offer an adjustable detail for odd-sized walls.

Installing exterior doors

For an exterior door, the process is similar, except that there will be an integral threshold to shed water and seal the door at the bottom. Before putting the door in place, check the floor for level at the bottom of the rough opening, and add shims as necessary so that the door will sit on a level surface. The door may come with installation instructions, but as a rule you have to caulk the door at the bottom to keep water from running under the door. If the door is exposed to heavy weather, it might make sense to install a flashing over the shimmed base, and out over the wall, before putting in the door.

I install the frame without the door because most exterior doors are heavy. If the door comes with exterior trim attached, it will be easier to get into proper alignment, but otherwise the procedure is as with an interior door. Again, make sure it operates well before finally nailing it off.

Sometimes you will be replacing a door, but using the existing door jambs. Take the new door, and test-fit it in the opening. Shim it up on a shingle at the bottom to position it at the right height. In many older homes, the door size will be nonstandard or the frame no longer level, and you'll have to saw or plane the door to size. Use a circular saw if you have to remove ¼ in. or

more (run the saw along a fence for a straight cut; score the cutting line with a utility knife if the saw tends to chip out along the cut.) To shave small amounts, use a sharp handplane. When the door fits right, put it in place, and, with a knife or very sharp pencil, mark the hinge locations on the new door. Old door frames may not be plumb. With the new door in place, see if it closes uniformly. In the photo at left on the facing page, with the door in tight top and right, it stuck out ½ in. on the bottom left. A partial correction can be made when the hinges are installed.

There are many ways to cut the recess for the hinge, known as a *mortise*. The photos on the facing page show the old-fashioned way. A simple gadget known as a mortise gauge is aligned with the marks that locate the hinge. A hammer blow

When replacing a door in existing jambs, put the door in place to see where it must be trimmed.

Door Jambs

Split jamb (adjustable): The split-jamb type can accommodate some variation in wall thickness, but it's not as rugged as a one-piece jamb.

Site-built jamb: Building a jamb on site makes sense for doors of odd thickness or size. You can also order jamb stock separately for making jamb sets.

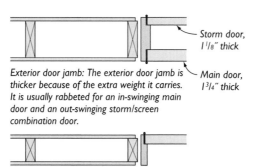

Storm door, 1¹⁄₈" thick

Exterior door jamb: The exterior door jamb is thicker because of the extra weight it carries. It is usually rabbeted for an in-swinging main door and an out-swinging storm/screen combination door.

Main door, 1³⁄₄" thick

One-piece interior jamb: This typical interior door jamb is rabbeted for a standard 1³⁄₈-in. interior door. Although they usually come 4⁹⁄₁₆ in. wide for standard 2x4 walls, they can be ordered wider. Suppliers will rip the stock down to your desired width before setting up a prehung door for you.

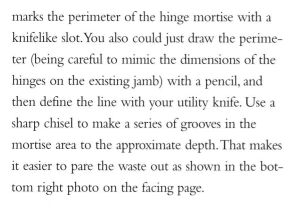

A butt (or mortise) gauge marks all three sides of the hinge mortise at once.

Chop the mortise to depth, then pare it out, all with a sharp chisel.

marks the perimeter of the hinge mortise with a knifelike slot. You also could just draw the perimeter (being careful to mimic the dimensions of the hinges on the existing jamb) with a pencil, and then define the line with your utility knife. Use a sharp chisel to make a series of grooves in the mortise area to the approximate depth. That makes it easier to pare the waste out as shown in the bottom right photo on the facing page.

In the example, the mortises were adjusted to compensate for the fact that one side of the door frame tilted outward ½ in. The top mortise was made about ³⁄₁₆ in. *wider* (moving the *top* of the door *outward*) a bit, and the bottom mortise was made ⅛ in. *narrower* to move the door *in* at the *bottom*. Along with some judicious sanding, the crookedness will be much less visible. Carpenters call this *splitting the difference*. The idea is to make a large discrepancy into several small and nearly unnoticeable discrepancies.

Mechanical Rough-In

The mechanical rough-in might be defined as any plumbing, wiring, heating, ductwork, or gas work that must go in before the finish walls, ceiling, and floor are applied. Typically it is the part

of the work that is never seen once the job is done, but it can represent a big part of the cost. The *finish* wiring and plumbing are usually done almost at the end of the job.

Think carefully about doing your own wiring. Wiring seems easier than it really is. The tools are simple, and it's easy to make things work. As long as a circuit is complete, the light will probably go on or the dishwasher will operate. But making it function safely requires knowing and following all the rules. If you take on wiring, get good books and videos, study them, and have a pro or the building inspector go over all of your work.

Rough wiring

The rough wiring includes removing any incorrect wiring and installing the new wires and boxes you need. I try to reuse any wiring or circuitry that is in a reasonable location and in good condition. If an outlet is in a functional location, there is no point in pulling it out. Rough wiring in renovation isn't just taking out the old and adding the new, but reconfiguring what is there as simply and effectively as possible.

On the other hand, with your walls and ceilings open, you may find unsafe or illegal wiring

PRO TIP

Wire one circuit completely, so that you'll have enough safe outlets to use during construction, and light to work by.

TRADE SECRET

To avoid any ambiguity, I mark right on the wall or ceiling surfaces where new electrical boxes will go.

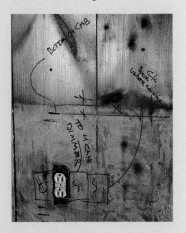

This box removed from a ceiling contains about three times as many wires as the code allows.

A maze of unprotected, incorrect wiring in an attic. This should be sorted out, properly routed, and replaced as needed.

Where the wire comes within 1¼ in. of the edge of the stud, a metal plate prevents nails from damaging the wire.

Tuck the wires neatly out of the way, all ready to hook up to the switch or receptacle.

that should be replaced. Old knob-and-tube wiring (with ceramic insulators through the studs) should go. I've seen extension cords buried in the wall as part of circuits. You may find boxes with too many wires stuffed into them. All unsafe and noncompliant wiring should be removed.

In an open wall, the usual practice is first to attach the boxes, nailing or screwing them in place flush with the eventual finish wall or ceiling. Then, where needed, holes are drilled in the studs, plates, or joists in order to run wires through, locating the holes near the center of these members, so that nails used to attach drywall or other materials

won't damage the wire later. Then wires are stripped (with just enough wire left to make connecting them convenient), fed to the box, and clamped firmly to the box (different types of boxes have different clamping requirements). The wires are tucked neatly into the box, labeled, if necessary, to avoid confusion later.

In renovation, where some walls haven't been opened up, wires often have to be *fished* behind existing plaster, drywall, or paneling to a hole made for the new box. Then, after stripping the plastic jacket, the wire is attached to the box and shoved back into the wall. Where there is no stud

Fishing Wires

Sometimes wires are fed directly behind enclosed wall surfaces, but for longer fishing expeditions a stiff wire known as a *fish tape* is used. The tape is easier to fish than the wire. When the route is established with the fish tape, the actual wire is secured to the fish with electrical tape and pulled back through. A thin chain is sometimes used for vertical fishing. Fishing wire works best with two people, one to push the fish tape and another to listen for its progress and pull it out when it's close to the new outlet's hole. This is one of the higher mysteries of the electrical trade. I've seen an electrician fish a

tape into the ceiling of one room, slowly work it along above the ceiling across the room and a large hallway, and then to an opening in a third room, thereby saving a great deal of time that would have been spent replacing or patching the ceiling.

After the box is rough-wired, it's shoved back into its hole. Since it can't be fastened to the wall studs, it has to be secured directly to the wall finish material. This box has plastic tabs that clamp the box to the drywall when tightened.

The steel fish tape is threaded through the wall to the new box location. Then the wire is taped to the fish tape and pulled back through. A special box has built-in clips that secure the box directly to the drywall.

to attach the box to, it can be attached directly to the drywall or plaster. Any electrical supplier can provide boxes with built-in clamps for that purpose.

Most new circuits are left off at the breaker for safety. But some lighting and outlets are needed for construction, and it's not safe to run the whole job off of one outlet with six extension cords. Any circuits left live should be safe. Unattached wires that must remain live should be

joined with wire nuts, taped, and tucked into their boxes.

Most lighting fixtures are wired from a box similar to those used for outlets. But recessed lights are wired directly. After marking the recessed light locations on the ceiling, cut out the appropriate-sized openings with a reciprocating saw. The fixtures can be installed from above if there is access to the area above the light.

WHAT CAN GO WRONG

In cold climates like here in Vermont, we try not to bury water lines in exterior walls. They can freeze and burst with disastrous results. Lines can be run through cabinets or through the cabinet kickspace to avoid the cold. When pipes must run along or even in an exterior wall, it's essential to provide some sort of access panel in case of a freezeup. It also helps to take extra pains with the insulation behind the pipes. If your installation is at all questionable, talk it over carefully with your plumber. Hydronic heat lines can be protected with antifreeze if necessary.

WHAT CAN GO WRONG

If pipes are buried in the wall, locate them where they are unlikely to get hit by a nail. It is very discouraging to have to open up a brand-new wall to fix a plumbing leak caused by a nail or screw. Where pipes are notched into a stud, protect them with nail plates. If installation is at all questionable, talk it over carefully with your plumber.

Cutting a hole for a recessed light.

This recessed light is being installed from above. Other types of recessed lights can be installed from below.

Rough plumbing and heating

As with wiring, if you do your own plumbing, get a good reference book, follow the codes, and get your work inspected. It's quite reasonable to do much (if not all) of your own plumbing, and a lot of the newer plumbing products are designed with the do-it-yourselfer in mind. If you are significantly changing the lengths of sink drains or the ways they are vented, make sure your solution is up to code.

If the sink location isn't being changed significantly, as shown in the top left photo on p.137, the sink plumbing may require little change. The drain (temporarily supported by a string) and dishwasher connections would be reworked later, during the finish stage. The supply lines were capped above the shutoffs, which would be used again.

Sometimes existing drains, supply lines, or hydronic heat are left exposed by the new layout and have to be rerouted out of the way. Pipes and wires can be hidden in walls, floors, or ceilings. In the top right photo on the facing page, supply lines leading to another part of the house were relocated tight to a wall, where a pantry cabinet would cover them (while making them accessible if necessary for repairs). In the bottom photo on the facing page, a hydronic baseboard was removed, and the pipes tucked down into the floor, where they will be covered by finish flooring.

The rough plumbing for this sink was almost unchanged because the sink was relocated only a foot or so from its previous location. A string provides temporary support for the pipe.

These pipes were tucked back to avoid interfering with the pantry.

Ductwork

Ductwork for heat distribution or stove venting should also be done now (see pp. 92–94 for information about kitchen vents.) Ductwork isn't difficult and requires relatively simple tools: a couple of kinds of tin snips and a cordless drill fitted with a special tip called a nut driver that will quickly install self-tapping sheet-metal screws.

Some electricians will do your ductwork, but doing it for yourself may avoid having to engage yet another subcontractor. If you do run some ducts, get the instructions and specs from the company that provides the hood or exhaust fan. Make sure the ductwork is firmly supported, free of vibration, and free of leaks, which would depreciate the efficiency of the unit. Also, be sure to insulate any heating duct that goes through a cold space or any air-conditioning duct that goes through a warm space.

Baseboard convectors were removed and the heat lines rerouted under the floor to make room for cabinets. The rest of the heat work will get done later.

Construction

It's unlikely that you will do all of the work on your kitchen project yourself. There is simply too much to do, too many separate skills involved. But many readers will take charge of major chunks of the skilled work described in this chapter, such as finish carpentry or flooring. The trick is to figure out which aspects of the work to take on. I'd suggest picking the projects you'll enjoy most, have confidence in doing, and realistically have time to get done.

Even if you hire out the major construction specialties, there are plenty of ways to contribute and keep costs down, including design, researching and obtaining products and materials, painting, and regular cleanup. Such tasks add up to a lot of work, representing savings of several thousand dollars. Make the choices that suit your skills and the time you have available.

1 Wall Prep, page 140

2 Insulation, Infiltration, and Vapor Barriers, page 141

3 Drywall and Other Finishes, page 143

4 Finish Carpentry and Flooring, page 151

When installing 1x3 strapping, two fasteners at each joist or stud will keep the strapping from cupping as it dries and popping the drywall fasteners.

TRADE SECRET

Keep a couple of clamps handy. It's often easiest to clamp awkward pieces before fastening them. Loose or floppy pieces may be fastened with screws rather than nails.

Make sure there is good support for drywall at all joints. Clamping the block makes it easy to nail or screw it on.

IN DETAIL

If you're going to install 3-ft. or 4-ft.-high wood wainscoting later on, you'll need to add continuous blocking between the studs to support it and the bottom of the drywall above. You also might provide blocking to hang upper cabinets. And you should provide blocking for any grab bars or railings (even if they might not be needed until later on). Install these on the flat so that there is more surface to support fastening and more room for error.

Wall Prep

Before insulating and covering up the walls, there are several important jobs to do that will avoid problems later. Gypsum wallboard goes up best when it is well supported, particularly at the joints, and when it goes up in as large sheets as possible. Sheets that are 10 ft. or 12 ft. long may be harder to put up, but they have fewer joints to tape. It also helps if the wall and ceiling surfaces are relatively flat, plumb, and level, and failing that, not so far out of whack as to be glaringly obvious.

I take a careful tour of the whole site, trying to imagine myself putting up large, heavy sheets of wallboard, and identifying all the places where I need to add or adjust nailing surfaces. Another useful exercise is to take a straight 6- or 8-ft. board and place it randomly against walls and the ceiling to see if the studs or joists are in plane. If you put

Construction Sequence

Although it can't always be followed perfectly, there is a logical order of work that often will help things go smoothly and save time:

- Prepare walls: strapping, nailers, etc.
- Seal around windows and doors
- Install insulation and vapor barrier
- Hang and tape drywall
- Paint drywall, particularly if a different color or finish than trim
- Install wood flooring; sand and apply first and second coats (resilient flooring or ceramic tile can go in now or after the cabinets)
- Install cabinets and counters
- Finish wiring, lighting, plumbing, heat
- Apply trim to windows, doors, walls
- Apply final coat of finish on floor

your straightedge across three or four wall studs or joists at a time, an unusually crooked, protruding, or recessed one should be evident. Use a 4-ft. level to identify walls that are particularly out of plumb.

Strapping

On a ceiling, it's best to support the drywall on 16-in. centers. In many older buildings, ceiling rafters are widely spaced and not particularly flat. As a result, it would be hard to put up drywall, and the results would be wavy. The traditional solution is to put up 1x3 strapping on 16-in. centers. Strapping can be attached with 8d common nails or 2-in. drywall screws, though the process is a lot faster if you have a pneumatic nailer. If the joists are misaligned, strapping can be shimmed with shingles to make it more flat, or a protruding joist can be notched.

Returns

Any added nailers that provide support for drywall, and any shims that will make a surface more flat are often called *returns*. Before beginning this task, I like to gather together a collection of usable scraps. Without knowing exactly what I'll end up needing, I collect ¾-in. scraps, plywood pieces of different thicknesses, maybe narrow strips of ¼-in. plywood, some shingles, a few scraps of 2x4, and any other odds and ends that might come in handy. I also get out a selection of fasteners, perhaps some 8d and 16d common nails and a selection of drywall screws. I've found it's often easier to screw returns or other small things together than to nail them. I'll grab my cordless power saw, an electric jigsaw, or a handsaw so I can quickly cut things to length. Since all this shimming will be buried, good looks aren't important.

With your kit nearby, check the walls for flatness. If there is a stud that is recessed but basically parallel to the others, add plywood about the right thickness to build it up. Check inside corners to make sure there is fastening, and add a stud if needed. Check around electrical boxes, new beams, windows and doors, and any place where framing has been changed to make sure there is something to secure the edges of the drywall to. If not, find something from your scrap pile and put it up.

Protecting pipes and wires

Make sure wires and pipes are not going to be damaged by the nails or screws used to hang drywall or cabinets. Wires should be set back at least 1¼-in. from the stud edge. If that isn't possible, they need to be protected with thin steel nail plates, sold at electrical-supply houses, hardware stores and home centers.

Iron pipe will resist nails, but a nail or screw will go right through plastic or copper, often without you even being aware of it. Unfortunately, in renovation work it's sometimes necessary to locate pipes where they could be damaged if they aren't protected. If so, as the drywall goes up, mark exactly where the pipes run so you can avoid putting screws or nails there.

Insulation, Infiltration, and Vapor Barriers

The effectiveness of your insulation depends both on what type you use (see the chart below) and how it is installed. Thermal performance of a wall is proportional to the thickness of the insulation.

Insulation Values

	R-value (per inch of thickness)
Fiberglass	3.5
Expanded polystyrene	4.0
Extruded polystyrene	5.0
Polyisocyanurate	7.2

Plumbing Walls and Leveling Ceilings

Some builders straighten and plumb every wall and level all ceilings. I must admit that it is a lot easier to hang cabinets on a wall that is flat and plumb. But my bias as a builder from Cambridge, Massachusetts, where it seems that every wall is out of whack, is to leave the walls alone in most cases. If you change them, you can end up having to redo wiring, replace trim, or even rehang doors. No matter how many changes I've made to a wall, I try to keep the finish wall surface in its original plane. Usually, once everything is complete on a project, imperfections in the walls will be hardly noticeable. In short, by all means make minor improvements, but think through the implications of major changes.

Similarly, some pitch to a ceiling will usually go unnoticed, unless there is a level line nearby—such as the top of a row of new cabinets. In an old farmhouse, where everything has settled, leveling a ceiling could make other nonlevel elements—such as the head casings on doors and windows—look worse.

There are some cases, though, where correcting a wall or ceiling makes good sense. The basic question is, what is there to compare the crooked wall or ceiling to? If it's near a new, perfectly plumb door, or 2 in. from the end of a beautiful new pantry, it might be a good idea to straighten things out.

Ceilings are best corrected by adding strapping and then shimming between the strapping and the ceiling joists as needed. To plumb walls you must either make tapered shims out of 2x4s (cutting them with your portable circular saw) or, if it is easier, nail a second 2x4 to the side of each wall stud in the correct plane (this is called *sistering*). If you do this, it may help to clamp the sister studs in place as you nail them up. Or, you could attach them with 3-in. drywall screws. Another procedure would be to strap the wall as you would a ceiling. This might be faster but uses up ¾ in. more of your interior space.

Inexpensive 1x3 strapping, screwed or nailed to ceiling joists on 16-in. centers, can be shimmed as needed to provide a flat, convenient surface for installing drywall.

PRO **TIP**

Photograph or video-tape your open walls, recording the location of framing and vulnerable pipes and wires for the next time the house is worked on.

WHAT CAN GO WRONG

There are two basic types of spray urethane foam: *expanding* and *minimal expanding*. Expanding foam is good for filling cracks and cavities, but don't use it to seal around a window or door. Besides making a mess, it will push against the jambs and probably cause an unwanted bow that will make the window or door difficult to operate. Even with minimal expanding foam, you may want to use a few scraps of wood to brace between the opposing door or window jambs, keeping them straight as the foam sets.

When applying foam, be sure to wear disposable plastic gloves (often they're included in the package), and use up the whole can in one session. The nozzles tend to gum up after the first use.

Twice the thickness means twice the R-value, or half the heat lost.

Controlling infiltration (actual air movement through the wall, or drafts) is equally important. In a drafty house, infiltration can account for half of your heat loss. By tightening up such a house, it's possible to save 25 percent or more of the heating bill, without adding any new insulation.

Installing insulation

Fiberglass is the most widely used insulation because it has a good R-value per dollar and can be installed quickly. Standard widths are 15 in. and 23 in., to match framing intervals of 16 in. and 24 in. on center. Although it comes with paper and foil backings, I much prefer *unfaced* insulation because it is easier to cut and handle. Insulation with a backing is stapled in place, but unfaced insulation is simply cut to a snug fit and placed in the opening, where friction keeps it in place.

When working with fiberglass insulation, wear eye protection, a dust mask, long sleeves, and a hat. I like to put a piece of plywood up on sawhorses to make a cutting table, and then use a board as a straightedge to compress the insulation as I cut it with a sharp utility knife. I cut the pieces just oversize so that they completely fill the cavity. A neat job with no voids is essential. It may help to split the insulation to get around pipes and wires.

Sealing around windows, doors, and electrical boxes

The gaps around doors jambs and windows are among the worst avenues for air infiltration; seal them carefully. These cracks vary in size, ranging from tiny slits up to 2-in.-wide gaps, though usually they seem to be 1 in. or less. The best method for sealing them depends on the size of the crack. Larger cavities that are sealed off from the outside

Unfaced batts, which don't have to be stapled in place, are much quicker to install than faced fiberglass. A snug, void-free fit is important.

Make sure the space behind electrical boxes is insulated. Cut away some of the thickness of the fiberglass to avoid compressing it and reducing its insulation value.

can be filled with fiberglass insulation. Minimal expanding spray urethane foam is great for cracks of perhaps ¼ in. to 1½ in. It expands enough to make a really tight seal, and also has good R-value. For finer cracks, use caulk.

There can be a lot of air leakage around electrical boxes. Some states (such as Wisconsin) now require the area behind and around boxes to be sealed up with spray foam. When the drywall goes up, the gap between drywall and the box is caulked. This is probably the best way to seal the gaps at outlets. While you are at it, foam around any pipes or wires that penetrate the bottom or top plates of the wall.

In cold climates, it's best to keep water lines out of outside walls. If you must put them there, pay careful attention to insulating and airsealing. I like to put as much rigid foam as I can behind the pipes, then seal the seams with spray foam or caulk to eliminate the possibility of drafts. I don't insulate between the pipes and the interior side of the wall, which would isolate the pipes from the warmth of the house.

Air and vapor barriers

There is some debate about air and vapor barriers. The most common approach is to staple large sheets of 4-mil or 6-mil clear polyethylene sheeting over the walls and ceiling after they have been thoroughly insulated and sealed. Poly comes in a variety of widths, so it's often possible to cover an entire wall with a single piece. The ceiling poly goes up first, then the walls, with the poly over-lapping onto the floor (the excess will be trimmed off later). Joints are best handled with generous, folded overlaps.

The theory is that the polyethylene prevents air (and moisture borne by the air) in the room from migrating into the wall. However, recent research indicates that most of the moisture that gets into walls does so by leaking through gaps in the wall

rather than by migration through wall materials. Some experts now recommend foregoing the plastic and concentrating on making the drywall airtight by using gaskets and special techniques. Because of this debate, practices that builders follow vary widely. Our choice is to use the plastic, install it with care, and seal up all of the openings.

Drywall and Other Finishes

It's almost magical to watch a professional dry-waller "hang board." In the morning, there is bare framing. By 2 P.M. the board is hung, and the place looks completely different. By 5 P.M., the first coat of compound has been applied. I once asked Walter Scott, a great drywaller I worked with for many years in the Boston area, how he did it so fast, particularly since he never for a moment seemed in any hurry. "You look at the board, look at the wall, and go!" he told me. You may never achieve Walter's speed, but the principle is the same: Start early, clear everything out of the work area, turn on the radio, and keep going.

Hanging drywall

As a rule, ceilings are done first, using the longest pieces you can handle to minimize butt joints. Twelve-foot- to 16-ft. long lengths of drywall are heavy, so you'll want help (or a rented panel-lift) to hang them. You'll also want them to go up right the first time, so don't measure or fit too tightly. Buy a drywaller's 4-ft. T-square for square cuts, and use a chalkline for marking longitudinal or angled lines. The edges of ceiling drywall typically aren't screwed in place at all but are supported by the wall pieces and allowed to float. This allows for differential movement between the ceiling and walls and helps to keep the fasteners from "popping."

Spray urethane foam seals the side of this window. Either foam or fiberglass would work at the bottom.

Where there isn't room for thick insulation, or where extra protection is essential, rigid foam is a good alternative. Its effectiveness is dependent on a tight fit. Fit the material carefully, and fill any gaps with caulk or spray foam.

TRADE SECRET

I don't recommend hanging ceiling drywall by yourself, but
walls are another matter. The
sheets are shorter and lighter,
and you can use gravity to your
advantage. Having the drywall
stacked conveniently minimizes
handling. Run the sheets vertically rather than horizontally,
forcing them up tight to the ceiling by jamming the tip of your
flat bar under the sheet and
stepping on the hooked end to
lever it up.

TRADE SECRET

Keep a cordless drill handy,
already loaded with a
screw. You can simply set the
drill on a stepladder or any
nearby surface, but many drills
have holsters (or get a Bigg
Lugg™, made by Prazi®—800-
262-0211—a hook that goes on
your tool belt and conveniently
holds a cordless drill.)

First, mark the line on the face, then follow the line
by eye with a utility knife to cut through the paper.

The sheet will easily snap back, then you can cut
through the paper on the back. It may be easier to
reposition the sheet for this.

Cutting drywall is easy. Just cut along your
marked line with a utility knife to cut the paper
on the face (you don't have to cut all the way
through). Then snap the sheet back, and cut
through the paper on the back. For an L-shaped
or U-shaped cut, use a drywall saw to cut out two
sides of the cut. Then use the knife-and-snap
method for the last cut.

Perhaps the trickiest part of hanging drywall is
locating electrical outlets or other holes or
notches in the sheet. There are at least three methods by which you can do this. One is to measure
over and down from a known line—perhaps an
adjacent sheet that is already in place. Here is
where a carpenter's framing square or a big T-
square come in handy. You might also use your
level to establish a measuring line. Another
method is to put a generous helping of colored
chalk from your chalkline on the edge of the electrical boxes, put the sheet in place, and press it

Large sheets of drywall are heavy. Get help holding them in position as the first screws are placed. To save time, lines on the drywall show where screws go. The cleat on the wall at the lower left provides support for the piece as it is positioned.

You can usually hang wall pieces by yourself, but get help when you need it.

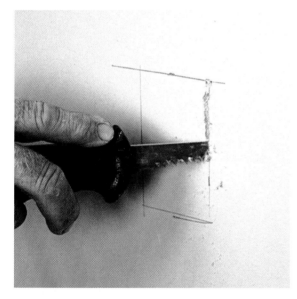

For notches or holes, use a little drywall saw.

Laying Out Cuts in Drywall

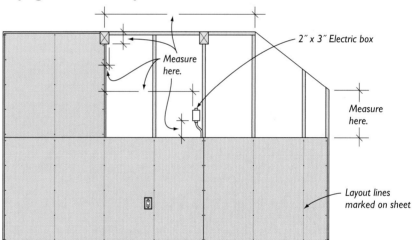

2″ x 3″ Electric box

Measure here.

Measure here.

Layout lines marked on sheet

Measure over and down (or up) to locate outlet boxes and notches, and angles. Then use your 4-ft. drywall T-square to find the same points on the sheet of drywall. It's often a good idea to mark lines on the drywall to show where the fasteners go.

against the boxes. Then you can take the sheet down, find the box outlines on the back of the sheet, and cut the holes with a drywall saw.

Most professional drywallers use a third approach. They measure and mark the *approximate* center of every electrical box or opening on the face of the sheet before they hang it. After it's hung loosely with a few screws, they use a special router with a short, skinny bit to make a plunge cut into the sheet at each mark. The router bit has a guide bearing, so it cuts to the inside edge of the box, hops over to the outside, and cuts around the perimeter of the box to make the hole, using the box as a guide. If you use this method, be sure to tuck wires well back in the box to keep them out of the way of the spinning router bit.

IN DETAIL

Metal corner bead is usually nailed to the outside corners, though there are now a great variety of new plastic bead materials for odd angles, rounded corners, and other special applications. When you're installing a corner bead, use a straightedge (a 6-in. drywall knife works great) to make sure that the nailing flanges, nails, or screws don't stick out beyond the plane of the wall. A corner bead is among the easiest joints to coat because the metal edge provides a smooth track for the trowel to follow.

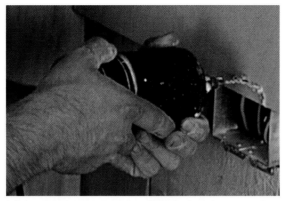

It's hard to locate cuts for electrical outlets exactly. This special router allows the cuts to be made after the sheets are hung.

Use the shortest drywall screws that will work to attach the sheets to the framing. Normally, 1¼-in. screws spaced about 8 in. o.c. work fine, unless you are placing drywall over another material, like plaster or rigid-foam insulation. You can use a cordless drill to drive the screws. The screw has to be driven in far enough to dimple the paper, without tearing it. This allows you plaster over the screw later.

The difficult part is simply holding the sheet in place long enough to get the first few screws in. This is particularly trying when you are holding up a long sheet on the ceiling. It helps to have at least one helper when you are hanging drywall.

Taping drywall

Sometimes people approach taping in a dabbing, fussy way, working over the same joint several times to get it perfect. They'll apply tape here, do a corner there, then sand another joint, then tape a different joint. This way, the task will take months. The best drywall tapers I know use large sweeping movements; the work should be rhythmic and flowing.

The first step is to bed the paper tape that bridges the gaps between sheets using a small drywall knife or trowel. I like the 6-in. Hyde knife because the blade is nice and flexible. You don't work directly from the 5-gallon pail of joint compound, but instead use a hawk or a large trowel to hold the mud.

First, put a ⅛-in.-thick bed of compound over the joint, making sure to leave no gaps. Then lay the paper tape into the compound, as straight as possible. Using your 6-in. knife, press the tape firmly into the compound, smoothing it so that there are no bubbles or globs of compound. If

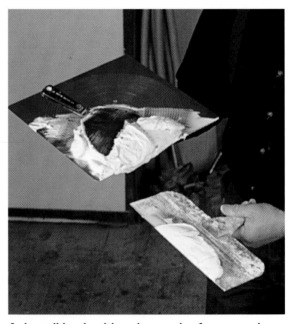

A drywall hawk, with a nice supply of compound on it. I usually use the long knife for smoothing flat joints. The 6-in. knife is my favorite all-around drywall knife.

Applying compound to a corner bead is easy.

Apply a bed of compound over a joint.

Set the tape into the compound.

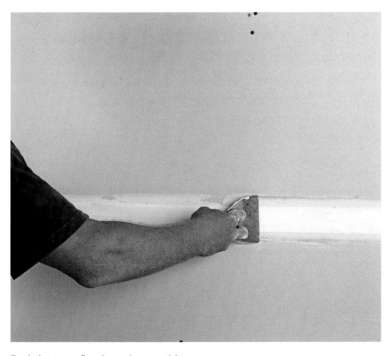

Bed the tape firmly and smoothly.

When the first coat is dry, apply a second coat of compound, using a wider knife.

necessary, make a second pass to remove the excess completely. Typically, I go around and bed all of the tape first, particularly on big jobs. When the compound is dry (usually the next day) you can go ahead and apply the next coat. Apply a wide band of compound with a wide knife, then in one smooth, continuous, forceful motion, smooth it out and remove the excess. A good job here depends on having the right amount of pressure, the right (quite low) angle, and a smooth movement. You'll have to experiment to find the right angle and pressure.

PRO TIP

Each time you put a coat of compound on your seams, hit all of the nail holes, too. Compound shrinks as it dries, so you'll have to do each nail three times.

TRADE SECRET

Different people like different sizes and types of knives; experiment to find the ones that are right for you. I recommend a 6-in. flexible knife for bedding the tape, applying the second coat, and plastering screw holes, though some prefer a narrower 4-in. knife for bedding the tape. Many pros will use a wide trowel-like knife that is stiff and slightly convex for the final coat, so that the compound crowns somewhat (see the bottom right photo on p. 147). That way, as the compound shrinks and is sanded, you end up with a flat seam. Others like a more flexible flat knife for their final coats (see the bottom right photo on p. 146).

It's always a temptation to try for a perfect joint. But it's better to make one smooth pass, maybe go over it once more if you are unsatisfied, then move on to the next joint. Where joints intersect, it's a good idea to let the first joint dry, then come back the next day to do the second.

Expect to make a total of three passes over each joint to get a smooth, correctly built-up result. Before each coat, I take the edge of my 6-in. knife and quickly scrape off any bumps in the surface.

When you do inside corners, you'll have to fold the tape (it has a crease in the middle) before bedding it in the joint compound. You can use a special 90-degree corner trowel to coat both sides of the corner, but I prefer to coat one side on one day, then coat the other side the next with a regular flat knife.

Sometimes the drywall will butt up against an exposed wooden beam. There are several ways to handle these joints, including a variety of plastic or metal beads that can be used to bridge the small

gap between the drywall and beam, and which are then coated like outside corner bead. Another approach is to fill the space with Durabond 90, a fast-setting joint compound that doesn't shrink or crack. If your beams shrink a lot, you may want to come back to the joint later with paintable caulk.

Another effective method for handling a gap against wood beams or trim is called *flat taping*. First the beam is masked with masking tape to protect it. Then joint compound is applied and paper tape bedded into it. The tape is put up flat and tight to the beam instead of being folded into the corner, then coated like any other joint. Later, after painting, carefully cut the masking tape at the corner and peel it away.

You may have some patching to do. This could be repairs to old plaster, gaps between your new drywall and the existing plaster, or holes caused by drywalling errors.

If I'm making a large patch in old plaster, I'll usually put a slightly larger scrap of ⅜-in.-thick

Inside corners are best coated one side at a time, allowing the first side to dry before doing the other.

Filling larger gaps with Durabond 90. Here the adjacent wood is protected with masking tape so that the 90 will not soil it.

drywall up against the hole and draw its outline on the plaster. Then I cut along the line with my utility knife and use the claw of my hammer to strip out the plaster up to the line. After screwing the patch in place, I fill the gaps with Durabond, then finish the patch with regular compound.

A similar method can be used to patch a hole in drywall. First, cut an oversize patch piece, mark the wall, then widen the hole to match. Take a couple of scraps of wood (strapping cutoffs work well here), fish them into the hole, carefully hold them in place, and secure them with screws. Then you can attach the patch. Cracks in plaster or old drywall can simply be filled with Durabond but also can be bridged with tape as you would a regular drywall joint.

The Magic of "90"

USG's Durabond 90 is described as a "setting-type joint compound." Regular compound is soft, water soluble, relatively weak, and comes ready to use. It dries overnight and shrinks as it dries. Durabond 90, by contrast, is hard, nonsoluble, and very strong. It comes bagged in powder form and is mixed with water. It is nonshrinking, and it dries rock hard in 90 minutes (there are also faster-setting versions).

Durabond does many tasks that regular compound does only poorly. For example, you can fill thick cracks and it won't slump. If you use it next to a beam, it won't shrink away and leave a gap, though the beam may shrink. Some tapers I know use Durabond to bed tape, mixing up large batches with a mixing paddle mounted in an electric drill. Durabond 90 is also great for patching large holes in plaster and for filling gaps between sheets of drywall.

Flat taping works well up against a wood beam.

Finally, the joints get sanded. This is nasty, dusty work that definitely requires a dust mask. A hat also helps. You'll want to use a half-sheet pole sander, which not only speeds up the job but also keeps your face and body a bit away from the stream of dust. I use ordinary 120-grit sandpaper, but a special mesh paper is made for the purpose; it clogs more slowly. When you're done, sweep down the walls, and vacuum up the dust immediately with a shop vac.

TRADE SECRET

Fiberglass mesh tape, which was developed for skim-coat plaster systems, has a couple of handy features. It is self-sticking, so it doesn't have to be bedded in compound but can be applied directly to the wall. Joint compound (either regular or Durabond) penetrates the holes in the mesh and adheres to the drywall or old plaster. It's handy for patching tasks, and some people use it for regular joints in drywall. I use it for patching, but I use paper tape for most drywall work because I think it is stronger, smoother, and easier to coat.

To patch a hole in drywall, first square off the hole, using a precut patch as a template. After cutting out the hole, attach tabs of scrap wood with drywall screws, then screw the patch to the tabs. Finish as any drywall joint.

Sanding drywall joints goes faster using a stick sander.

Finish Carpentry and Flooring

Finish carpentry—including window and door trim, baseboards, moldings, and perhaps shelving projects—and flooring is one of the most satisfying parts of building. It's relatively clean, there's little heavy lifting, and you get to use neat tools of all sorts. But it is careful work, and there are a lot of techniques and tricks to getting good results efficiently that are gained only with experience. Still, if you are patient, work carefully, and are willing to look for professional advice when you come up against a stumbling block, there's no reason why these tasks aren't within your capability. I recommend hiring a finish carpenter to work with you for a day or two to get you started in the right direction.

Favorite Tools

Cordless drills and drywall screws can be used to fasten almost anything to almost anything else, with a quick, strong, reversible connection. I keep one set up with a magnetic bitholder and a Phillips driver tip, and another with a pilot bit for predrilling screw holes. (If you have just one drill, get a convertible driver tip, which has both functions built in and converts quickly). Nearby is my parachute bag, which carries several sizes of drywall screws. I also use clamps to hold things in place for cutting or fastening things. They remove a lot of uncertainty and awkwardness from carpentry. While I have quite a collection of clamps, my Quick-Grips® (from American Tool Company®) are the ones I usually reach for first. Another tool I love is the Swanson Speed® Square, which does the job of an ordinary square but never goes out of square. I use it to mark or read angles (either in degrees or in terms of roof pitch), and it also serves as a handy saw guide. I keep it in my tool belt or back pocket at all times.

Some favorite tools: cordless drills with pilot bits and a handy collection of drywall screws; a cordless saw with a Swanson Speed Square and Quick-Grip clamp; and a jack plane.

IN DETAIL

What you'll need for finish work:

- Good hammer
- Levels
- Scribes for marking irregular cuts
- Variety of drills and drill bits
- Squares
- Bevel square to measure angles
- Chisels
- Handplanes
- Handsaws (I like to use a Japanese-style pull saw)
- Circular saw
- Table saw
- Chopsaw (or sliding compound-miter saw)
- Block plane
- Sanders: belt, half-sheet orbital, random orbit

Laying wood flooring

There's a right time and a wrong time to lay a new wood floor, but it depends on the individual project. For instance, a strong argument can be made for putting down the floor *before* the trim and cabinets go in because it saves a lot of fitting. You won't need precise fits at the base of the cabinets as long as the flooring runs a few inches beyond the front of the cabinet kickspace. You won't need precise fits at the walls because the baseboard and door trim will cover up to ¾-in. gaps there. On the other hand, your cabinets and trim will take a bit more fitting, and you'll have to be careful not to damage the new floor as you work.

When laying hardwood flooring, it helps to work as a team. One person selects the flooring, cuts it to size, and lays it out, while the second person does the fitting and nailing. The person laying out the pieces tries to select them so that the joints are adequately staggered, the long and short pieces are evenly distributed, and the color and grains are thoughtfully arranged. This is demanding work, so you may want to take turns nailing (kneepads are a big help, too).

Strip hardwood tongue-and-groove flooring is nailed down with a special nailer that plants a nail through the tongue of the piece, where it will be concealed by the groove of the next piece. In the

A pneumatic flooring nailer takes the hard work out of nailing tongue-and-groove flooring.

To integrate a new section of hardwood flooring, slide the new boards in among the old flooring.

Drive nails for the first few rows by hand, predrilling the holes. Then use a nail set for the last few strokes to avoid damaging the edge of the board.

A drum floor sander requires a gentle, consistent touch. To avoid gouging, lower the drum carefully, advancing the sander as soon as it touches the wood.

photo on the facing page, the carpenter is using a pneumatic flooring nailer, which is the easiest to use if you have compressed air on the job. The special mallet has a soft head for activating the nailer and tapping the flooring into place, and a hard hammer end designed to tap the ends of the flooring strips into place. If you don't have air on site, you can rent a similar flooring nailer that is powered by a larger version of the mallet. This works well but is hard work, and it takes considerable strength. In this example, the new floor is being woven into an existing field of flooring (see the bottom photo on the facing page). With either type of nailer, the last few courses have to be hand-nailed with finish nails, driven through the tongue, because the power nailer runs into the wall. Use 6d finish nails and predrill for each one with a bit just a little smaller than the nails. When the nail is about ¼ in. up, finish the job with a nail set.

The floor shown was sanded with a *drum flooring sander* rented locally. Since it's a new floor, only two grits, 60 and 100, were needed. With an older

floor in worse shape, we would have needed to begin with coarser grits. The goal was to avoid having to refinish the living room floor, which was sanded and refinished only recently. For that reason, only the finer grit was used near and on the old section.

The big sander won't reach the edges; for that we used a smaller sander called an *edger*, which is basically a heavy disc sander on wheels. I also like to use my half-sheet orbital sander and small belt sander in tricky places, while I know others who have had good luck with random-orbital sanders, particularly in corners.

The floor finish was three coats of oil-based satin polyurethane finish. The keys to a good job are sanding lightly between coats, a thorough vacuuming before each coat, and very good light so that you don't miss any spots. Because the floor area shown in these photos was relatively small, the finish was applied with a large brush, but we also could have used a lamb's wool applicator.

TRADE SECRET

Dust and small bubbles in the finish will leave minute bumps in the finish, particularly after the first coat. Between coats, we used a floor buffer fitted with a sanding screen to smooth off the bumps and make sure the next coat would adhere properly.

A floor polisher, fit with a fine-mesh 150-grit screen, is used to sand lightly between coats of finish.

Laying other types of kitchen floors

In my experience, resilient flooring, ceramic-tile flooring, and the new click-together laminated floorings are reasonable projects for the home-owner. I can't provide detailed instructions here but will give the basic idea. See Resources on p. 196 for books and videos with more detail. Flooring vendors are always eager to help out with advice and equipment rental.

Resilient flooring could be vinyl tile, new types of laminate flooring that are installed in a similar way, or "sheet goods"—vinyl that goes down in large sheets.

With any flooring that goes down in tiles or small sections, layout is half the battle. The goal is a field of pieces that minimizes cutting while avoiding tiny slivers of flooring, looks basically parallel to the walls, and has attractively proportioned borders. You have to visualize the tile pattern over the entire floor. Sometimes I make a large-scale drawing to develop the best layout. It's also crucial to get the first row or rows of tiles *very* straight.

With resilient flooring, the quality of the floor is dependent on the quality of the surface it is being glued down to. A layer of plywood called underlayment, with a void-free top interior, is thoroughly nailed down to the old floor with nails or screws in a 4-in. or 6-in. pattern. The thickness here is ¼ in., but a thicker layer could be used for strength or to align the tile with another floor. Floor-leveling compounds can be used to flatten the floor if needed, either before or after the underlayment goes down. The mastic is spread with a notched trowel. The size of the notches regulates the amount of mastic spread. Often a large area, perhaps a quarter of the floor, is done at once, laying full tiles first.

Some types of mastic are designed to be tiled immediately, and some work more like contact cement; the tiles are set when the mastic dries. At the appropriate time, it's easy to drop the tiles into place if the mastic job is neat. Vinyl tile can be scored easily with a utility knife and snapped back.

Sheet goods also are bedded in mastic. Unless the room is very simple and the edges will be

Lay out vinyl or ceramic tile to be parallel to walls, to minimize cutting, and particularly to avoid skinny slivers of tile if possible.

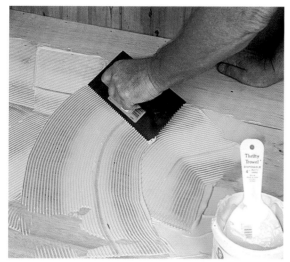

A large area is covered with mastic using a notched trowel, which regulates the amount of adhesive.

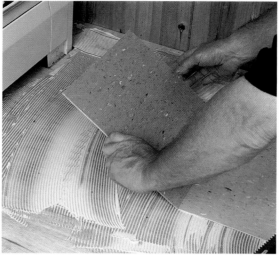

When the mastic is spread neatly, it's fairly simple to drop the full-size tiles into place.

Straight cuts in vinyl tile can be made by scoring with a utility knife and then snapping the tile. For complex cuts, soften the tile with a heat gun or small torch.

covered with baseboards later, a full-size pattern of the floor is made using brown kraft paper. The pattern is taped to the flooring, and the flooring cut out to match. The piece or pieces are test-fit before applying the mastic. This is tricky if the shape is complex. In this case, you may want to watch this being done, or get some expert help, before doing this yourself.

The new click-together laminated flooring is perhaps the easiest for the homeowner to install. It can be installed over any reasonably flat surface. Instead of being nailed or glued down, the pieces are attached to each other and float on a base consisting of a thin foam pad with a slick upper surface. A ⅜-in. gap is left at the edges of the room to permit expansion and contraction. This gap is covered by baseboard or a small molding. The joint between pieces is a tongue-and-groove joint. As a piece is lowered into place, an added notch in the joint acts as a hook to lock the two rows together. Although the joint is tight and strong, the floor can be removed by reversing the process.

Installing ceramic tile is similar in some ways to installing vinyl tile but uses different materials. Instead of plywood, ½-in. or ¼-in. cement board is the substrate. But as with plywood, it has to be very securely nailed or screwed down. The tiles are

cut with a snap cutter (if the cuts are straightforward) or a wet saw, either of which can be rented from a tile store. Instead of mastic, the tiles are bedded in thinset mortar, a very strong adhesive that provides the tiles with more support than mastic while bonding them firmly.

The separation between ceramic tiles varies. Uniform, machine-made tiles can have relatively narrow joints, ⅛ in. or smaller. Rougher, larger tiles often have ¼ in. or even larger grout lines. The

With the new laminate flooring, each piece interlocks with the previous row as it is tilted down into place.

PRO TIP

One way to visualize how your proposed trim will look is to mock it up, using scraps to play with the widths and thicknesses. Live with the mockup for a while.

IN DETAIL

Most windows and doors can be ordered to fit standard 2x4 or 2x6 walls. But for nonstandard walls, jambs will usually have to be extended to match the thickness of the wall. Many windows are now designed on the assumption that jamb extensions will be added to customize the window to the wall, in which case they can be ordered along with the window and ripped to width on site. The other option is to order a standard window or door and rip and attach your own jamb extensions on site.

Spread thinset mortar with a notched trowel. Photo by Charles Bickford, ©The Taunton Press, Inc.

Ceramic tile cuts easily with a wet saw, which is readily available from rental centers. Photo by Charles Bickford, ©The Taunton Press, Inc.

grout varies similarly. Wider grout spaces call for a more concrete-like grout with more sand, called *sanded grout*. Some tiles are quite porous and have to be sealed before grouting. Many glazed tiles can be grouted directly. Normally the grout is essentially smeared over the whole surface and forced into the spaces between the tiles with a rubber trowel or squeegee, then the excess is wiped off with a large, damp sponge.

It's usually best to install ceramic- or stone-tile floors after the cabinetry and finish work have been completed, particularly if the tiles are thick or irregular. It's very time consuming to fit baseboards and other trim to uneven tiles.

Window and door trim

There are many styles of window and door trims, varying from narrow "clamshell" molding to more complicated, molded treatments. The detail you choose will have a big influence on the overall look of your house. In an older home, you'll probably want to match the rest of the trim in the house.

Ceramic tiles are set one at a time in thinset mortar. Photo by Charles Bickford, ©The Taunton Press, Inc.

Grouting fills the spaces between the tiles and secures them. Photo by Charles Bickford, ©The Taunton Press, Inc.

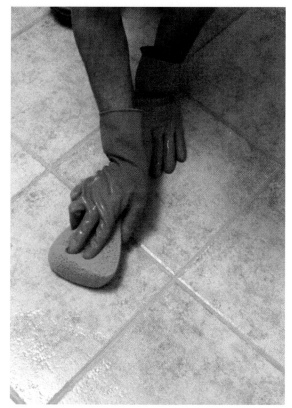

Large sponges are used to clean up the excess grout. Photo by Charles Bickford, ©The Taunton Press, Inc.

It's best to sand trim elements before installation, particularly if you will be using a varnish or other clear finish. I usually use a half-sheet orbital sander with 120-grit paper for this.

In a simple window treatment, 1x4s (which are actually ¾ in. by 3½ in.) are used for side and head casings. They're typically set back about ¼ in. from the window jamb or jamb extension. This setback is called a *reveal*. It looks good and introduces a small tolerance that makes casing the window much easier. Sometimes, the head casing overhangs the side casings slightly, which also looks nice while again introducing a tolerance. Varying any of these dimensions is a simple way to adjust the style of your finish work. For example, in the photo above, the side casings are a full 4 in. wide, and the head casing is made of thicker 5/4 wood, which (when finished) is a full 1 in. thick. The

Interior Window Trim Elements

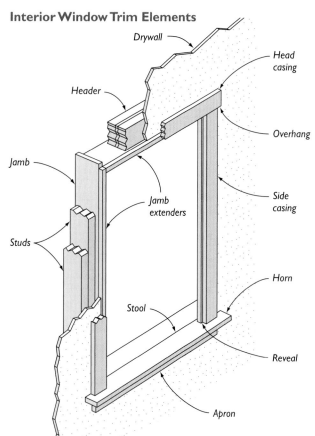

WHAT CAN GO WRONG

Occasionally a door or window jamb is slightly proud or slightly shy of the wall plane. If the jamb sticks out more than about ⅛-in., it can be trimmed with a handplane. If it is recessed even as little as ¹⁄₁₆-in., it can cause trouble. Sometimes it is possible to carve away a bit of the drywall (behind the casing where it won't be seen) enough so that the casing can sit flat against the wall.

On this window trim detail, the head is made of thicker stock and is rounded over. The sill also is thicker and has a bullnose edge.

interior sill, or *stool,* also is made of this thick stock and rounded is over with a "bullnose" profile. This gives the window a bolder, more definite appearance. In the photo below, some beading and a peaked head casing give the trim a more traditional look. Although much dressier, this style doesn't have to be much more difficult to do than a regular flat casing.

For window casing, the first step will often be installing jamb extenders, strips of wood that bring the window jambs out to the plane of the drywall or other wall finish, or just a hair beyond. If you are fortunate, these strips (they are supplied with some brands of windows) will be of uniform width. In some older homes, you may have to vary them to obscure wide variations in wall thickness. Although it's ideal for the jamb extenders to be either exactly flush with the wall or perhaps ¹⁄₁₆ in. proud, it's okay to project up to about ⅛ in. They can be nailed to the jambs with finish nails.

Next comes making the stool. This has to be notched to fit around the wall, such that it fits tight to the wall and tight to the bottom of the window. In the top right photo on the facing page, the stool stock is held in place and marked left and right to indicate where the notch begins. At the same time, the carpenter measures back to the window to determine how deep the notch will be. The notches can be cut with a handsaw, sabersaw, circular saw, or table saw. I like to round over the front edges of the stool, but it's not necessary.

Side casings come next. With the stool square with the window, measure up to the head (top) jamb, and add ¼ in. for the reveal. Cut the sides to length. While any saw can do this, a chopsaw or

Beaded details, made with a router, and a peaked head casing give this window casing a more traditional, old-fashioned look.

Mark the stool-cap stock for where the notch begins, and measure back to the window sill to determine how deep the notch must be. The scraps below the sill support it as measurements are made.

Jamb extenders may be needed to bring the jambs flush with the wall plane.

Cut the ears on the interior sill, or stool, using a sabersaw, handsaw, or table saw.

A router with a roundover bit can dress up the edges of the stool or other trim elements.

PRO TIP

PRO **TIP**

A threshold, notched as needed, can bridge floors of different heights. If the floors align, eliminate or minimize the threshold.

IN DETAIL

Baseboards are among the last details. Tips: Mark stud locations lightly on the wall or on your baseboard stock. Narrower boards—1x4 or smaller—are easier to force-fit tight to the floor. Surprisingly, few baseboard cuts will be exactly square. Cut a piece of baseboard stock about 2 in. overlong, put it in place, and scribe one end to fit. Cut the piece, test-fit it, and trim as needed. Only then mark the other end for cutting.

A sliding miter saw makes cutting casing and other trim a snap.

Install the side casing, nailing in a neat pattern.

Screw the stool to the sides for a tight fit. Predrill.

Installing the head casing.

Clamp the apron to the stool, then nail it to wall studs and framing below the window. Before removing the clamp, nail the stool down to the apron.

sliding miter saw is ideal. After test-fitting the sides, nail them to the jambs with 6d finish nails and to the wall stud with 8d finish nails, using a neat nailing pattern. I find the hardest part is to nail through the casing into the jamb. You have to nail at a slight angle so that the nail catches the jamb without the point coming out the side of the jamb. This just takes care and practice.

For a tighter fit, I then put a 1⅝-in. drywall screw (predrilled) up through the stool, into the bottom of the side casings. The head casing is next. With a normal flat casing, just cut the piece to length, with the overhang you have decided upon, and nail it up as you did the sides.

Finally, add the *apron,* which supports the trim above and closes the gap below the window. It usually looks better to make the apron a little narrower than the casings. Clamping the apron to the stool while fastening it makes for a tighter fit. When you're all finished, drive the nails below the surface with a nail set.

Your finish work may include custom elements you have designed for special situations. Left, a low slotted bootrack, positioned over the hydronic heat, dries out winter boots. Below, a simple bench with a hinged top provides a place to sit while taking boots off and plenty of economical storage, too.

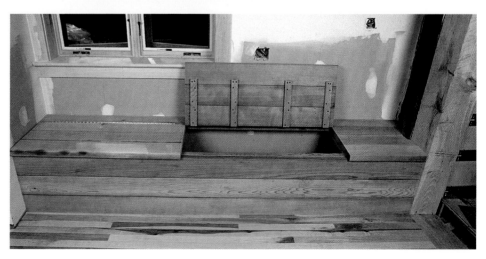

Cabinets

CHAPTER EIGHT
and Counters

The installation of the cabinets and counters is often the most exciting part of a kitchen renovation. It's the time when the ideas you've developed over weeks and months take shape. As the end of your project comes into view, you can begin to enjoy the design you've created. The work itself is gratifying also, because the carpentry techniques you will use are both interesting and challenging.

I'm always a bit nervous here, because this is when I discover any errors or unanticipated difficulties in my design, or in the cabinets I've ordered or built. Though it's great when everything goes in without a struggle, I've learned that even if something isn't quite right, there is always a way to make it work. This chapter reviews some of the methods cabinet installers and carpenters use to achieve a clean, professional-looking installation, whatever problems may crop up.

PRO TIP

For some tasks, a stiff folding rule is easier to use than a tape measure. That's why I always carry both with me on any finish carpentry job.

IN DETAIL

What you'll need:

- Finish nails and screws
- Good levels
- Cordless drills and pilot bits
- Big rafter square
- Stepladder
- Chopsaw or sliding compound-miter saw
- Table saw
- Shim shingles
- Kneepads

WHAT CAN GO WRONG

I don't necessarily try to get the counters on wall A at the same level on another wall. A difference doesn't usually show (unless they are connected), and in a crooked old house, you could end up throwing the counter heights way off.

Layout

By this point, a building site can look like a war zone, with materials and tools everywhere. Before starting to install, do a thorough cleanup. Tack a clean copy of the drawings on the wall, and lay out the tools and supplies you'll need. Make sure your chisels and sawblades are sharp. Cabinet installation demands working in a careful, thoughtful way.

With your work area set up, the next step will be to determine the exact location of all cabinets and counters and to mark these locations on the wall or floor. The process doesn't take too long and makes the actual fitting of the cabinets as simple as possible.

Establishing wall lines

I start by defining the height of the countertops. If all floors were flat and level, this would be easy. I could just measure up the standard 36 in. and make a mark on the wall. But floors aren't level. It's not unusual to find an inch or more of

Before you begin installation, do a thorough cleanup, sharpen your tools, and set up your work area.

variation along a run of cabinets. Cruise the entire floor with your 4-ft. level to see how crooked the floor is, which way (or ways) it pitches, and where the high and low points are.

But if the floor slopes considerably, you'll have to decide *where* the counter will be exactly

Assess the levelness of the floor throughout the area to be covered with cabinets. Find the high and low points. Photo by Roe A. Osborne, ©The Taunton Press, Inc.

If your floor is basically flat and level, you can simply measure up the wall to find the counter height, typically 36 in. If you are working on the subfloor, be sure to add the thickness of the yet-to-be-installed finish floor. Photo by Roe A. Osborne, ©The Taunton Press, Inc.

right and where a bit high or low. As a rule, I try to establish the counter height at the most frequently used work stations. When the main work stations are in different runs of cabinets, it's okay to have the runs at slightly different heights, if it makes the counter height correct. If your work stations are connected in a continuous run of cabinets, you'll have to compromise. Your food-prep counter might be a bit low, and your cooking center a bit high.

Make sure you leave enough height for your dishwasher. Dishwashers are nominally 34½ in. high, to go under a 1½-in.-thick counter. There is some leeway in the adjustable feet, but if your sink counter is more than ⅜ in. low, the machine might not fit. Look at the dishwasher itself or its spec sheet to see how much variation from the norm is possible.

In many old houses, there can be as much as a 1-in. difference in height at the wall and just 2 ft. out where the fronts of the cabinets will be. If so, measure up for the counter height not at the wall but 2 ft. out. Use a folding ruler (or a stick cut to 3 ft.), then level back to the wall.

After establishing the counter height (or heights) on the wall, measure down to mark a level line that represents the top of the cabinet *boxes*. Typically this would be 34½-in. up, which is the standard 36-in. counter height minus the 1½-in. thickness of a typical counter. Use your 4-ft. level to make a line along the entire run of cabinets. If the wall is very long, or if you want to transfer the height to another run of cabinets, you could consider using a water level.

Installing the Cabinets

Next, draw lines on the walls to indicate where all the cabinets and appliances go. It's a good way to remind yourself of the layout and make sure everything will fit. You can use a little story pole, aligned with your cabinet height line, to

If the floor is very uneven along the wall, measure up from 2 ft. out to find the counter height on the wall above. Mark a level line on the wall representing the top of the cabinet boxes (right). They will be shimmed up or trimmed down to this line. Photo at right by Roe A. Osborn, ©The Taunton Press, Inc.

Water Levels

A water level—basically a plastic jug plus about 25 ft. of ¼-in. i.d. plastic tubing—is simple, inexpensive, very accurate, and easy to use. Just fill the jug with water, stick one end of the tube in the jug, and suck on the other end to fill the tube (I use tape or wire to keep the tube from coming out of the jug). As long as the jug stays put, the water level in the tube will remain the same regardless of where you take it. (Add a little food coloring to the water to make it easier to see.) To establish cabinet lines on walls, you'd make a series of marks on the walls even with the water level in the tube. Use a story pole to record the difference between these lines and the cabinet height. With the story pole, mark up to the cabinet height at each of your water-level marks. Then connect the marks with the long level or straightedge.

TRADE SECRET

Shimming the cabinet level is easier using a small flat bar, which lifts the cabinet gently without moving it out of position.

A story pole establishes the line for the upper cabinet.

Use shim shingles to raise the cabinet up to the line. Photo by Roe A. Osborn, ©The Taunton Press, Inc.

mark the bottom edge of where the upper cabinets go. As you install, you may find final location will depart slightly from the marks you've made. While marking the walls, mark stud locations just above your wall line, so you can find solid fastening when you need it.

Installing base cabinets

Your wall line makes installing the boxes relatively straightforward. Usually there is a logical place to start. If there is a lazy Susan or other inside-corner cabinet, start there. Slide the cabinet into place, and compare it to the line on the wall that represents the top of the cabinet box. In the example, the finish floor hasn't been applied yet, so all the cabinets will be shimmed *up* to match the wall line, using wood shims. Special shim shingles are made for this, but regular shingles used for siding are fine also.

Use your levels to check the cabinet for plumb and level in all directions. Slide the shim in and out until the top is level in both directions and the face of the cabinet is plumb. If the cabinet itself seems out of square, it will be squared up later as the cabinets are secured to each other, the counters, and the walls. When you bring in the next cabinet, you won't be able to reach in to shim up the rear corner where the two cabinets meet. So add that shim now, tacking it to the floor.

Bring in the next cabinet, and follow the same procedure: Shim it to the line, check for level, and adjust the shims. Before moving on, connect the two cabinets by screwing them together at the front. Some cabinets will come with special screws or other hardware for this. If not, use drywall screws of the appropriate length. Predrill with a pilot bit. If it's hardwood,

When the first cabinet is level, bring in the next. Photo by Roe A. Osborn, ©The Taunton Press, Inc.

As you shim, check cabinets for level in all directions. Photo by Roe A. Osborn, ©The Taunton Press, Inc.

Continuous Kickspaces

Some European cabinets, and many custom cabinets, are designed to install on a continuous, level kickspace on which several cabinets rest. The kickspace has to be carefully scribed to the floor and leveled. This system works well for odd shapes or where ductwork, wiring, or plumbing will be run in the kick.

Drawer bases are positioned according to plan and screwed down to the kickboard. The door cabinets—really just bottom shelves—are built in place.

IN DETAIL

When the cabinet is higher than the wall line, you'll have to cut the kickspace down rather than shim it up. Level it carefully. Measure exactly how much above the wall it falls. Set your scribes (or compass) to that amount, and mark all sides of the kickspace. Cut on the line. Where you can't reach to scribe, estimate by measuring down from the wall line or by comparing to the previous cabinet.

With the cabinets shimmed level, run the scribes along the kickspace to mark the cutting line.

Fasten the cabinets together at the front with screws. Often, clamps help in screwing the cabinets together. Photo by Roe A. Osborn, ©The Taunton Press, Inc.

soap the screws. It helps to have one drill set up with the driver bit and another with the pilot bit. It also helps to clamp the two cabinets together to fix the relationship as you install screws.

Install the whole run of base cabinets in the same way. At the end of a run, you may have to add a filler between a cabinet and the wall. In some cases, you can place and level the cabinet, and then measure directly the width to which the filler must be cut (it could vary top and bottom). Cut the filler strip with a table saw, circular saw, or sabersaw.

Sometimes the filler will need to be scribed. One way to do that is to attach the filler to the cabinet, slide the cabinet into position, and then measure how far out of position it is. If your layout indicates the cabinet should be ¾ in. further, set your scribes to ¾ in. and run the point of the scribes down the wall, making a line on the filler ¾ in. from the wall. With the filler still

If the cabinet is ¾ in. out of position, set the scribes to ¾ in. to mark the filler for cutting. Photo by Roe A. Osborn, ©The Taunton Press, Inc.

attached to the cabinet, cut the line with a sabersaw or circular saw.

Make sure your run of cabinets is fairly straight end to end. If the wall is crooked, the cabinets could be out of line a bit. Eyeball down the row of cabinets from one end. Alternatively, stretch a string along the top front corner of the run of cabinets, or use a straightedge along that line. If they're perfect, great. However, a little variation—say up to ¼ in.—will become invisible when the counters are installed. A larger discrepancy should be corrected by slightly repositioning the base cabinets. Sometimes, though you've leveled and plumbed the base cabinets carefully, the front faces won't plumb up. Later, when you install the countertop, you can push or clamp the cabinets into the correct position, then screw the top of the cabinet to the counter to hold it where it should be.

Shim any gaps, then screw the cabinets together at the back. Use the same method to secure the cabinets to the wall studs. Photo by Roe A. Osborn, ©The Taunton Press, Inc.

Specialty Base Cabinets

A great variety of base cabinets are made for special situations. Tall cabinets are made to conceal refrigerators or to accommodate wall ovens. The unit in the photos shows a cabinet that surrounds a refrigerator and provides some storage above it. It consists of a deep door cabinet, plus two side panels. These elements are assembled on site, then installed as a unit. It's important to make sure it lines up properly at the top; it should align with adjacent overheads. When a maze of plumbing would make installing an assembled sink base awkward or impossible, you can order the sink cabinet in parts and assemble them in place.

Assembling the refrigerator cabinet from stock elements. Photo by Roe A. Osborn, ©The Taunton Press, Inc.

Tilting the refrigerator cabinet into place. Make sure the sides are plumb before securing it. Photo by Roe A. Osborn, ©The Taunton Press, Inc.

If there are two adjacent runs of cabinets meeting at a corner, use a rafter square, perhaps extended with your 4-ft. level as a straightedge, to see if the two runs are at right angles. A little discrepancy is okay, but if you can reposition the cabinets a bit to square them up, it will make counter installation easier. I usually prefer to leave the discrepancies at the back of the cabinets, where I can hide them with splash detail. (see "Installing Counters" on p. 173 for more on this).

With a run of cabinets in place, secure them firmly. At the back, slide shims into the gaps between them, and screw the cabinets together with short screws. Use the same method to secure the cabinet to the wall studs. If you omit

PRO TIP

I prefer to install base cabinets first because small adjustments in the base-cabinet locations can alter the position of the uppers.

IN DETAIL

To mount cabinets securely, you'll have to locate the wall studs. Often with new drywall, the screw or nail heads may be visible. I pound in a finish nail (at a height that will later be covered by the cabinets) to verify where the studs are. A simple battery-operated studfinder often works well too. You also can locate studs by trial and error, making a row of holes with the finish nail until you locate a stud. Once you have found one, the likelihood is that the next ones will be 16 in. away or, less often, 24 in.

Island and Peninsula Units

Islands and peninsulas often consist of a group of cabinets and perhaps a sink or stove. Installation is similar to cabinets against a wall. Attach 2x4 blocks to the floor to locate and support the cabinets. Position these to fit just inside the kickspace. After the cabinets are shimmed or trimmed level, put a few screws into the 2x4s to secure the cabinets.

Some cabinets will come with finished sides, and the vendor can provide matching stock to finish off the back of the cabinets. But you also can make site-built panels or shelf units that fit the décor of the kitchen or adjacent spaces.

Two-by-fours screwed to the floor provide extra stability for an island or peninsula. Photo by Roe A. Osborn, ©The Taunton Press, Inc.

After leveling, screw the cabs to the reinforcing blocks. Photo by Roe A. Osborn, ©The Taunton Press, Inc.

the shimming step, you could distort the cabinets and throw them out of plumb. Finally, put a few toescrews into the floor through the kickspace, predrilling first. Be sure you don't move the cabinet as you drive these screws home. Then cut off the excess shim material using a sharp utility knife.

Installing upper cabinets and shelf units

The upper cabinets are attached to the wall by screws through the cabinet back, near the top of the cabinets. Mark stud locations on the wall if

you haven't already done so. If the walls were open during construction, you may have installed blocking to support the cabinets, in which case screws can go anywhere as long as they are at the right height.

What's the right height? Upper cabinets are typically placed so that their bottom shelves are 18 in. or 20 in. above the counter. I often locate them 15 in. or 16 in. up, a lower height that makes the shelves much easier to reach for most people. Cabinets above stoves have to be relatively high because of the heat from the stovetop. For electric stoves, 24 in. of *clearance to combustible surfaces* is

Support the upper cabinet on 2x4 props as you fasten it to the wall. Photo by Roe A. Osborn, ©The Taunton Press, Inc.

Sometimes an upper cabinet or shelf unit can be supported on a permanent wall cleat.

often required, and for many gas stoves, 30 in. In most cases, a ventilation hood can be mounted below that cabinet (consult the specifications that come with any stove or hood you purchase).

Before lifting the cabinet into place, predrill holes for each screw. If there is a board or cleat just below the cabinet top, I drill the holes there for extra strength.

It's awkward to hold a cabinet to a level line on the wall as you screw it in. Instead, devise a way to hold the upper cab at the perfect height as you fasten it. One simple way is to cut a couple of short 2x4 props of the proper length to support the cabinet, as in the photo above.

Two other methods also work well in some cases. Sometimes I install a permanent level cleat to the wall to position and support the upper unit. The face frame of the cabinet may conceal the cleat once the cabinet is up. For an open shelf unit, this wall cleat can be located right under the top shelf. More often, I nail together a little self-standing prop, which gives the upper cabinet full support during adjustment and installation.

When an upper cabinet meets a wall, you may have to trim the face frame or add a filler to position the cabinet correctly. Prop the cabi-

Use a temporary prop (cobbled together from plywood) to position an upper cabinet for fastening. The cabinet is attached through a 2-in.-wide pine cleat inside the cabinet at the top, which also serves to strengthen the cabinet.

net in place (with the filler, if any, attached) and scribe at the wall as in the top photo on p. 172 for a perfect fit.

Attach a whole run of uppers with the minimum number of screws that will keep them in

IN DETAIL

With European-style frameless cabinets, you can adjust the fit of the doors by adjusting the hinges. One adjustment on the hinge moves the door in or out, while another moves it left or right. By making these adjustments, you can make the doors flush with each other and with a uniform gap between them.

To fit a cabinet to a wall, position the cabinet (supporting it as necessary) and scribe the filler piece. Photo by Roe A. Osborn, ©The Taunton Press, Inc.

place safely. At this stage their positions are still somewhat variable, and you can make some adjustments to improve the fit markedly. First use your level on the cabinet sides to make sure they are plumb as you face the cabinets. That is crucial. Also see if they are plumb as measured on the face of the cabinet, which is sometimes less crucial. Next, clamp the cabinets together and fasten them to each other at the front, as you did for the base cabinets.

If the cabinets were perfect, and the wall both flat and plumb, your cabinets would now look perfect. They'd be plumb in both directions, doors would close evenly, and nothing would look crooked. If you had European-style frameless cabinets or face-frame cabinets with inset doors, the gaps around doors would be uniform and everything would look perfect

In the real world of remodeling, though, both walls and cabinets have imperfections.

I don't worry too much if the wall is a bit out of plumb, as long as it is consistently, uni-

A shingle behind the left-hand upper corner of the cabinet plumbs it where the wall is crooked. Photo by Roe A. Osborn, ©The Taunton Press, Inc.

formly out of plumb. The wall cabinets may look good and operate well. But if the wall is twisted, the cabinet also will twist as it's attached, and nothing will fit right at the front. (You can get the same effect if the twist is in the cabinet.) If so, shim between the cabinet and the wall to force the cabinet into the correct position.

When a kitchen is all done, one or two crooked doors, particularly at eye level, can spoil the effect. Although I don't expect perfection, I like to take pains to get the best fits possible. If I have to reposition a hinge or plane or sand something down, I will. When you've made every adjustment you can, add the remaining screws to secure the cabinets to the wall, being careful not to change the cabinet location while you do so.

Use the same approach to tune up the doors of the base cabinets, if necessary. I might mention here that there are many little techniques professional installers use to solve seemingly impossible problems in a kitchen installation, and I can't cover all of them here. In a pinch, I've made a 30-in. cabinet into a 27-in. cabinet, rebuilt broken doors and drawers, and repaired seemingly ruined finishes, for example. There's almost always a way. If you get stumped, get help.

Installing Counters

I think of counter installation as one of the more risky and difficult tasks. Errors in fit are difficult and potentially costly to correct. Although counter surfaces are supposed to be tough, they're surprisingly easy to scratch during construction when there is a lot of abrasive grit around. Such blemishes can be quite noticeable and hard to repair. The bigger, heavier, and more awkward the counters are, the more susceptible to damage in transit, storage, and installation.

Therefore, before beginning, I do a thorough cleanup and vacuum any grit or dust that might cause trouble. During installation I vacuum again whenever grit gets on the counters. So that tools I'm using don't end up scratching the surfaces, I cover the counters with clean plywood scraps or cardboard.

Strategies for easier installation

There are several useful strategies that can make your counter installation simpler while minimizing the number of times you have to handle each section of counter.

Templating. When counters are large, oddly shaped, complex (built-in drainboards, for example), or made of costly materials, make full-scale templates *after* the base cabinets are in place. I use ¼-in. lauan plywood. You can just cut a large piece to represent the counter and label it unambiguously to show sink holes, drainboards, finished edges, and other details. When the shape is very complex, it may be easier to make the shape up from a collection of scraps. In the photo on p.174, the wall is curved at the back,

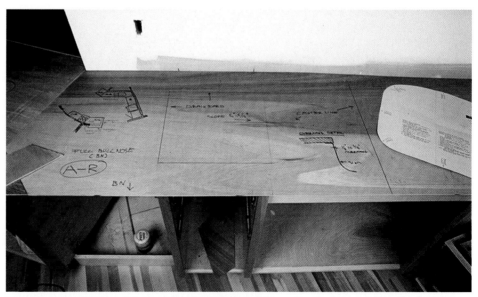

The template for the sink counter has sink centerlines, the drainboard location, labels to indicate which edges receive bullnoses, and a sketch of the floor plan, so fabricators can understand how the counters will go together.

PRO TIP

Mask the counter carefully when grouting a tiled splash. Otherwise, the abrasive sand in the grout will scratch the counter.

TRADE SECRET

If the particleboard used for a laminate core gets wet and stays wet, it will swell. One vulnerable location is where the counter meets the splash. Be sure this area is well caulked and the caulk repaired when necessary.

Most susceptible to water damage is the edge of the sink cutout, even though sinks are caulked here. Enameled sinks have visible caulking that can be maintained. This isn't possible with stainless steel drop-ins; the caulk is underneath the sink's lip.

The best precaution in either case is to coat the particleboard edge of the sink cutout with at least two coats of oil-based polyurethane varnish before putting in the sink. This seals the edge and prevents swelling.

Narrow strips, hot-melt glued together, make a quick, accurate template.

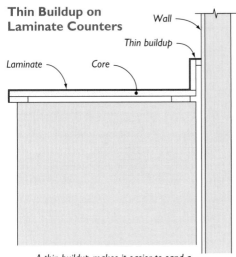

Thin Buildup on Laminate Counters

A thin buildup makes it easier to sand a counter to fit a wall, if necessary.

and there's an angle on one end of the counter. It was easy to fit each side of the counter individually, then assemble the pieces with hot glue. If you are having a solid-surface, stone, or stainless steel counter fabricated by someone else, have him come in to make his own template. That way, it's his responsibility to get it right. If you make the template, label it thoroughly, and provide a floor plan of the kitchen so the fabricator (even if that's you) can keep straight how things go together.

Build laminate cores on site. If you are fabricating laminate counters yourself, build the core of the counter on site like a template, after the base cabinets are in place (see the sidebar on pp. 177–178). Make up the core, apply any edgings, and fit the core to the cabinetry as if you were installing it, including cutting out for the sink. Then apply the laminate or tile. The counter will fit perfectly the first time.

Simple splash details. No splash detail is perfect for every situation, but if you visualize the entire process of handling, installing, and

securing counter and splash, you can usually find methods that will make it easier rather than harder. With stock laminate counters, the *buildup* where the splash meets the wall will typically be thin, so that if you do have to sand a bit off with a belt sander to fit the wall, you'll be sanding something ¾ in. thick, which is easy, rather than something 4 in. tall, which would take forever. You can use the same principle with counters you make yourself.

It's a lot easier if the counters themselves don't have to fit perfectly at the back as you install them. I usually accomplish that by having a separate trim cap above the splash, which I can easily scribe to the wall after installing the counters. It's much easier and less risky to trim a lightweight wood strip than to remove the entire heavy counter, perhaps several times, to trim the counter itself. You can accomplish the same end by designing the splash to be installed after the counter is in place. A wood splash, matching the cabinets, can be nailed or screwed to the wall after the counters are in. If you do this, caulk the seam with a caulk that matches the color of either the splash or the counter. The same thing can be done with tiles, applied directly to the wall or to a plywood backer, as in the top photo on the facing page.

Cap Detail

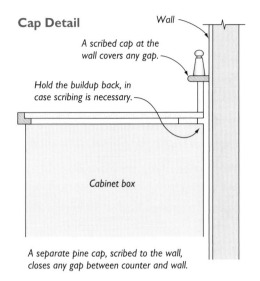

Wall

A scribed cap at the wall covers any gap.

Hold the buildup back, in case scribing is necessary.

Cabinet box

A separate pine cap, scribed to the wall, closes any gap between counter and wall.

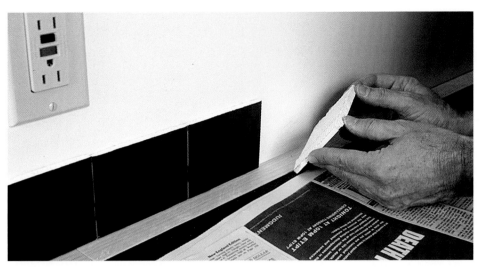

A tile backsplash looks great and also closes any gap between counter and wall. The wood strip creates a uniform caulking gap below the tiles.

Installing laminate tops

In many cases, most of the work of installing a laminate top is in the preparation. In the example here, cutting the sink hole is the biggest job. Most new sinks come with a marking template for marking the hole, but you can turn the sink upside down to use it as a template. It's usually easiest to put the counter in place to locate the sink. That way you can center the hole in the sink base. When positioning the template or upside-down sink, I try to locate it as far forward as possible to put the sink near the user. On the other hand, if the sink is too far forward, the cabinet doors may bang on the sink, or you may end up cutting away too much of the base cabinet. And if the sink is too far back, water will be trapped against the splash. Use a rafter square to make sure your template or upside-down sink is square on the counter.

If you are using the sink as a template, mark around it with a pencil. Remove the sink, and make a second line ¼ in. to ½ in. in. (Inspect the sink to see how much to measure in.) This is the cutting line. Drill holes inside this line at perhaps two of the corners. Cut the hole out using a sabersaw. I use a piece of cardboard under the saw to prevent the saw vibration from scratching the laminate (see photo on p. 178).

Use a new, very sharp blade to minimize chipping out along the cut, and use clamps (or get a helper) to support the sink cutout as you finish the cut.

Attach the splash next. The same method can be used with a wood or laminate splash.

Put a small bead of silicone caulk along the back of the counter. You also could use a water-cleanup caulk that roughly matches the laminate in color. Clamp the splash in place, and check it for squareness with the counter. Predrill from

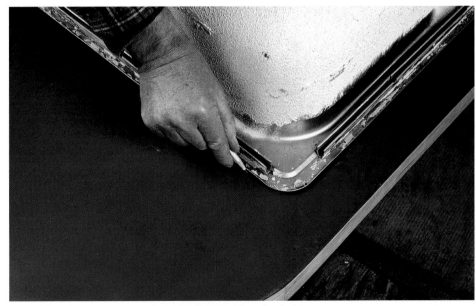

The sink can be used as a template for marking the hole.

TRADE SECRET

If you are going to use a lot of laminate, consider investing in some of the special tools made for working with it:

- A laminate shear, similar to tinsnips, is great for cutting laminate with minimum damage.

- A fine dust brush is helpful for cleaning the surface before applying the contact cement.

- Old venetian blinds are perfect for separating the cement from the laminate.

- A flush-cutting bit is essential for trimming the laminate flush—a carbide-tipped bit with a ball bearing will last longer and work better.

- The router bit made for beveling back the edge of the laminate produces more consistent results than a file or sander.

Make Your Own Laminate Tops

Here's the way I like to make laminate tops. I think a wood edge looks better than a laminate edge and is easier to do. The wood can match the cabinets or other wood counters. A biscuit joint and glue is a great way to connect the edge piece to the core. You could use screws or even nails. You must get the edging exactly flush at the top; if it sticks up, sand it flush using a belt sander.

The laminate is cut oversize, ½ in. to 1 in. more than the core. The excess will be trimmed off later. You can cut it on a table saw (using a fine-toothed blade), with a sabersaw, or with a hand shear made for the purpose. Whatever tool you use, support the laminate well, go slowly, and make sure the laminate isn't fracturing too much along the cut.

The laminate is attached to the core with contact cement. I use latex-based, water-cleanup cement. You may be able to find this in spray cans. Follow the directions to the letter. The basic idea of all contact cements is that you apply the cement to both surfaces, let it dry thoroughly, then mate the surfaces.

Once the surfaces touch, they can't be adjusted. Use thin wood strips, dowels, or clean venetian blinds at about 4-in. intervals to support the laminate over the core, making sure there is overhang on all sides. The next step goes better with two people. Working from the middle out, one person removes a support while the other presses the laminate down smoothly, always pressing from the middle toward the end. When all the supports are out, use a hard rubber roller to complete the mating of the surfaces. A clean pine block and a hammer will also work.

Trim off the excess laminate using a flush-laminate-trimming router bit. Eye protection is crucial here, as well as a dust mask. Use a belt sander to clean up and smooth the edge, then an orbital sander to sand it smooth. Bevel the top edge slightly with the orbital sander, with a large file, or with one of the 10-degree router bits made for the purpose. Finally, finish the wood edge with three coats of satin polyurethane finish.

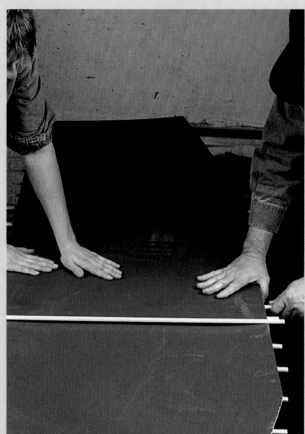

1. Apply a hardwood edge to the particleboard core using a biscuit joiner.

2. Apply contact cement with a roller.

3. Sticks or dowels separate the two surfaces. Working out from the middle, remove the sticks as you press the laminate to the core.

4. Secure the contact-cement joint either by rolling the laminate with a rubber roller or hammering it with a softwood block.

5. Use special router bit to trim off excess laminate.

6. Sand the edge smooth, then varnish the wood.

IN DETAIL

Tight-joint fasteners are a strong and stable way to join two counters of any material that can be drilled or worked with ordinary tools. They're mounted from underneath using a marking template and a special drill bit.

IN DETAIL

Tile your tile counters in place: Build the core, dimensioning it to minimize tile cutting. Fit and install the core, and varnish the wood edges with three coats of finish. Then install the tiles. Mask the wood parts before grouting.

Cut the sink hole on the inner line, protecting the laminate from scratches.

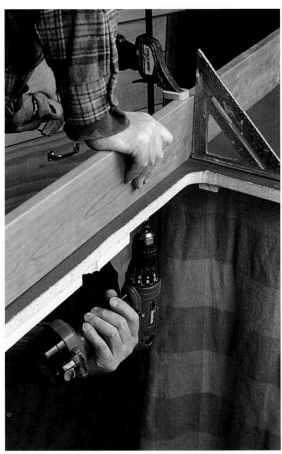

Clamp the splash in place, predrill, then install 1⅝-in. or 2-in. screws. Seal with a small bead of silicone.

below, and install 1⅝-in. or 2-in. drywall screws. Skim most of the excess caulk with a sharp chisel (gently), then use the appropriate solvent and a rag to remove the rest.

Finally, put the counter in place. Just a few screws up into the counter from below is all it takes to keep the counter in place. Some cabinets have a solid top, while others have wood corner blocks or metal brackets to screw through. Be sure the screws aren't too long. It can be very discouraging to get to this point and have a screw come up through the top of your new laminate.

Installing wood tops

Wood counters are typically commercial butcher-block or custom-made wood-plank tops made by cabinet shops. In general, the installation

Remove the excess caulk with a sharp chisel, then use a rag dampened with thinner to remove the last of the squeeze-out.

procedure is similar to that for plastic-laminate tops. But there are some additional considerations.

If you have to cut a wood top, I suggest cutting from the back, with the counter upside down, using a circular saw with a very sharp blade. Cutting from the back will give you a cleaner cut on the face. Clamp a fence to the counter to guide the saw.

Any exposed end grain should be sealed with polyurethane varnish, two coats, even if the top surface is oil finished. This will minimize small cracks, called *end checks,* which sometimes appear as wood seasons.

The counter will be screwed to the cabinet from underneath like a laminate top. But unlike a laminate top, wood counters shrink and expand a bit seasonally. A stock 25-in. counter might vary from 25⅛ in. in the summer to 24⅞ in. in a dry winter. The holes for the screws have to allow for that kind of movement. The drawing on p. 67, shows how this should be done. Predrill the screw holes, and soap the screws. Otherwise, the screws will shear off in the hard wood.

Installing stone, Fireslate, and other heavy tops

Granite, Fireslate-2, and other monolithic, heavy counters are easy to install in that they are held down simply with caulk. A few large dabs of silicone caulk are placed on the top of the cabinet box, then the counter simply laid in place. The weight of the counter keeps it from moving. Handle the counter gently, particularly if there is a sink hole in it. The sink hole is a weak point, so fully support the counter as you manipulate it. Sometimes we have clamped a 2x4 to the counter, across the sink hole, to protect the top during transport.

Undermount sinks are often included with this type of counter. There are basically two approaches to installing undermount sinks. First, you can fully support the sink on the cabinetry. In the top photo on p. 180, I've built a stout frame to support the sink. The trick here is to

Wood tops are screwed in place from below.

locate the sink accurately. Then the counter simply drops over the sink, caulking where the sink meets the top. After doing it this way for years, I've come to think a better method is to fasten the sink directly to the counter. On a recent project, the sink came with inserts designed to be drilled into the bottom of the counter. We used a masonry bit to drill a ½-in. hole in the counter, then screwed the threaded insert into this hole. Small brackets, bolted to the threaded insert, hold the sink firmly to the counter. Consult with the counter fabricator and the sink supplier to find the best method in your situation.

Even counters that have been templated may not fit perfectly. If a wood top is a bit too big, you can saw it or sand it down. If a laminate top is too big, you can sand it down or trim it with a router. But it's not as easy to trim heavy stone or stonelike products. Fireslate is not as hard as granite, and it could be trimmed using a belt

PRO TIP

Store your yet-to-be installed counters in a clean, out-of-the-way place, and cover them with tarp to keep them clean.

IN DETAIL

If a kitchen has a wood treatment or paneling on the wall, I like to use that same material for the end panels or for the backs of islands or peninsulas. If the walls have 3-ft.-high beaded wainscoting, for example, using that same material for the end panels unifies the whole design and makes the cabinets look more built-in. Doors or narrow shelves can be incorporated easily into this where needed.

This undermount sink is supported on a wooden frame attached to the cabinets.

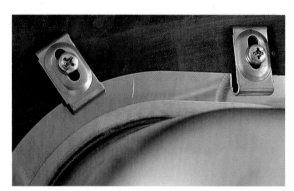

Brackets screwed to threaded inserts drilled into the bottom of the counter hold the sink in place.

sander. It would take a long time to trim ⅛ in. off of a Fireslate counter and forever to trim a granite counter that was too long. Cabinet installers will go to some length to avoid having to do that. Sometimes it's easier just to cut a little channel in the drywall so a bit of the counter can be discretely tucked into the wall to make it fit right. It's also possible to carve a bit of wood away, if that will allow the counter to slide into place.

It can be tricky to make a clean, waterproof joint where two stone or Fireslate counters meet. If such a joint is necessary, the counter vendor should provide the materials and clear instructions for making the joint. Epoxy is sometimes used. On a recent project with Fireslate counters, the vendor provided an epoxy mix, plus Fireslate dust to mix with it to get a color match. Clear instructions described the method. If you are using old stone counters or haven't been provided with materials or instructions, it should work fine to fill the crack with a vinyl adhesive caulk such as Phenoseal® or Polyseamseal®. Such caulks are somewhat resilient, adhesive, and strong, and they clean up with water. They come in several colors. Unlike silicones, which are gummy, vinyl adhesive caulks develop a skin that is reasonably washable. Fill the crack, trim the excess with a sharp chisel, then use a wet rag or scrubby to tool the material with a slight depression.

For stone or stonelike counters, it's often easier to relieve a wall or carve away an obstruction, when necessary, rather than to trim down the countertop.

Cabinet Trim

The cabinet trim elements may include end panels (which cover unfinished ends or exposed backs of cabinets), finished kickboards, fillers, and moldings at the tops of cabinets. These features deserve as much thought as the cabinets themselves. The cabinets, even if custom-made, are a set of matching but separate units. The trim closes gaps around cabinets and ties everything together into one composition.

End panels

All cabinets of course are finished on the face. The sides and backs often are concealed and don't always need to be finished. Different kinds of cabinets provide different ways of finishing off these surfaces when they do show. Most face-frame cabinets come with finished sides. While some frameless cabinets can also be supplied

with finished sides, others, particularly European brands, are designed for exposed sides to be covered with separate end panels matching cabinet styles. These are glued or tacked to the cabinet with small brads. Some applied end panels come oversize, so they can be scribed to close any gaps between the cabinet and the wall. Alternatively, a molding can be added to close such gaps.

Islands and peninsulas will need finished ends and sides. In the top right photo on p. 182, the cabinet was supplied with a beaded end panel, and the back panel is a site-applied sheet of matching beaded plywood. The total effect is to make the separate cabinets appear to be a single unit.

Site-built storage units can sometimes be used in place of or in combination with end panels to cover exposed ends or backs of cabinets. A set of thin spice shelves are easy to build, and

IN DETAIL

There's no reason you have to use factory-supplied materials to enclose islands. I often like to use contrasting materials, which match the décor in adjacent spaces rather than mimic the cabinets. Wallboard, painted plywood, varnished hardwood plywood, or any sort of wood paneling can make a good surround for island or peninsula cabinets.

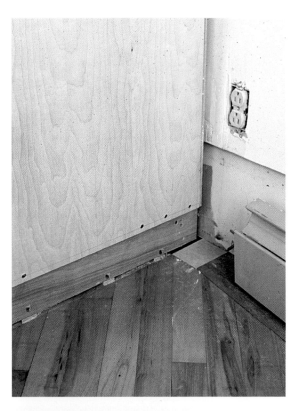

When there is a gap at the wall, a molding of matching wood can be glued in place to close the gap. The little stick wedged against the window apron works like a clamp to position the piece as the glue dries.

The cabinet vendor supplied the island cabinet with a beadboard side panel and a matching panel to cover the cabinet backs, making the island seem like a single unit. Photo by Roe A. Osborn, ©The Taunton Press, Inc.

can be applied like an end panel to an upper cabinet, adding variety while adding useful storage.

In the top left photo on the facing page, a pine bookcase covers the back of two base cabinets. A cherry plywood end panel covers the joint where the bookcase meets the base cabs and makes the whole set of cabinets seem like a single unit.

Kickspace trim

Most domestic cabinets have the kickspace built into the cabinet. After shimming, this has to be covered with some trim material as a finish. Although a rubber base is sometimes used, it looks better to apply thin pieces of plywood or solid wood that matches the cabinets. Since the material is thin, it's fairly easy to trim it with a

An end panel and molding connect the drawer base and bookcase.

A wide shelf for large pottery, with bullnose crown molding, ties things together.

block plane to fit the floor. A little gap at the top won't be seen.

Crown molding

Some cabinets, particularly modern styles, look nice and clean with no trim at the top. In other cases, trim at the top finishes off the cabinets and ties them together. In the top right photo, the client had large plates and other pottery she wanted to display so I devised a wide shelf to sit on the upper cabinet. The shelf has a slot to position the plates and is trimmed with a bull-nose crown molding.

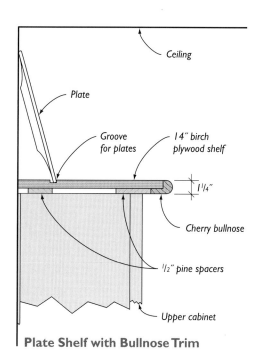

Ceiling

Plate

Groove
for plates

14″ birch
plywood shelf

1¼″

Cherry bullnose

½″ pine spacers

Upper cabinet

Plate Shelf with Bullnose Trim

Finishing Up

CHAPTER NINE

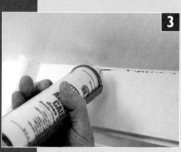

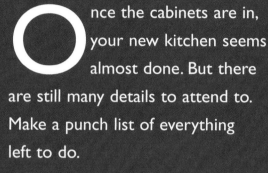

O nce the cabinets are in, your new kitchen seems almost done. But there are still many details to attend to. Make a punch list of everything left to do.

Do a careful inspection of fits and finishes. Nothing's perfect. My goal at this stage is to correct defects that will be noticeable. I don't worry about a drip in a dark corner or a scratch on a shelf that will be covered with cookbooks. But I will fix a scratch in a varnished counter that will be highlighted by a splash of sunlight every morning or by the new lighting; I know it will bother me if I don't fix it.

Do the inspection in bright light. Also figure out which surfaces your new light fixtures will call attention to. If these fixtures haven't been installed, use a clip-on light to simulate the effect. Put anything important you find on your punch list.

IN DETAIL

Just in the last year or so, our shop has used pulls from many sources. On one kitchen, we used brass sash lifts from the local lumberyard. We've used beautiful loop handles made by local blacksmiths; amazing handles cast in the forms of shells, each one different; and brass nautical hardware. You might begin with something simple, live with it awhile, and dress up your kitchen later by replacing the pulls with a fortunate find.

WHAT CAN GO WRONG

The screws that come with drawer pulls are usually designed for ¾-in.-thick drawer fronts. Thicker or double-front drawers will require longer screws with the right thread.

Completing Final Cabinet Details

Inspect your new cabinetry with particular care. Check the finishes as described above. Operate every door and drawer. Drawers should operate smoothly and doors close firmly. Make sure all the screws for hinges and drawer slides are in place. Check alignment and fit of doors and drawers. Step back, look at a rank of cabinets or drawers, and look for any sloppy, out-of-parallel fits. These final adjustments are easier if the cabinet pulls or knobs are in place. If not, now is the time to install them.

Knobs and pulls

Your cabinets may have come with pulls or knobs and with installation holes for them already drilled. With European or custom cabinets, drilling for hardware is often done on site. Sometimes this task is left to the end because people haven't selected the hardware they want until the last minute. While there is a wide range of options that can make this choice difficult, most often we use simple round knobs or D-pulls bought locally or purchased through catalogs.

Pulls located low on the upper doors are easier to reach. The pulls line up with the bead on the door.

If you are locating the pulls now, do it carefully. First, they should be located to minimize reaching. That means upper door pulls should be low and lower door pulls high. Drawer pulls, particularly on bottom drawers, should be high on the drawer front to minimize leaning over.

Locating the hardware properly makes a surprising difference in how graceful and *right* the kitchen looks. Hold the hardware in place and try different alignments to find what looks best to you, while also being convenient. Have a helper hold the pull in place so you can stand back and gauge the effect.

When you've decided where to put things, make a simple plywood or cardboard template to locate holes, as shown in the top left photo on the facing page. Use a center punch to mark the locations so that the drill bit centers accurately.

Mark the drawer fronts using a plywood template.

Getting the pull locations just right makes a big difference. On long drawers, a longer pull may look better proportioned.

On drawers, I find it often looks right to center the pull for the top drawer, then place the remaining pulls at that same distance from the top edge of the drawer front, or perhaps just a sliver more. In the top photo at right, the top drawer was about 5½ in. wide. After holding the pull in several positions to see how it looked, we decided to set them about 2¾ in. down from the top edge.

Final tune-up and touch-up

Cabinets are never perfectly straight or square. The idea is to make them look that way. This could mean readjusting a drawer, moving one last hinge position, planing an edge, or sanding something. As with finishes, imperfect fits will be more noticeable at eye level or in bright light.

As you are looking closely at all of the cabinets, this is a good time to touch up the cabinet finish if necessary. Begin by repairing any areas damaged during installation. Sometimes scratches

These cabinets were finished with three coats of oil-based satin polyurethane. The parts that will get the most use or the most exposure to water, like this shelf, might benefit from a fourth coat.

IN DETAIL

Fillers and color putties are available to fix dings and dents in wood. You also can make your own by mixing sawdust with glue or epoxy. Often you aren't trying for perfection, just for enough improvement that the spot doesn't call attention.

TRADE SECRET

To repair a ding, take a sewing needle and poke a bunch of tiny holes in the depression. Then wet the spot for 30 to 45 minutes. The water will soak into the wood, causing the wood to swell back into shape. This method, which can be used with either unfinished or finished wood, will usually bring the surface at least halfway back. After the surface dries, it can be lightly sanded and touched up.

and dings are truly unrepairable, but it's surprising how many *can* be eliminated or moderated.

It usually doesn't make sense to sand out dents or holes; you'll likely end up with a blotchy, mismatched finish. Instead, try filling them. Take a sample of your kitchen finish—perhaps a scrap from a filler strip or a small drawer—to a hardware store, lumberyard, or home center to find the filler closest in color. Then fill according to the product directions. I recommend experimenting to see how a given wood filler will look. Experiment on a spot that doesn't show.

Having patched dings as well as possible, touch up the finish as needed. If you are working on cabinets you built or finished yourself, you would sand lightly with 180- or 220-grit paper, then refinish lightly with the same polyurethane (or paint) used on the cabinets. If you are touching up factory-finished cabinets, you may be able to get a small amount of finish from the cabinet supplier for touching up. However, on most wood cabinets a little touchup with ordinary polyurethane will usually work fine. Again, do a sample in a corner to make sure. While a perfect match is ideal, a close match will typically be fine.

Counter repairs

Solid-surface, Fireslate-2, and stone counters can be sanded to remove problems. The risk here is that the surface texture will change, and you will get a blotchy look that is more noticeable than the original scratch. You might have to resand the whole top. Try to touch up using the same grit that was used to surface the counter as a whole. Consult the instructions that came with your counters, or call the people who sold them to you. In addition, a test repair with a scrap, or in an obscure spot, might be a good idea.

Oiled wood counters that people chop on will inevitably get marked up; this becomes part of their patinas. But *stains* don't look that appealing. Most food stains, such as beet juice or grape, may seem impossible to remove but will go away by themselves in a few weeks. Rust stains, though, are more of a problem. They occur when an iron object is left in a wet spot on the counter for a while. Most oiled wood counters have a black mark or two showing where a carbon steel knife, wet with food juices, sat for a half hour. These can be scraped or sanded out, but try to avoid them by cleaning up as you work and picking up or drying off any iron implements as you cook. Some counter problems will cure themselves. For example, a white ring in a varnished counter, caused by leaving a wet flowerpot on it overnight, may disappear once the sun hits the counter for a couple of hours. Or try wiping an alcohol-damp rag over the spot; it may displace the trapped moisture.

While I can't say there is *always* a way, there is *often* a way to fix something that at first seems hopeless. Don't be afraid to experiment (although you should do it on an unobtrusive spot). Also, wait a while. Something that really bothers you the day you move back in may be forgotten a week or two later.

Accessories

Sometimes the accessories are what really make a kitchen personal. The nicest cabinetry looks a lot better accented by elements that introduce visual variety while performing a task. I love a good pot rack, a nicely divided drawer, or a special shelf that can't be found in any catalog. I love to see pictures on the wall. Often kitchen utensils, dishes, or equipment become part of the décor, particularly if there are open shelves or glass doors.

A pot rack, custom pulls, and some round shelves in the corner make this kitchen unique.

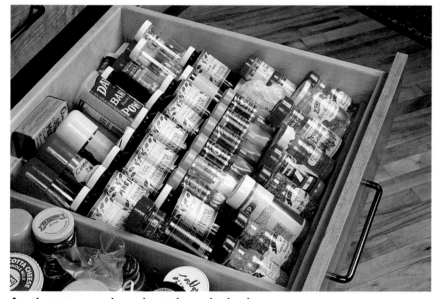

Another accessory is a spice staircase in the drawer.

Wire baskets provide good storage and add variety.

The plates on the top shelf are an important part of the design.

A bookcase can be a valuable accessory in a kitchen.

TRADE SECRET

I know of no way to remove scratches in laminate counters, but you can improve the situation with a discreet application of nail polish or paint of just the right color, neatly brushed into the slit and quickly wiped with a rag.

IN DETAIL

Domestic dishwashers are 24 in. wide. Make sure the opening is 24⅛-in. wide. Protect the floor with cardboard while the subs are at work. Make sure the dishwasher is pushed all the way in. Also make sure the machine is plumb at the front by adjusting the adjustable feet. Finally, secure the dishwasher to the counter. There are normally tabs provided for short screws up into the counter.

Completing Mechanical Systems, Installing Appliances

You know you are almost done when it's time for the final plumbing, wiring, and gas work. They are among the last things to do because the appliances have to be ready to put in place and because it's easier to paint before light fixtures, cover plates, and such are installed. Give your subcontractors as much notice as possible.

Dishwasher Connections

A dishwasher has three hookups. The first is the hot-water supply, which typically comes from the water supply under the sink. Each leg—the water for the sink and the water for the dishwasher—should have its own shutoff.

The second hookup—the drain connection—is typically a flexible hose that connects directly to the sink drain below the basket strainer. If there is a garbage disposal, it will have a connection on the side for the dishwasher drain. Some plumbing codes require an air-gap inlet, a device mounted next to the faucet on top of the sink that prevents waste water from back-siphoning into the sink. In that case, the dishwasher drain connects to the air-gap inlet, which in turn connects to the drain or disposal.

The third connection is the electrical hookup. The dishwasher should have its own 20-amp circuit. The dishwasher line is often connected to an outlet at the back of the cabinet so it can be unplugged for service. If it is hardwired, you may be required to provide a switch under the sink.

Plumbing

The plumbing finish will include hooking up the sink (or sinks), installing the dishwasher, and usually completing the heating, since on small projects the plumbing and heating are often done by the same person.

Undermount sinks will have been installed already. With a laminate counter, or any counter where the sink mounts from above, begin by attaching as much of the plumbing as possible to the sink; it's very awkward to work from below, inside a dark, small cabinet. In the example pictured we attached the faucet and water lines. As the sink was being reused, the basket and tailpiece (connecting the sink to the trap) were still attached. Bed the sink in the caulk that comes with it. In this case, we put a bead of silicone caulk around the opening and set the sink in place. Stainless steel sinks like this are held down by little clamps that fit into a channel attached to the sink underneath. With a good light to work by, lie on your back under the sink to fit these in place, at least three per side. Have a helper make sure the sink stays straight as you tighten it down. I like to use a sharp chisel to lift off most of the excess caulk. Then I use the appropriate solvent on a rag to remove the rest.

Cast-iron sinks don't have little clamps. They are held in place by their own weight and by the caulk. The sink will typically come with a caulk that matches the color of the sink. Generally these will be water-cleanup caulks such as Phenoseal or Polyseamseal. Put a bead of caulk around the opening, and carefully let the sink down into place. The caulk will squeeze out. If the sink rocks a bit, put a tiny wood shim underneath to stabilize it. The caulk for these sinks will show, almost like a molding or gasket. Where the gap between sink and counter isn't full of caulk at this point, add more, being sure to tool it and clean it up neatly.

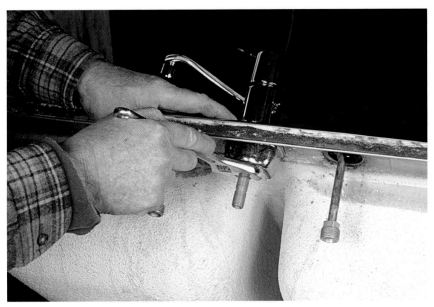

A single large nut in the middle secures the faucet to the sink. A built-in gasket seals the joint. Some faucets are held down at two points.

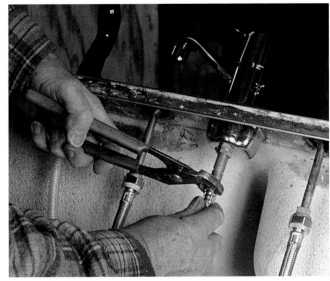

The new flexible water-supply lines make hooking up the sink much easier. Some can be tightened by hand with paddlelike wing nuts.

No-Sweat Plumbing

Plumbing has become much easier in recent years, as manufacturers have created products that are easier to use and that require few tools. Most lumberyards, hardware stores, and home centers can help you figure out which pipes, fittings, and supplies fit the sink and faucet you choose, and most tie easily into your existing house plumbing. Most of the plumbing can be assembled with simple gasketed or compression fittings and tightened down with wrenches, large Channellock pliers, or even by hand.

Chances are, your sink's supply lines are copper or chrome-plated brass, and you can still use these types of lines, either with sweated or compression-type fittings. But braided stainless steel supply tubes are becoming increasingly popular because they are so quick and easy to install. There's no cutting; all you do is tighten the connection at either end using a wrench.

Again, use a chisel at a low angle to lift the worst of the excess. Then tool the caulk with your finger, nice and wet to ensure a smooth job. Usually there will be a residue of caulk on the counter and sink. Use a nonmetalic kitchen scrubby—also kept wet—to retool the joint and remove this excess at the same time.

Now it's time to hook up the drain. Often the 1½-in. tailpiece (which comes down from the sink—some have a branch for the dishwasher), drain arm (running to a second bowl), and the trap are finished in chrome-plated brass, all assembled with threaded fittings with rubber gaskets. However, regular PVC drainpipe also is used, glued together with PVC solvent. Your supplier can help you figure out which will be simplest and easiest to join to the drain coming out of your wall or floor.

If the supply lines have been attached to the sink, they are dangling and can be attached to the angle stops located either on the wall or on the bottom of the cabinet. If the copper supply lines coming out of the wall or floor have been capped off, you will have to sweat *angle stops* there as a transition to your flexible supply lines.

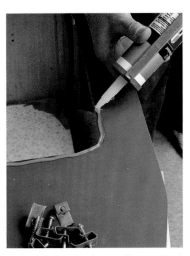

Bed the sink in the caulk supplied with it. I like to trim the excess with a sharp chisel, then clean up the last bits with the appropriate solvent.

WHAT CAN GO WRONG

The risk with a rigid cast-iron drop-in sink is that it won't sit quite flat on the countertop. If it's off by 1/16 in. or perhaps 1/8 in., the discrepancy will be taken up with caulk. If it is more, probably the sink is warped. If you've checked the countertop with a straightedge and it's flat, I'd suggest exchanging the warped sink for another.

IN DETAIL

Make sure there is room for the clips that hold a stainless steel sink in place. A thick countertop can get in the way of the clips. If so, you may have to climb under the sink and drill upward at the edge of the sink hole with a 3/4-in.- or 1-in.-diameter spade bit to make a small recess where the clip can grab hold.

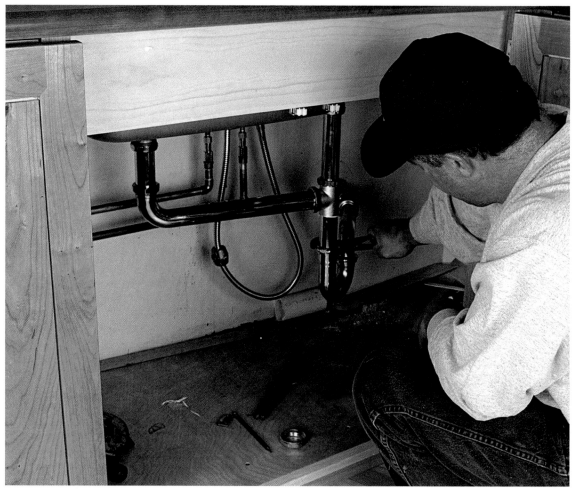

Hooking up a sink.

Finish wiring

The finish wiring is often quite simple. Recessed lights require only a bulb and the attachment of the trim. Track lights can be mounted to conventional ceiling boxes but are sometimes wired directly.

The outlets and switches also are simple, at least if you remember which box does what. Often the tricky part for the amateur electrician is judging how much wire to leave. Too little, and the switch or receptacle will be hard to attach. Too much, and the wires crowd the box. Folding and positioning the wires in the box so that they will tuck out of the way as the switch or receptacle is pushed in is another trick. Perhaps the most important point is to get a secure connection and to make sure the grounding or *bond* is complete.

You can use an ordinary circuit tester to make sure your boxes are grounded, but a special outlet tester also is a good idea. Remember that counter outlets, or others near water, must be GFCI protected, either at the receptacle (the one closest to the panel will protect those that follow it) or with a GFCI breaker.

The track light was wired directly to a wire that had been neatly drilled through the ceiling beam.

The trim on recessed lights is typically secured with simple spring hooks and installs very quickly.

Installing appliances

Normally the gas company will install a gas stove and an electric stove will simply plug into a special 220-volt outlet. But it is up to you to get it ready. It's just as important to level the stove as to level the cabinets. You don't want the oil in your frying pan to run down to one corner of the pan. The bottom of the stove normally has threaded adjusters. Remove the bottom drawer, if possible, and adjust them up and down as needed. The instructions with the stove will describe exactly how this works, but adjusting the feet is usually rather uncomfortable. A new safety feature is a little bracket, screwed to the floor, that interlocks with one of the rear adjusting feet. It keeps the stove from tipping forward dangerously if too much weight is put on an open oven door. The stove should come with a template for locating this antitip bracket.

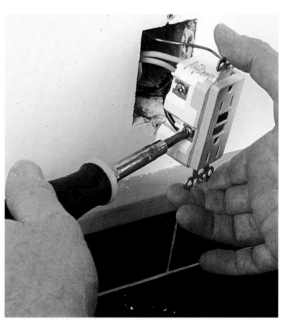

Positioning the wires neatly makes hooking up the box easier. Turn off the circuit at the panel before you work on it.

An outlet tester tells you whether an outlet you have wired is live, wired properly in terms of polarity, and grounded.

The hinges and door handles on most refrigerators are reversible. The dealer will set up the door swing as you wish, but be sure to let him know. The new fridge will almost always ride on little wheels. These can be adjusted up and down with setscrews to level and plumb the unit.

WHAT CAN GO WRONG

As you move large appliances like the stove or refrigerator into position, protect your floor from scratches and dents. Often you can use a large sheet of cardboard cut from the appliance's packing material.

TRADE SECRET

It's a big help to have a good caulking gun. In cheaper guns, the caulk keeps coming out, even after you stop pumping. Look for a gun with a pressure release. Another nice feature is a built-in spike for puncturing the inner seal of the caulking tubes. Some guns have a little cutter, like a cigar cutter, to snip the end of the tube off, but I prefer to do this with a sharp utility knife.

Built-In Cooktops and Wall Ovens

Fitting a wall oven, cooktop, or drop-in range into stock cabinetry is usually not too complex. Cooktops typically drop into a cutout in the countertop, like a drop-in sink. Wall ovens are installed in tall cabinets that are properly dimensioned and ordered according the wall oven's requirements. A drop-in stove may fit between adjacent cabinets (in which case fillers will close in the space below it) or have its own specialized cabinet. In each case, the appliance's spec sheet will describe the required dimensions and clearances.

The problems tend to come with hooking them up. Electric models will have dedicated 220-volt lines and are usually hardwired, with enough slack to permit installation or servicing. Codes may require a lock-out device at the breaker when the electrical panel is not within sight of the appliance. This device allows anyone servicing the unit to lock the breaker open while working.

Gas models can present more problems, primarily finding a route for the gas line—usually black iron pipe—to be routed to the appliance in a way that won't obstruct the cabinetry. In one recent project, I had to cut down the drawers below a cooktop to make room for a gas line coming up from the basement. Study spec sheets and installation instructions carefully as the cabinetry is being set up to minimize such problems.

Final Finish Details

There are usually a number of little carpentry details, seemingly trivial tasks that don't show much when you stand back and look at the whole space but make a big difference up close.

Filling nail holes

Although I don't mind neatly done finish nails in wood trim, most people prefer to fill nail holes. In trim to be painted, spackling compound, sanded lightly, works well. Nail holes in varnished or stained wood trim can be filled with wood filler in a matching color. Fill nail holes after varnishing or staining trim. If you do it before, the filler will reject the finish, and you will get a noticeable blotch at each nail. Sometimes the nail holes look almost invisible when first filled but stick out glaringly a year later. That's because wood darkens from exposure to sunlight, but the wood filler does not. For that reason, use a slightly darker color of filler, or better yet, fill the holes after six months to a year, when the wood has had a chance to darken.

Caulking cracks

Small cracks between the painted wall and adjacent trim elements or cabinets are unavoidable. Some are caused by wood shrinking after installation. Wallboard walls are never perfectly flat, so there are often cracks along baseboards or behind casings. Many of these don't show much, but where they do, they can be filled with caulk of a nearly matching color. I use Phenoseal, a vinyl caulk that is adhesive and water-resistant, washable, and paintable when cured. At the same time, it can be cleaned up with water when you apply it. It's somewhat resilient, which means it's unlikely to crack as things around it move. But unlike silicone products, which remain somewhat gummy, its surface is hard enough to be cleaned.

First, put a small bead into the crack, as neatly as possible. A small, angled hole in the caulking-cartridge tip makes this easier. Then wet your

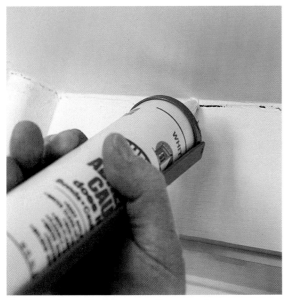  

Apply caulk, tool with a wet finger, and remove any excess with a scrubbie and water.

finger with water, and run it down the joint to smooth it. Finally, if there is excess, use a wet dishwashing pad to scrub away as much as needed. After it dries, it can be painted if the color doesn't match.

Moving in

Paradoxically, some important design work happens after the project is complete. As you move into your new kitchen and put things away, remind yourself of some of the design principles introduced in the early chapters of this book. Locate things in the *work centers* they belong in. Put the things you use most often in the *optimum reach zone*: the top two drawers, the margin at the back of the counter, the lower overhead shelves. Remember the idea of *one-motion storage.* Put things at *point of first use*: the spot where you will be standing at the moment you want to use them. If you follow these rules in the main, you'll be surprised how different your new kitchen will be to work in. It will be easier and more efficient but also more pleasant and agreeable.

On a more prosaic note, establish a file somewhere of all the important kitchen information, such as warranties, spec sheets, Web addresses,

contracts with builders, and a full set of the kitchen drawings. If you took photos or a video of the walls before they were covered up, include them. Also, set aside a place in the basement for all the leftover paints and finishes—clearly labeled—plus any spare parts, such as extra cabinet pulls, which might come in handy later.

Finally, don't forget to put some pictures on the walls, and perhaps a vase of flowers somewhere, some snapshots on the refrigerator door, and perhaps a couple of decorative plates where they can be enjoyed. These things are part of the design, too.

Now put up the decorative plates, paintings, and other artwork to complete the project.

Resources

There is a huge amount of literature on the kitchen, which includes books, periodicals, catalogs, and online resources. Here are some of my favorite recent books:

The Kitchen Idea Book, Joanne Kellar Bouknight, The Taunton Press, 1999. Full of ideas, great photos, and practical information.

Kitchens and Baths 1-2-3, Meredith Publishing Group, 1999. Project editor John P. Holms. This is Home Depot's kitchen book. It has a wealth of useful information, including design methods.

Building Traditional Kitchen Cabinets, Jim Tolpin, The Taunton Press, 1994.

Kitchens: The Best of Fine Homebuilding, Kevin Ireton, ed., The Taunton Press, 1997. Key articles from *Fine Homebuilding* magazine on both design and building topics.

Fine Homebuilding Kitchen and Bath annual issues. The magazine publishes a kitchen and bath issue each year. Particular topics from the magazine can be searched through the magazine's website.

The Independent Builder, Sam Clark, Chelsea Green Publishing, 1996. This is a general book on building. It has chapters on house design, basic wood-frame engineering, heat-loss calculation, and all aspects of house building. It would be helpful if your project includes major changes to your house.

Chelsea Green Publishing Company (800-639-4099, www.chelseagreen.com) has published a wide variety of excellent books on sustainable building, alternative building, and other environmental subjects. Some of their titles: *The Natural House,* Daniel D. Chiras, 2002; *The Solar House,* Daniel D. Chiras, 2002; *Serious Straw Bale*, Paul Lacinski and Michael Bergon, 2000; *The New Independent Home*, Michael Potts, 1999.

Classics: Some of the best books on the kitchen are classics published quite a while ago. Here are my picks:

Management in the Home, Lillian Gilbreth, Dodd Mead and Co. This book went through many editions in the early '50s and is a great introduction to research kitchens and the Motion Study approach that lies at the heart of ergonomics. The novel *Cheaper by the Dozen*, by Frank Gilbreth, Jr. and Ernestine Gilbreth Carey, is a funny treatment of the same subject.

Small Kitchens, Robin Murrell, Simon and Schuster, 1986. A great book with innovative ideas about kitchen layout.

The Motion-Minded Kitchen, Sam Clark, Houghton Mifflin Co., 1985. This is hard to find but is a good source on early ergonomic and kitchen research, inexpensive kitchens, and building cabinets in place.

A Pattern Language, Christopher Alexander, et al., Oxford University Press, 1977. This isn't about the kitchen in particular, but I think it is probably the most powerful and useful book on how to make a home warm, inviting, and beautiful.

Videos: The Taunton Press markets a variety of videos on building topics, including one on making kitchen cabinets by Paul Levine and one on installing cabinets and countertops by Tom Law.

Catalogs: We obtain a lot of what we need from print or online catalogs. Many catalogs sell both hardware and tools. Among the most useful are: Lee Valley (800-871-8158; www.leevalley.com); Woodcraft Supply (800-225-1153; www.woodcraft.com); and Toolcrib (800-635-5140; toolcrib@amazon.com). Renovators Supply (800-659-2211; www.rensup.com) specializes in old-fashioned products and hardware for renovation. Real Goods (800-762-7325; www.realgoods.com) sells environmentally friendly products, including books. Duluth Trading Company (800-505-8888; www.duluthtrading.com) has great tool bags, toolbelts, kneepads, parachute bags, and similar accessories. Also don't forget IKEA (800-434-4532; www.ikea-usa.com), which sells affordable flat-pack cabinets and well-designed furniture, lighting, and other household products.

Kitchen design on-line: Check out these sources if you're interested in getting more information about computer-aided design:

•Advanced Relational Technology, Inc. (301 North 3d. Street, Couer, d'Alene, ID 83814, 800-482-4433) makes Chief Architect for professionals and 3D Home Architect for home use. Chief Architect: www.chiefarch.com

•Twenty Twenty Technology program, called 2020 Kitchen Design (Twenty Twenty, 1867 Berlier Street, Laval Quebec, Canada H7L 3S4; 514-332-4110). The company makes a program tailored for kitchen design, which can be used by both design professionals and homeowners. 2020: www.2020design.com

•Planit-Autograph, by Planit-AG (699 Perimeter Drive, Suite 300, Lexington, KY 40517; 800-234-5089) is a similar web-based program. There also are a variety of design programs for the homeowner available through software vendors. Planit-Autograph: www.planitautograph.com

Kitchen Layout Templates

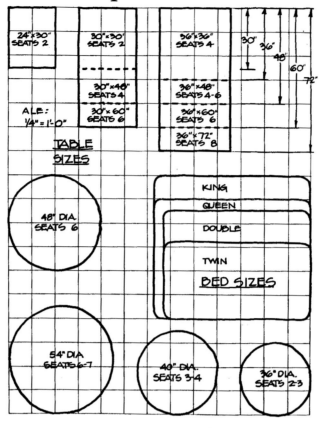

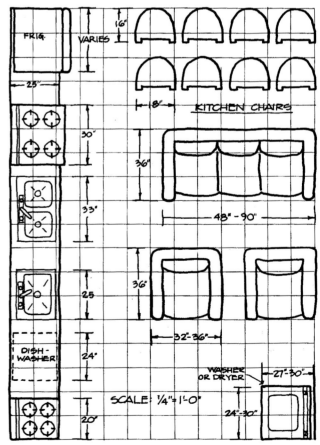

1/4" = 1'

From *The Motionminded Kitchen,* by Sam Clark, Houghton Mifflin Co., 1983

Index